# The Nature of Nurture

# The Nature of Nurture

Rethinking Why and How Childhood Adversity Shapes Development

JAY BELSKY

The Belknap Press of Harvard University Press

CAMBRIDGE, MASSACHUSETTS · LONDON, ENGLAND · 2026

EU GPSR Authorized Representative
LOGOS EUROPE, 9 rue Nicolas Poussin, 17000, La Rochelle, France
Email: Contact@logoseurope.eu

Cataloging-in-Publication Data available from the Library of Congress
ISBN: 978-0-674-29719-7 (alk. paper)

*To my two granddaughters, Ida Rose and Noa Mae, and my two stepdaughters, Alexandra and Christina— may you (eventually) be fruitful and multiply.*

*To my fellow evo-devo travelers, Bruce, Marco, and Willem, and to Marinus and Marian, who have played such an important role in my thinking, research, and writing.*

# Contents

# Preface

THE TRUTH is that I am quite surprised to be sitting where I am today, as I submit the final draft of this book to Harvard University Press. If someone had asked me when I was graduating from high school what the chances were that I would become a scientist and a teacher, I would surely have said "zero." Yet here I am, a recently retired college professor, after a longer than four-decade career in teaching and researching child development. Whether or not these "developments" surprise you, they most certainly astonish me.

I say this because I spent my entire childhood and adolescence with a singular goal in mind, one that affected almost everything I did up till high school graduation, and this was to attend the United States Military Academy at West Point. Yet, once I was admitted, I realized West Point was not the place for me, for a variety of reasons. So I began my college career at Georgetown University's School of Foreign Service—in part because it had no science or math requirements. When that, too, proved a bad fit, I succumbed to a classic adolescent identity crisis. "Who am I," I wondered, "and what will my future be?" I was lost. Fortunately, a chance encounter with a teammate on the varsity soccer team led me to volunteer at the university hospital day care center. It was this experience that would eventually lead to this book, though the path was by no means straightforward. My first child-development ambition was to become a nursery school teacher, to light a candle rather than curse the darkness. It was, after all, the early 1970s. Eventually, though, enrollment in graduate school at Cornell University fostered a fascination with and love of science, motivating a career doing child- and family-related teaching and research at the college level.

In any event, there I was one day, some thirty-plus years ago, sitting in my office during my first academic job at Penn State University, rifling through a sizable stack of manuscripts that I kept for occasions when I had some free time on my hands. There was no internet back then, or even a personal computer, let alone a smart phone. The paper I picked up, not quite at random (it had been left with me by a future departmental colleague), would dramatically alter—and deepen and enrich—my understanding of child development. Its anthropologist authors, Pat Draper and Henry Harpending, cast my own area of research, the effects of early life on later life—that is, the role of nurture—in an entirely new light. The paper underscored that evolution by natural selection shaped children's responses to their developmental experiences while growing up, influencing who they became.

This, to be honest, was something I had never thought about—not as an undergraduate psychology major, not through the course of earning a master's degree in child development and PhD in human development, and still not in the first decade or so of a career as a professor at a major research university. This, no doubt, is why it blew my mind. As I make clear in the early chapters of this book, I was not by any means immediately persuaded by what I read about evolution shaping children's developmental responses to their early-life experiences, however intriguing I found it. But it did set me on a wonderful intellectual journey, changing how I thought about nature, nurture, and human development. I hope *The Nature of Nurture* will do the same for its readers.

I was a student of nurture through and through—and I still am, as this book attests. But stimulated by this one paper, my thinking about and understanding of human development, as well as what I taught my students about it, was radically transformed. This was especially so with respect to the focus of this book, the short- and long-term effects of early-life experiences on later development. No longer would I be able to embrace the "perfectibility-of-man" developmental perspective that I cut my teeth on, now that I appreciated that such thinking represented an idealized and romanticized view of human nature.

This is probably why I find it so dismaying that the ideas and arguments advanced in *The Nature of Nurture* have exerted so modest an impact on the study, understanding, and treatment of children, especially given that many of these understandings are foundational to the study of all other living things on this planet. As I say in the opening chapter of this book, it is high time that those of us who are interested in and care about children, families, and societies moved beyond the prevailing view of how children come to develop as they do.

Central to the Darwinian perspective at the heart of *The Nature of Nurture* is the idea that we have to look at our own species in the same way we view all other forms of life on this planet. That means recognizing how natural selection works and what it achieves—which is not always health, wealth, and happiness, or even longevity. These *can* be means to fundamental evolutionary ends, but only under certain conditions, which unfortunately don't always characterize human experience. In consequence, natural selection has shaped human development to respond to other conditions in strikingly different ways, which is what the first part of the book is all about.

Evolutionary insight also challenges the assumption, so often made, that children are inherently developmentally plastic, shaped by their lived experiences. This is not to say that early-life conditions don't affect all children. (Clearly, for example, children pick up only whatever languages they are surrounded by.) What the second half of this book makes clear, however, is that some children are more receptive and susceptible than others to what they are exposed to in their early years when it comes to who they will become.

As I trust I make clear throughout the book, the Darwinian perspective does not imply a nihilistic view of human development. Having said that, I do understand—and even respect—that some hesitate to embrace the evolutionary nature-of-nurture view advanced herein. After all, it took me a while to get on board, too, with such a new way of thinking about whether, how, and why early-life conditions shape child (and even adult) development. These are topics of great personal, familial, and societal importance.

What has proven so surprising to me as I have moved from viewing development in perfectibility-of-man black and white to seeing it in evolutionary color has been the discovery that putting on modern evolutionary lenses does not require a wholesale rejection of the standard developmental canon about the effects of nurture on human development. Just to be clear, then, this is not a book that repudiates the view that sensitive, supportive care can foster much of what most of us value: emotional security, psychological autonomy, a caring social orientation, and a capacity for intimacy and relationship commitment that supports rearing children in a manner that promotes such well-being. Nor is it a book that denies the undermining effects of early-life adversities that foster the development of insecurity, advantage-taking, antisocial behavior, and insufficient care for offspring (all too often passing sins perpetrated on parents during their own childhoods to subsequent generations). *The Nature of Nurture* also embraces the view that genetic differences between individuals influence how they develop—but at the same time recognizes that, just as the effects of nurture have been exaggerated, the same is true of the effects of DNA.

As I have become ever more enamored with the insights that modern evolutionary thinking affords, and conducted and advocated for research testing such insights—the scientific imperative—I have long thought about writing a book on the topic. Two things have impeded that ambition. The most important, no doubt, has been the question of whether such a task was beyond me. Decades of scholarship have taught me that, unlike certain colleagues I admire, I am principally a writer of scholarly articles, not book-length manuscripts. The second, of course, has been the challenge of finding the necessary time. In that regard, my somewhat earlier-than-expected retirement has proved to be a blessing in disguise. I hope readers will find my time well spent.

# The Nature of Nurture

# Introduction
## *Biological Gravity*

It is generally accepted that the more bad experiences one has while growing up (such as being exposed to domestic violence), and the fewer good experiences one has (such as being cared for by devoted parents), the more likely it is that one's development will go awry. In other words, children with difficult childhoods—and the adolescents and adults they become—are more likely to manifest dysfunction and dysregulation, if not diagnosable disorder. And this is presumed to be true even if a substantial role in who each of us becomes is thought to be played by genetics.

I share these widely embraced observations not so much to herald the importance of the conditions that characterize children's lives (though this will be a major focus of *The Nature of Nurture*), but rather to highlight the common belief captured in them, which I suspect most readers found perfectly unremarkable: the notion that development "goes awry" in the face adverse childhood experiences, so-called ACEs.

The very idea that development can go awry more or less presumes that there is a non-awry—and thus correct—way to develop. Things turn problematic, then, when conditions of adversity block the way that nature intended humans to develop. These are widespread and fundamental ideas about the effects of children's experiences and exposures that this book challenges, upon viewing development through modern evolutionary lenses.

Many find it difficult to accept that humans and their development have been influenced by the same evolutionary forces that shape all living things on this planet. I am speaking here about my fellow academics who study children's development, about those who make policies or engage in practices designed to foster the well-being of children, and about the families and communities affected by those policies and their underlying ideologies. My intent in this book, then, is to challenge this avoidance or ignorance of modern evolutionary understanding by sharing what such a perspective reveals about why, how, and for whom early-life experiences shape later life.

It is well past time the study of children's developmental responses to the nurture they experience moved into the twenty-first century, surrendering what I have come to regard as idealized and romanticized views of who we humans are, and why children and adolescents develop the way they do. We are a form of life that functions in accord with the same evolutionary principles that guide all other living things on the planet. The refusal decades ago to accept and embrace this reality was responsible, at least in part, for separating the social sciences from the life sciences, a schism that by now should be seen as a huge mistake. In making this claim, I am just rephrasing the famous and controversial view advanced by the great evolutionary biologist E. O. Wilson in the final chapter of his 1975 book, *Sociobiology*.[1] Time has proved his argument for the incorporation of biological, and especially evolutionary, understanding in non-biological fields to be prescient. The fact that, for the most part, this has still not occurred in developmental science is the motivation behind this book.

To be clear, I write these words as someone who for quite a long time rejected the very evolutionary insights that are central to this volume. Why? For the same reason that many others did: I simply didn't like what they seemed to suggest, because I erroneously believed they implied that biology is destiny. Eventually, as a scientist, I came to see my intellectual resistance as unsustainable. Scientists studying virtually all other forms of life take evolutionary considerations for granted as a starting point in their efforts. Could we humans really be that different? If not, as I will argue, then why do child development textbooks still have so little to say about evolution (beyond spurious references to "survival of the species" and, perhaps in passing, to John Bowlby's theory of attachment)? This lacuna becomes especially evident when we turn to the widely discussed issue at the heart of this book: whether and how children's early lives shape who they become.

What I have come to appreciate is that the process of evolution by natural selection, Charles Darwin's world-shattering insight, served to change individuals—and thereby species—in ways that increase their chances of flourishing, meaning *surviving to reproduce* and thus produce descendants. That is why those changes are referred to as *adaptations:* They better fit the organism to the environment in which it finds itself, thus increasing its chances of such (reproductive) flourishing. It is important to recall that Darwin did not know about genes and thus could not explain *how* adaptations are passed on to future generations; he knew only that there must be something that would account for the process. One cannot but wonder how much further he might have developed his theory had he been familiar with George Mendel's famous work—which apparently sat unread on his bookshelves—on the inherited traits of smooth and wrinkled peas.

A groundbreaking extension of Darwinian evolutionary thinking that is central to this book is still not widely appreciated by many, perhaps especially in developmental science, even though the theoretical insight dates back to 1964.[2] It was made by an English biologist, William Hamilton, while he was still a PhD student. Hamilton realized that it is not just children and grandchildren who carry—and can thus pass on—an individual's genes into the future, but siblings and more distantly related kin, as well. The closer the biological kinship to an individual, the more this will be the case. Full siblings and offspring share on average 50 percent of an individual's genes, nephews and nieces less (25 percent), and first cousins even less (12.5 percent). Natural selection thus involves *kin selection,* referring to the fact that what are subject to natural selection are genes shared by oneself and one's blood relatives. A related term, *inclusive fitness,* refers to the sum total of the genes passed on by a person and that individual's kin who also carry them. On average, then, someone who has lots of siblings and a large extended family will likely have more of their genes present in future generations than someone else who has only one or two siblings and few relatives. This generalization, of course, comes with the important qualification *ceteris paribus,* meaning "all other things being equal"—which they rarely are.

This book relates the story of two evolution-inspired and quite original predictions that I advanced over the years—in an effort to test the utility of evolutionary analysis—about *why, how, and for whom* early-life conditions might influence children's long-term social, emotional, and behavioral development. As more and more evidence has emerged that is at the very least not inconsistent with these hypotheses, I remain surprised and disappointed that, although the empirical fruits of this work have been widely embraced by developmental scientists, its theoretical evolutionary foundations have not. Lamenting this fact, I have sometimes used an analogy: Imagine entering a dark house with many treasures behind locked doors, and happening upon a flashlight that allows you to find the key to enter a first room and enjoy its riches—but then discarding that illuminating tool, making it less likely that keys to other rooms, also filled with hidden treasures, will be found.

This book is structured in two parts, each devoted to one of the hypotheses that radically changed my view of human development as they received empirical support. Part I tells the story of the *puberty hypothesis,* a theory of how early-life conditions affect development from childhood through adolescence to adulthood, from the first ideas that formed the hypothesis to the evidence that emerged consistent with it. Part II does the same for the *differential susceptibility hypothesis,* which adds nuance to what is asserted in the first part by noting that effects of early-life conditions vary across individuals, and clarifying which children are most and least affected by them. In telling this story of the development of my own and others' evolutionary-developmental (evo-devo) thinking, I make a concerted effort to give our critics serious consideration, as I trust will become apparent. I emphasize questions and challenges that have arisen in the minds of others, as well as in my own mind.

IT IS IMPORTANT to flag that, in the text that follows, the term *nature* is used in at least two ways. The first, much more the focus of popular attention than the other, is the usage referring to what I will call *Mendelian nature*—that is, how differences in genetic makeup, or DNA, help to account for variations in how individuals think, behave, and develop, as well as in aspects of their health and many other areas. Hardly a week goes by without an announcement on social media or in the popular press that some feature of human development, a phenotype, has proven to be heritable, the result of an individual's genetic makeup. Most of us have seen such stories, be they about intelligence, obesity, or mental health problems.

While taking Mendelian nature seriously, this book will emphasize more what can be thought of as Darwinian-Hamiltonian nature, which for simplicity's sake will be labeled *Darwinian nature* in these pages. It refers to how the ancestral history of our species shapes who we are, and how and why we develop as we do within the varying contexts of our early lives. For the most part, such evolutionary analysis focuses not on differences among individuals in the traits (such as height and athletic ability) that are the concern of Mendelian genetics, but on commonalities of our species as a whole—for example, that we have two arms and two legs, we tend to form families for rearing children, and we develop through "stages," from infancy to early childhood to adolescence and so on.

Of course, Mendelian genetics play a critical role in all of this, because genes that have been selected for over the course of our evolutionary history are responsible for why we all share so much in common and why, at the same time, we differ from one another in so many ways. With regard to the latter, we also need to appreciate that different populations can be genetically—and phenotypically—different because of their ancestral histories. For example, people whose ancestors lived high up in the Andes are typically more barrel-chested because, across many generations, individuals born with greater lung capacity were better equipped to thrive in a relatively oxygen-poor environment. Just as important to appreciate is that, even among such populations, individuals vary in their abilities to oxygenate the hemoglobin cells in the blood that carry oxygen throughout the body. In fact, among women living at high altitudes, those with the greatest levels of oxygenation produce, as a group, the largest number of live births across their lifetimes, thereby passing on more of their genes.[3]

Elsewhere I have written about how the understanding of human development is disconnected from the perspectives of *both* the Darwinian and the Mendelian traditions.[4] What I find particularly surprising about this disconnectedness is that it flies in the face of the so-called Modern Synthesis that emerged in biology in the early to mid-twentieth century, quite some time ago now.[5] This intellectual revolution succeeded in integrating what had been separate ways of looking at evolution—specifically, Darwinian natural selection and adaptation with Mendelian genetics. It created a comprehensive framework for understanding, among other things, how evolution works at the molecular level—via the selection of genes that contribute to adaptations.

This integration of Darwinian and Mendelian natures, despite how historic and fruitful it has proved to be, seems not to have influenced how developmental scientists think about the widely studied effects of early-life conditions on later psychological and behavioral development, especially with regard to Hamilton's insights. Indeed, as I think back to when I first began to consider the possibility that evolution influenced how children are shaped by the contextual conditions to which they are exposed, I knew of only one developmental psychologist who considered both Darwinian and Mendelian nature as he sought to illuminate effects of nurture. This was David Rowe, who sadly died at a rather young age. While he was an early—and most reasonable—critic of the ideas that are central to the first part of this book, he unfortunately never got to see what future research would reveal.

One of the goals of this book, then, is to move developmental thinking and inquiry toward its own, much delayed, modern synthesis by considering Darwinian adaptation by natural selection, Hamiltonian kin selection and inclusive fitness, and Mendelian genetics, all while primarily focusing on early-life environmental influences on children's later development. Perhaps I should have titled this book in the plural: *The Natures of Nurture*. While David Rowe certainly would not have abandoned the view that genetic differences matter a great deal (nor should he have), I think that, given his open-mindedness and commitment to empirical inquiry and theoretical integration, he would have come to embrace the very kind of developmental synthesis this book is all about.

BECAUSE THIS BOOK is also very much about *nurture,* let me make clear how that term will be used. Nurture will refer to more than just how parents bring up their children, or fail to. It will also encompass other *developmental experiences,* as well as *environmental exposures* within and beyond the family. Whereas the former term refers to the actual "lived experiences" of a child—like receiving sensitive care from parents, being bullied by a sibling, or having supportive friends—the latter refers to the broader context of development. These more distal conditions—like living in a dangerous neighborhood, growing up on a farm, or attending an overcrowded public school—also have been referred to as "social addresses" because they are only probabilistically (that is, imperfectly) associated with more "proximate," lived experiences. For example, two children could grow up in the same violent neighborhood, but its effects might be manifested in the behavioral development of only one of them. Thus, more distal exposures are presumed to be less tightly tied to (and less likely to influence) how children develop than more proximate ones.

In the terminology of this book, then, environmental exposures are most likely to shape development when they also affect developmental experiences. For example, it is principally when life in a violent neighborhood (the environmental exposure) results in parents' being stressed and engaging in severe discipline (the developmental experience) that we might expect a child growing up there to be prone to antisocial behavior. If a set of parents in a violent neighborhood can provide supportive care, as many certainly do, this could override distal risk and prevent otherwise anticipated problematic developments.

Another way of thinking about this relation between distal and proximate sources of influence is in terms of *protective factors,* a term introduced to the study of child development by my friend and colleague Dante Cicchetti of the University of Minnesota. Protective factors can mitigate the influence of adverse distal conditions, buffering development so that perhaps expected problematic developmental sequelae do not materialize.[6] Sensitive-supportive parenting and the establishment of a secure attachment to the parent have been found to buffer otherwise anticipated adverse effects of negative contextual conditions.[7] But there is every reason to presume that many other protective factors can operate in the same way—including, for example, high-quality childcare, a special uncle or aunt providing the nurture and support lacking in a nuclear family, or close friends supplying psychological nourishment. This would account for why plenty of children who grow up in high-risk contexts do not develop problematically.

By the same token, growing up in conditions of affluence does not ensure the absence of developmental risk, and especially not when socioeconomic advantage (an environmental exposure) coincides with the developmental experience of insensitive or neglectful family relationships.[8] The implication of all this, and a theme that will run through this book, is that development is complex, shaped by multiple factors and forces. Simplistic explanations of influence will thus be avoided—such as claims that it's just the genes that matter, or just the environment, or the early years and not the later ones, or peers rather than parents who are influential. I know from years of teaching about child development that complexity and conditionality can be frustrating to those looking for simple answers to complex questions; the same goes for the levels of uncertainty and ambiguity that must be tolerated in any serious inquiry into why development operates as it does and particular children develop the way they do.

In a prior book, *The Origins of You,* I compared human development to the weather. On any particular day or week or year, the weather is multiply determined. It is not a function of just wind speed, for example, or humidity, temperature, or precipitation. It is the complex interaction of many factors that makes it virtually impossible to predict precisely and with complete certainty what the weather will be, especially over longer periods of time.[9] This reality is nicely captured by the meteorologist Edward Norton Lorenz's image of a butterfly flapping its wings in Brazil and producing a first movement of air that goes on to spin up a tornado in Texas.[10] Of course, this does not mean that prediction is hopeless, only that it is limited and constrained. And if that is so in the case of weather forecasting, a science much more advanced than the study of human development, we have to be humble about any claim to understand how a particular child—or children more generally—will develop. But that should not stop us from continuing our scientific efforts to do so. This book tells the story of one such effort to do just that, which I helped launch and have been involved in for quite some time now.


MY TITLE FOR this book is cribbed from the title of a groundbreaking 2011 paper by a friend and one-time departmental colleague, Robert Plomin, now of Kings College, London. (Thank you, Robert!)[11] That paper illuminated the role of Mendelian genetics in shaping the nurture or lack thereof which children receive, a subject addressed in detail in Chapter 6. This book seeks to do the same by underscoring how children's developmental responses to the support or adversity they experience while growing up are shaped by natural selection in service of *the same fundamental goal of all living things.* And what might that goal be? It is the passing on of one's genes to direct descendants and other kin—that is, *inclusive fitness* via *kin selection.*

Having said that, let me repeat something stipulated earlier. Given how genetic inheritance works, closer blood relations—like parents, siblings, and children—carry more of each other's genes than do more distant relatives, like nieces and cousins. This is why one famous biologist, J. B. S. Haldane, said the following to illustrate the fundamental importance of inclusive fitness: "I would lay down my life for two brothers or eight cousins!"[12] The fact is that, because Haldane's eight first cousins, just like his two siblings, on average collectively carry 100 percent of his own genes, the genetic impact of losing his life while saving either set of relatives would be the same. With 100 percent of his genes retained, the elimination of his own life would not represent a genomic loss at all. Laying down one's life for less would be less likely, *ceteris paribus*. In sum, kin selection is the process by which inclusive fitness is fostered; the former is the means to the latter end.

Difficult as it may be to embrace this gene-centric worldview, this is how so much of life on this planet works.[13] In light of this insight, this book addresses the following evolutionary question: *If being developmentally plastic—that is, susceptible to environmental influences—in childhood heightened the chances of passing on one's genes to future generations, thus increasing reproductive fitness, how would natural selection have shaped children's development?* In other words, do the developmental responses of children to their early-life conditions influence their later lives in ways that make (or at least once made) evolutionary biological sense—meaning that they spell greater success in passing on genes?

Despite what has just been stipulated about the fundamental purpose of all life on this planet, many object—just as I once did—to claims that the evolutionary history of our species has much explanatory power when it comes to accounting for how humans develop, think, and behave, to say nothing about their developmental responses to experiences and exposures encountered while growing up. So, before proceeding to develop the nature-of-nurture ideas at the heart of this book, it is imperative that I address some of these concerns. The remainder of this Introduction first tackles the contention that evolutionary analysis embraces the view that biology is destiny. Then it moves to consideration of the widespread claim that we as a species are special and different from all others—that the laws of evolution applying to other species are not as applicable to us humans. Next to be addressed is another frequent claim, that evolution is first and foremost about survival. All this leads to consideration of whether non-evolutionary explanations of human behavior and development—focused on psychology, physiology, and sociocultural forces—constitute *alternatives* to Darwinian ones, as many seem to believe. Subsequently, attention shifts to the subjects of childlessness, small family size, and abortion, each of which might appear at odds with the claim that the core purpose of life revolves around transmitting genes to future generations. Lastly, the common view that childhood adversity induces developmental disturbance, dysfunction, and disorder will be challenged by considering what else might be going on.

Readers already familiar with evolutionary understanding of these issues and thus the purpose of life—to make more life—should feel free to skim the following sections. But before moving on to Chapter 2, be sure to read the final section of this one, which outlines how the story to be told will unfold and what I would like readers to get from this book.

## Biology as Destiny

Throughout *The Nature of Nurture* the case is made that we need to think about the passing on of genes, the fundamental goal of all living things, as a constant and pervasive source of pressure on child development—a kind of biological gravity that exerts influence on how children respond to nurture broadly conceived. Just as almost nothing goes into the design and manufacture of an aircraft without taking physical gravity into account—so that the plane can fly safely, its fundamental goal—it is useful to think about human development having a similarly essential consideration. Without an understanding of physical gravity, there can be no engineered flight. Is the same true of biological gravity and the understanding of whether and how the nurture that children encounter while growing up shapes who they become? I have come to think so.

The point to be made, though, is just the opposite of how many respond when informed that people develop, think, and behave in certain ways because of how human evolutionary history has shaped our species. Rather than implying that "biology is destiny" and thus there is nothing we can do if we want the world to look different, the insight about biological gravity and human development can lead us to the exact reverse of that conclusion. To appreciate why this is so, consider, as an analogy, that as a species we cannot fly as birds do. But we can and do fly, because airplane designers, going back at least to the Wright brothers at Kitty Hawk, took physical gravity—and so much more—into account and *engineered around these forces*. Because they designed machinery that could overcome gravity—making use of lift, thrust, and aerodynamics—people today enjoy travels that were once unimaginable. The same goes for human development. If we don't want development to proceed in certain ways due to the legacy of evolution, we can enhance our chances of success by taking biological gravity into account and engineering around it.

One of my favorite examples of this is the work of a longtime friend, David Olds, now of the University of Denver School of Medicine. Half a century ago, he developed from scratch a program for poor, young, single mothers that is now world-famous, implemented across America and many other parts of the globe. Appreciating that the life conditions of these mothers would place their own and their offspring's development at risk, he undertook to engineer around various adverse forces to foster well-being. Even though he was not guided by an evolutionary mindset, Olds nevertheless realized that "early intervention" beginning at the age of three or four was already too late for many children growing up in disadvantaged circumstances. He also understood that parenting efforts in the absence of strong social supports often made bad situations only worse.[14]

For these reasons, Olds's program enrolled young women during pregnancy and kept them participating until their children were two years of age, with regular support, encouragement, and expertise provided by specially trained home-visiting nurses with whom the young women could establish enduring and trusting relationships. These frequent home visits focused on myriad developmentally appropriate topics. During pregnancy, they emphasized overcoming unhealthy habits such as smoking and other drug use, and the importance of proper nutrition. Once the baby was born, topics included the benefits of breastfeeding, keys to early childhood nutrition, the importance of talking to the baby, and protecting oneself from an abusive partner. It was because of Olds's insights, devotion to purpose, and rigorous evaluation and documentation of the program's effects that his nurse home-visitation program has come to be regarded as one of the best models for how to "engineer" around adversity. Neither biology nor sociology need be destiny.

## We *Homo sapiens* Are Different

The claim is often made that evolutionary and other explanations that make sense in the case of meerkats, or birds, or even all other species are not as applicable to our own. We are too different for modern evolutionary thinking to apply to us, or at least for it to apply very much. We have culture, we have language, we engage in commerce . . . and so on. What we seem not to realize or appreciate is that the exact same case could be made for every species. Worms are different because they live in the ground, eat dirt, and sometimes survive when cut in half. Birds are different because they fly, build nests, and sometimes bear multiple clutches of offspring in a single breeding season. I could go on, but I won't.

What needs to be appreciated is that each and every species is distinct, which is what makes it a species, usually being able to breed successfully only with other members of the same species. Let's not forget that, whatever we think makes us different, we are not the most successful species on the planet. There are many more ants, mosquitos, and beetles than people. Moreover, there are many things that other living organisms can do that we cannot, such as survive when partially frozen or grow a replacement limb when one is lost. So why should a claim to being special depend more on the characteristics that make *us* different than on the ones that make some other species different? Many might claim specialness for a species whose individual members have consciousness, even free will, to behave in ways they choose, thus perhaps defying biological gravity. The counterargument is that these also reflect the legacy of evolution and are likely to have played a direct or indirect role in the passing on of genes. This will be discussed in detail in the "Alternative Explanations" section below.

The same claim that we humans are not so special extends to this book's subject of how evolution has shaped children's developmental responses to early-life conditions. Simply put, we are not alone when it comes to early-life conditions shaping future development in the service of reproductive ends, the passing on of genes, biological gravity. Indeed, what is striking about the nature-of-nurture theme central to this book is how well appreciated it is among scientists studying the development and behavior of other living things. Consider first in this regard a snail whose shell grows to a greater or lesser thickness depending on whether it, while still in the larval stage, senses chemicals in the water that indicate the presence of predators. A better defense against likely threats, in the form of a thicker shell, is obviously a step in the right direction when it comes to surviving and reproducing. Similarly, juvenile stickleback fish grow their bony defensive spines in greater numbers and sizes if they detect the presence of predators during their early development. As a final example, there is the familiar case of honeybees. Whether they become queens with many offspring or offspring-less workers—whose queen shares 100 percent of their genes—depends on what they are fed as larvae. A diet of royal jelly nourishes the development of a queen, whereas those provided with less nutritious fare become worker bees. In light of these examples, is it so strange a notion that natural selection could also have shaped humans' responses to early-life conditions in ways that promote the passing-on of genes to future generations? A central claim of this book is that the possibility is not so far-fetched!

## Survival Is Not the Goal of Evolution

Oft-repeated statements about "survival of the fittest" and "survival of the species" would seem to imply that evolution is first and foremost about survival. Surviving is important because it is highly useful when it comes to passing on genes. And this is exactly why not surviving is usually not the way to go. Not often appreciated, however, is that not surviving can sometimes be advantageous when it comes to passing on one's own genes, counterintuitive as that observation may be. In fact, *reproduction* of the fittest is a more accurate phrase expressing what evolution is all about. (Note, too, that the "fittest" individuals are those best equipped to succeed in their environment and who thus disperse more genes than others in future generations; the term is not being used in the popular sense of "most physically fit.").

When I became a father, I changed from a guy who was never worried about dying to one who developed what might be called a survival imperative. Why? Because I could imagine the pain and hurt that my children would experience if I were to pass away before they were much older. This was my evolved psychology's way of saying, "protect your genetic investment, Jay." And this is why parents will risk their lives to save their children from drownings or fires, or other mortal threats, à la Haldane. Without even knowing it, they have evolved to protect their—and their ancestors'—genetic legacy. This is not to deny the role that love and devotion play in situations like this, as well as in many others, but rather to underscore that psychological inclinations like these evolved because of their importance to passing on genes to the next generation, as means to that end.

This is also why an elderly Eskimo grandmother might go out to die on an ice floe if resources in her extended family proved limited. Better for her children and grandchildren, who share, respectively, 50 percent and 25 percent of her genes, to survive so they can pass them on—a service that for menopausal reasons she is no longer able to perform. It may even be why women, unlike some other female mammals, evolved to lose their ability to reproduce with advancing age. Theory and some evidence suggest that menopause evolved because grandmothers helping their daughters bear and rear the next generation of offspring succeeded in passing on more of their genes than they would have by bearing additional offspring of their own.[15]

Intriguingly, there is even a similar evolutionary case to be made for suicide. If killing oneself increases the likelihood that one's progeny and kin will survive to reproduce, then the inclination to do so under such conditions may also have evolved. Imagine an ancient Japanese warrior, a samurai, having erred in such a serious way that his disgrace could forever taint his family. He might engage in ritualized suicide by disembowelment, known as *seppuku,* as a means of erasing the shame on him-self—and his family. By protecting the reputation of kin and thereby preventing their being ostracized by the community, the suicide served to increase the chance that his genes, in the bodies of his relatives, would be passed on to future generations.[16] Please appreciate that there is no presumption in any of these cases that the actors are thinking in terms of passing on genes, though some might be.

As already noted with regard to parental love and devotion, it is important not to view such an evolutionary analysis as inimical to a psychological explanation. It may be that when kin resources are meager and individuals come to see themselves as more of a drain than a source of gain—like the previously mentioned Eskimo grandmother—depression is especially likely to increase and serve as a psychological mechanism inducing self-sacrifice. This brings us directly to the next subsection.

## Alternative Explanations

When attention is called to the role of evolution in shaping our species—and each of us as individuals—counterclaims are often advanced. Many contend it is not evolution, and perhaps not even genetics, that influences child development.

Rather, it is the economic status of families, the conditions of their neighborhoods, the availability of helpful friends and relatives, and family dynamics (such as family size and the presence or absence of domestic violence) that shape children's development. Explanations highlighting psychological processes—like attachment security, reinforcement learning, biased attributions, and sensory sensitivity—also get portrayed as alternatives to evolutionary accounts, as do mechanistic explanations involving the biology of the brain, the immune system, the epigenome, and even the microbiome. But what is often not appreciated is that these are not inconsistent with explanations based on evolution. Often, they are part and parcel of complex—and evolved—systems of causation. The aforementioned examples of parental love and devotion and of self-sacrifice illustrate this point.

A helpful way to acknowledge these indisputable sources of influence and avoid treating them as oppositional to evolutionary explanations might be to extend the earlier analogy of aircraft engineering. Which of the following is the reason the plane flies: the engine, the tail fin, or the flaps on the wings? The answer, of course, is that they all matter and must work together to get a flying machine from here to there. Unless it has all these components and subsystems, it cannot fly—they are all necessary means to achieve the desired end.

The same is true of human development and functioning. If the matter of interest is what causes healthy growth in children, understanding that eating matters does not mean denying that sleeping matters. Outcomes for most things, and certainly most living things, are multiply determined by varieties of factors and forces, just like the weather in my prior analogy. Psychological, biological, and behavioral processes are the products of natural selection. Living things could not survive and reproduce if the many parts that comprise them did not evolve to serve these and other functions. Without these mechanisms of influence, genes would be just DNA stuck inside a cell. As any molecular biologist will tell you, the paths from genotypes to phenotypes are long, winding, convoluted, and still not fully understood, even if great progress has been made.[17]

These mechanistic processes can also be thought of as proximate sources of influence, as opposed to ultimate ones. Proximate sources address the *how* of development, ultimate sources address the *why*. For genes to be passed on to future generations—the *why* of development—there must be one or more means to that end, providing the *how*. This is again why psychological, sociological, and physiological explanations of development are not alternatives to evolutionary ones. Consider, for instance, the role played by the psychological processes of attraction, love, and sexual arousal—again, the *how*—in the passing-on of genes to future generations, the *why*. Without these proximate processes, it would be an even greater challenge to produce offspring than it is already.

This critical distinction between *how* and *why* explanations, which will be a recurring theme in this book, also applies to claims asserting that we develop and function the way we do because of the society and culture in which we grow up. And this is because our societies and cultures, too, are means to the same reproductive end of passing on genes to future generations. Indeed, the argument can be made that differences in the organizations and operations of cultures reflect the fact that the best ways to succeed in passing genes on to future generations varied according to the conditions of the different economies and social systems that grew up in particular locales, and these in turn were outgrowths of those locales' unique geographic characteristics and ecologies. For example, people who lived near bodies of water typically fished, whereas those who lived inland made their living in other ways. In one culture, survival—and thereby reproduction—might have been enhanced by swimming ability, whereas in another it could have benefited from learning when in the year trees produced edible fruit. The point is that the ways of developing and behaving induced by a culture in its members—which can be strikingly different across cultures—fundamentally facilitate the passing on of genes to future generations, no doubt through a long and complex process. It is difficult to imagine much reproductive success happening without individuals sticking to the "scripts" stipulating what being a member of a particular society and culture entails.

Let me call attention to two lines of research that nicely illustrate the points just made. The first looked at differences in social orientation in societies depending on whether their main economic activity was rice-growing or wheat-growing. The evidence showed that these two economic mainstays, because of the different requirements to successfully raise these crops, gave rise to different social relations.[18] In the case of rice-growing, it was difficult to plant and harvest a crop on one's own, let alone maintain critical irrigation systems, and therefore farm families had to work together. Rice-based societies tended to have communal and interdependent social relations. In contrast, wheat farmers were far less reliant on other wheat farmers as they planted and harvested their product, so societies based on wheat economies valued autonomy and independence more than interdependent rice-growing ones did. An insight here is that, as explanations of how rice- and wheat-based societies (and many other societies) operate, geography, culture, and psychology are not alternatives—they are intertwined.[19]

The second line of research concerns psychological differences in individuals who live in places where water is scarce versus places where it is plentiful. Data collected from eighty-two countries revealed, for example, that people who live where water is limited place more value on thinking for the long term and less on living in the moment than do those who reside in water-rich environments.[20]

Critically, such tendencies in social relations and psychological orientation are not written in the different genes of those who reside in these contrasting contexts. Instead, humans evolved to create the psychologies and cultures that enable survival and reproductive success in the physical and economic circumstances in which they found themselves. In short, there is no one way to get the job of life done—although, as will be seen later in this chapter, there most certainly are ways not to.

What all this implies is that culture-making is also in our genes—in the Darwinian and Hamiltonian sense, not the Mendelian one. By that I mean that our species evolved to create and rely on culture because of its utility in passing on genes to future generations, in whatever ecology a population lived. This, of course, is not true of all creatures; mosquitoes and polar bears have developed instincts to guide their behaviors toward other members of their species, but lack the human capacity to make different decisions about how to structure family, community, and societal relations.

To repeat, then, the argument being advanced doesn't mean that the people who grew up to grow rice would not have learned to grow wheat if they had grown up in a different culture than the one they did because they lacked the genes for doing so. Rather, culture is very much like language (which, of course, is a central feature of a culture). Where we grow up and live typically determines the particular language we speak, so people around the world speak different languages. The capacity for language, however, is universal, a capability that evolved long ago.[21]

We thus need to avoid pitting proximate and more distal determinants of how we develop, think, and behave—family, economy, society, culture, and even history—against evolution by natural selection. When these systems and forces do not fit together, a culture either does not emerge or it eventually declines, because people fail to pass on their genes to the extent necessary to sustain it. Thus, it is how the many forces shaping us go together that enables cultures and populations to endure. This is because, rather than genes and reproductive success first and foremost serving culture, it's the other way around.

That said, it also needs to be appreciated that a culture, once it proves sustainable, can itself become a selective sieve, allowing for genes to be passed along or not according to their influence on ways of functioning that best fit important practices in that culture; this is referred to by anthropologists as "gene-culture coevolution." It operates this way: because individuals with certain genes tend to fit the culture better than those lacking those genes, the former are more likely to survive and reproduce, and perhaps the population eventually reaches the point that everyone carries the genes in question. Geneticists refer to this as a population being driven to "fixation" on a gene, with no alternative variants still existing.

## What about Childlessness?

Evolution by natural selection does not imply that every individual will develop, think, behave, and function in ways advantageous to passing genes on to the next generation. As noted above, biology is a probabilistic and complex system. In a deterministic system—the classic case being Newtonian physics—things happen in unvarying ways. The earth goes around the sun and rotates on its axis without exception. In a probabilistic system such as a biological ecosystem, on the other hand, perfect consistency is not the rule, and processes don't always operate as expected.

Thus, while natural selection regularly produces particular effects, this is not always so, sometimes for sound evolutionary reasons. Even if developing in a certain way proved in the past to be generally a better strategy for passing on genes in a given harsh environment, that was probably not the case all of the time, nor will it be today. Not every evolved way of developing in response to varying conditions of nurture, broadly conceived, ends up increasing an individual's reproductive fitness (again, defined as the spread of his or her genes to future generations). Yet this is not evidence that natural selection has failed to shape us generally to respond successfully to our particular early-life conditions.

Evolution, then, is like baseball. Just as even a great hitter does not get a hit every single time at bat, evolutionary adaptations do not always yield the fitness-enhancing results that allowed them to persist. That reality is not a disconfirmation of the theory of evolution by natural selection and its effects on behavior and development. We know that seat belts save lives, and the fact that they sometimes fail to do so, and have even occasionally caused a person's demise, is of course no reason to abandon wearing them.

The baseball analogy also applies, perhaps even more strongly, to the case of childlessness. It is rather common, when one advances the argument that the passing-on of genes is the fundamental goal of all living things (humans included), to have someone object by pointing to the incidence of voluntary childlessness. This is not an unreasonable issue to raise—but individuals who forego parenting, even as they represent exceptions, don't disprove the rule that evolution has shaped life first and foremost to achieve reproductive success. At least, they do not necessarily, given the theories about kin selection and inclusive fitness noted above. To understand why, consider a simple question: Do childless individuals with siblings, nieces, nephews, or cousins—some of which have children and others of which will someday—ever help those relatives in any way? If they do, then they are aiding and abetting the spread of their own genes which are also carried by these relatives.

Assistance to relatives with children can be direct or indirect. Providing direct support could include buying books for nieces, nephews, or cousins, counseling them about the best ways to behave, or contributing to their college funds. Indirect help could just involve being emotionally supportive of and available to relatives with children. Either way, the effect, whether appreciated or not, is to boost the prevalence of the non-reproducing person's genes in subsequent generations. We can compare this to some bird species whose offspring, under certain ecological conditions, forego their own breeding for a season to assist their parents in raising a next brood. These species evolved to feature such "helpers at the nest" because the effect of the additional care was to enable more of the helpers' genes—as shared by their siblings—to be carried forward to future generations than would be the case if they departed the nest earlier to breed themselves.

The point here is that glib dismissals of evolutionary analysis usually fail to acknowledge or understand the inclusive-fitness character of kin selection. Just to be clear, this is not to say that, for humans in the modern era, social processes of the helper-at-the-nest kind still yield the reproductive return that they likely once did. But again, and as will be stipulated repeatedly, even if such impulses no longer make much difference to the abundance of the helper's genes in subsequent generations, this does not mean the helping processes favored by past kin selection have ceased to be part of our psychological and behavioral makeup.

A good example of someone failing to appreciate the reality of inclusive fitness shows up in the 1992 movie *The Last of the Mohicans,* when an Indian warrior, Magua, threatens the English solider, whom he calls Grey Hair, in especially malevolent terms: "When the Grey Hair is dead, Magua will eat his heart. Before he dies, Magua will put his children under the knife, so the Grey Hair will know his seed is wiped out forever." What Magua could not have understood given the historical context of the story—set in a time two centuries before the evolutionary significance of inclusive fitness was recognized—was that even with the daughters dead, Grey Hair's seed (that is, his DNA) would still exist to a large extent in his siblings, nieces, nephews, cousins, and their offspring. It would hardly be wiped out forever with the killing of only Grey Hair and his direct descendants.

Before moving on from the subject of childlessness, one more fact of modern life must be noted, particularly for its impact in advanced economies, whether in Europe, Asia, or North America. Across the past several decades, the ecology of human development has been utterly transformed by the sciences and practices of controlling reproduction. Starting with the availability of well-manufactured condoms for men and contraceptive pills for women, today's options to avoid having children are now so widely understood, accepted, and reliable that the decision to start a family is now quite decoupled from the choice to enjoy sex. As a result, in many countries of the world, including the United States, birthrates have fallen below replacement level. America's population would be shrinking were it not for its ability to attract immigrants.

This is a situation that evolution has never confronted before—and perhaps the day will come when our species has been meaningfully reshaped by these technologies and their effects on natural selection. But again, for purposes of this book, the fact that we live in a world in which biological conditions have been fundamentally disrupted and sex need not have the reproductive consequences it once did does not mean that the physiological, cognitive, emotional, and behavioral machinery that succeeded best in passing on genes under the old laws of biological gravity is not still operative and detectable. This claim is in line with Richard Dawkins's reminder, in *The Genetic Book of the Dead,* that the "Darwinian sculptor's sharp chisels penetrate every internal cranny and nook of an animal," including its physiology and even down to "the sub-microscopic interior of cells and the high-speed chemical wheels that turn therein."[22]

## Small Family Size

Central to modern evolutionary thinking is the claim that living things seek to maximize their reproductive success, the spread of their genes through future generations. This would seem to suggest that being more reproductively successful is a simple matter of having more children—and nieces, nephews, and other kin. But this is not the case. Maximizing the pass-along of genes is more complex than that—starting with the fact that having more children than can be protected and supported can put all the children at risk. There is a delicate balance between the number of offspring and reproductive success. The challenge, then, is getting the number of children right, or as close to right as possible, a probabilistic process for sure given the inherent uncertainty of the future.

Having more children than one can provide tolerably decent care for can be risky when it comes to passing on genes. But when an environment is so dangerous that child survival to reproductive age is unlikely, it can make biological sense to "go for broke" and keep having more and more children. Short of this, in a somewhat risky developmental landscape it can make (reproductive) sense to produce an additional child or two to raise the odds of at least a couple of them reaching reproductive age and being able to pass along their genes—and their parents' genes. In much safer and more secure contexts, parents hoping for the same result might decide that having just two children would suffice.

Perhaps the best evidence of such strategic thinking by parents shows up in national population statistics, as societies reliably undergo what is known as the "demographic transition" from high birth (and death) rates to low rates as they attain higher levels of female education and technology adoption. Where great uncertainty reigns—as in conditions of poverty—families tend to be quite large. But family size shrinks dramatically when more women who would in the past have remained uneducated gain the skills to better control their own and their children's destinies. With training, they become more able to provide the protection and secure the resources needed to raise offspring to reproductive age. The children of more-educated mothers may be fewer in number, but by dodging child mortality and getting more parental attention and care, they grow into adults capable of competing socially and producing more and healthier grandchildren.

But the modern era raises an interesting conundrum. Why are family sizes in today's affluent societies so small, with so many having just one or two children? In all likelihood a big role in this is played by reliable contraception, a modern reality already mentioned. But other factors include the expansion of women's occupational opportunities outside the household; the reduction of help with childrearing that comes with fewer relatives and increased physical distance from them; and the scarcity of alternative childcare options.

It may even be that small family sizes under these conditions make evolutionary sense by the laws of biological gravity. Might many parents today have a sense, however unconscious, that the future will require more nuclear-family resources than were previously needed to bring children—and grandchildren—to maturity? Consider America's ballooning costs of housing, childcare, and education, for example. Could smaller families reflect, at least in part, a strategy of husbanding resources so they are not spread too thinly across too many (very likely surviving) offspring and even grandchildren? Of course the answer cannot be known—but this is the kind of speculation that evolutionary analysis affords, and in which we can certainly enjoy engaging. Having said that, it is critically important not to mistake speculation (or theoretically informed hypothesis) for established fact.

Whatever factors and forces have led to it, the decrease in family size may well explain, again via reproductive logic, the very high levels of parent involvement seen in many societies today. Think about so-called helicopter parenting. This may be the simple result of parents putting their eggs in so few baskets, even when risks to survival would appear minimal. If, for example, an only child dies or is rendered by disease or injury unable to reproduce, the transmission of genes to future generations is cut off; after a certain point, earlier for women than men, it becomes impossible to bear another child. So, what does one do? Make sure that child is safe and secure, even if that means overprotected.

## What about Abortion?

If the evolutionary imperative is to pass on genes, then rising rates of pregnancy termination might seem hard to explain. Abortion is wholly inconsistent with that objective, right?

Yes and no. Obviously, an aborted fetus cannot pass on genes. Yet humans have been aborting babies before birth and practicing infanticide after it throughout human history. Why? As the anthropologist Sarah Hrdy and others have pointed out, bearing and raising children is an "investment."[23] But because parental investment—the term used by evolutionary biologists to describe what most of us refer to as parenting and more generally nurture—doesn't always pay off, people have evolved to evaluate the yield it is likely to return. The way they think about this depends to a great extent on a mother's condition, health- and resource-wise, and therefore her expectations of the future.

From the standpoint of passing on genes to future generations, abortion or infanticide is the logical equivalent of removing a stock from an investment portfolio when its future value prospects are negative. Under conditions of adversity that threaten the eventual reproductive success of a fetus or newborn, it can be reproductively strategic not to squander limited resources and risk undermining the life chances of children already born, or potentially to come later. Perhaps there are already too many mouths to feed, the infant is unhealthy, or conditions for childbearing and rearing are expected to improve substantially. Why undermine the ability to take advantage of a potentially more promising future by committing resources to a risky investment now? Given the imperative to make such reproductively strategic calculations, Hrdy observes, mother love is not unconditional. And choices to cull offspring, however unethical or illegal they may be, can be recognized as consistent with the objective of maximizing the transmission of genes to future generations. That is why, Hrdy argues, infanticide has been a feature of the human condition for millennia. (Just to be clear, this should not be read to imply that either she or I condone it.)

Indeed, the most astonishing point to be made about abortion and infanticide, as viewed from the perspective of passing on genes to future generations, is that it can be in the best interest *of the very life that is taken* to be treated this way! To understand why this is so, recall again the ideas of kin selection and inclusive fitness. Imagine that a particular family is like an overburdened boat, not yet taking on water but at very high risk of doing so. One more person on board could bring things to the tipping point, causing the boat to founder and sending all family members into the drink. If that life were sacrificed and the effect was to avoid the tipping over, the siblings could grow up, have their own offspring, and pass on the substantial percentage of the victim's genes shared by each of them. Certainly, the genes of the terminated life would be more likely to be passed on than would be the case if the new addition lived to see the day that the entire family was plunged into the water and drowned. Thus, the pressure of biological gravity can cause practices like abortion and infanticide to be selected for in some measure, and be part of the evolution of how parents and families function.

## Disturbance, Dysfunction, and Disorder

A major objective of this book, which will come into greater focus in Chapter 1, is to encourage a different perspective on many ways of functioning that tend to be regarded as evidence of psychological, emotional, and behavioral disturbance, dysfunction, and disorder. The argument is that viewing them through the lens of evolution by natural selection and the passing on of genes may reveal them to be anything but that. One such condition is attention-deficit hyperactivity disorder (ADHD), which may not be a disorder at all when considered from an evolutionary standpoint.[24] Consider experimental research showing that individuals whose scores on a reliable screening measure put them in the ADHD category engaged in more efficient foraging than their peers.[25] Specifically, while playing an online game simulating berry-patch foraging, they were quicker than others to spot and move to nearby bushes offering more abundant berries than the one they had been depleting. This is clearly not a disturbed, dysregulated, or dysfunctional way of behaving.[26] Indeed, this is consistent with evolutionary optimal foraging theory.[27] Perhaps even more noteworthy, given the focus here on reproduction, is evidence that psychopathic traits like impulsivity, manipulative behavior, and lack of empathy, which are associated with parental neglect and neighborhood violence, are also associated with heightened sexual behavior, including greater numbers of dating and sexual partners.[28]

To fully appreciate these findings and others like them, we must embrace two ideas which together challenge the notion (widespread among professionals and citizens alike) that ways of functioning that are not valued in contemporary society necessarily reflect dysfunction and disturbance. The first idea, addressed just below, involves what will be referred to as hidden talents. The second idea, taken up in Chapter 1, involves the idealization and romanticization of child development in Western culture.

It is known that children growing up in adverse conditions (such as poverty, child abuse, domestic violence, and dangerous neighborhoods) are more likely to become aggressive, antisocial, uncooperative, and depressed, and to prove to be abusive spouses, harsh or neglectful parents, unfriendly neighbors, and unproductive workers. Recognizing this, most of us—certainly including myself, early in my career—have viewed these ways of developing as evidence of psychological, emotional, and behavioral "damage." Many child development theories and perspectives presume these are not the way humans are "supposed" to develop. As we will see in Chapter 1, they say that children develop this way when, because they have not received the care they should, they have not been able to realize their "potential."

A counterclaim central to this book is that humans—probably like many other species—have evolved the capacity to develop in a variety of ways depending on their particular contextual conditions early in life and on which ways yield the greatest pass-along of genes under those conditions. From this perspective, ways of developing that we don't value today, like the ones listed just above, can be just as natural and appropriate in some childhood conditions as their (societally preferred) opposites are in other conditions. How could aggression, abuse, and so on be part of a development path conducive to passing along genes? Because adversity has certainly been a long-standing feature of human experience on this planet, whether in the form of natural disasters, such as floods and fires, or conflicts with other groups of humans.

In other words, the so-called good and bad ways that humans develop and behave, especially in response to, respectively, supportive and adverse childhoods, can reflect human evolution in the service of inclusive-fitness goals. Additionally, there is no one best way to serve evolutionary fitness across all conditions of childhood. Implicit in this framing is an appreciation that growing up under different conditions results in different patterns of development, any of which might constitute a sound "strategy" for passing on one's genes. Thus, the experience of adversity has not so much disrupted psychological and neurobiological development as it has directed that development to function adaptively in the face of a stressful childhood. Consider, as a rather dramatic example of the point, evidence that among young men of known involvement with criminal justice, those who score high on measures of psychopathy tend to engage in more impersonal, precocious, and coercive sexuality—which of course is not unrelated to reproduction, even if that is probably not the conscious intent of such perpetrators.[29]

Appreciating that adversity might foster ways of developing that are psychologically, behaviorally, or reproductively strategic, even if not valued by mainstream society, has led some recent scholars to investigate the unique strengths or skills of those who have long been regarded as developmentally compromised. These capabilities have been labeled "hidden talents" by my friends and colleagues Bruce Ellis of the University of Utah and Willem Frankenhuis of the University of Amsterdam in the Netherlands.[30] The word *talents* reflects the view that developmental responses to being raised under conditions of adversity can improve children's fitness and thus chances of surviving and reproducing in the world they are likely— or once were likely—to encounter. *Hidden* refers to the general lack of recognition that some (and perhaps many) putative problems are actually developmental strengths given the context of a child's life.

Hidden talents research suggests that children experiencing early-life adversity can develop abilities that enable them to deal more effectively with challenging environments where risks loom large and potential rewards are rare and hard to secure.[31] An individual growing up in threatening and dangerous conditions could, for example, become especially able to identify imminent dangers, notice and keep an eye on quickly changing conditions, persist in pursuit of a reward, react quickly to negative emotions displayed by other people, and recover quickly from setbacks. It's a list that sounds more like strengths than weaknesses, yet certain behaviors induced by such hidden talents are routinely treated as problematic. They are presumed by psychologists and the lay public, to say nothing of the legal system, to reflect moral failings, dysregulation, and even disorder. In other words, the supposition is that something has gone wrong—awry—rather than right, that such behaviors reflect developmental damage, the opposite of realizing one's potential.

But consider the case of child abuse. Extensive evidence indicates that maltreated children are especially vigilant to threat, particularly in uncertain situations in which it is unclear why something happened, like being knocked over from behind by another child on the playground.[32] There is even research that indicates that the brains of children growing up under conditions of adversity respond in the same way to others' ambiguous and surprised facial expressions that they do to faces clearly expressing anger and threat.[33] Other children respond quite differently to such distinctive stimuli. Does it not seem perfectly sensible that children whose experience induces a general view that others can't be trusted, and that the world is an uncaring, dangerous, and painful place, would hit back first and ask questions later—that they might not wait for an explanation of, say, why they were being pushed from behind? After all, it might have been an accident.

It is not just in the rough world of our ancestral history—the "environment of evolutionary adaptation," as the English psychiatrist John Bowlby referred to it— that it would seem to make a whole lot of sense to respond in such antisocial manner. In dangerous communities today (including prisons), one's personal safety and thus survival is often enhanced by letting others know that one won't accept mistreatment from anyone, whether intentional or accidental. The alternative is to risk being regarded as an easy mark. That is not a great way to increase one's chances of passing on genes to future generations.

Recent work even suggests that, when children exposed to conditions of threat are engaged in problem-solving, it is the ones with histories of exposure to harshness that come up with the more original solutions—in one particular study, generating more novel ideas for improving happiness.[34] That research involved an experimental manipulation in which children were randomly divided into two groups. The first group viewed a five-minute video designed to elicit stress before being given a creative problem-solving task to complete, while the second, control group spent those five minutes sitting quietly in the lab before being presented with the same challenge. Notably, these experimental results were in line with those from a prior investigation carried out by the same researchers that was observational in design, thus more weakly positioned to detect causal effects. It is unclear how generalizable these findings are and how much they apply to broader considerations of creativity, but this work seems highly consistent with the claim that adverse childhood experiences can foster talents, skills, and capabilities that are overlooked when there is an obsessive focus on dysfunction, disorder, and dysregulation.

Looking at things through an evolutionary lens, I have often wondered if mal-treated children's tendency to become antisocial and hypervigilant to threat actually reflects the evolutionary logic underlying the maltreatment itself. Parents who mistreat their children typically themselves grew up, and often still live, under highly stressful conditions, ones in which it may be "a bridge too far" to cope suc-cessfully with a trying situation. Could their hostile or neglectful parenting, then, be an evolved response to such conditions that actually promotes their children's likelihood of passing on their own genes (and thus also their parents' genes)? Might maltreatment function as a way of conveying to a child that the world is a tough place and the parents lack the ability to foster the child's competence to succeed in it? If both things are true, the child might do better to become alienated from the parents and perhaps find guidance, care, and consideration elsewhere. Short of that, could the best way to succeed in this harsh world involve thinking about oneself first and taking advantage of others, while finding one or more mates in order to reproduce? I don't know if this is the case, but it might help explain why mistreated children don't tend to develop greater empathy, sensitivity, and caring, despite having come to know firsthand the pain and suffering of mistreatment. From a non-evolutionary standpoint, wouldn't that have been just as psycho-logical as what the evidence actually indicates?

## The Plan of the Book

Having addressed what might be regarded as some key challenges to an evolutionary worldview, especially as applied to human development and the role of nurture in shaping who children will become, let me outline how the pages to come will explore "why and how childhood adversity shapes development." The six chapters making up Part I address the issues of why and how; those in Part II address for whom this shaping of later life is likely to prove most and least influential.

Chapter 1 shares the semi-serendipitous story of how I came to entertain the evolutionary perspective central to this book—that is, the fundamental importance of passing on genes to future generations. Chapter 2 highlights what troubled me about the enticing ideas I encountered and how I eventually came to embrace the view of biological gravity shared here. It outlines the broader intellectual framework on which my nature-of-nurture thinking is based, while sharing the only real intellectual struggle of my career—along with the breakthrough insight that eventually resolved it and pointed me toward the ideas in this book. However fascinated I was by evolutionary analysis, I was not an immediate convert.

Chapter 3 focuses on the early research evidence that provided empirical support for that *eureka*-crying insight, resulting in the development of what I initially called an evolutionary theory of socialization. Chapter 4 does to my own thinking about the development of reproductive strategy just what Chapter 2 did to the foundational work that stimulated me to rethink my understanding of child development in the first place: it offers a critique of the work at hand—the nature-of-nurture thinking—and addresses various questions and challenges that have been raised about it. Then, in Chapter 5, having convinced myself—and I hope my readers—that the evidence should foster a further embrace of evo-devo or nature-of-nurture thinking, I consider other recent research about the effects of developmental experiences and environmental exposures on "biological aging," even in childhood, including some focusing on epigenetics. This is work that was not undertaken based on my own or anyone else's evolutionary thinking, but proved to be in line with such theorizing. Chapter 6 wraps up Part I by addressing the "elephant in the room," returning to the Mendelian-genetic perspective to consider the challenges it poses to Darwinian nature-of-nurture thinking and research.

Part II then substantially modifies the evolutionary, evo-devo idea laid out in Part I. The question addressed in Chapters 7 through 10 is whether the ideas advanced earlier apply to some children more than others. Evolutionary considerations are central to this part of the book, as well, explaining why such differential susceptibility to environmental influences should be expected and providing evidence that it exists. Finally, the Conclusion provides a succinct summary of the book's take-home messages, considers implications and applications of the ideas advanced herein, and highlights what might be called "unknowns" about the nature of nurture.

In closing this Introduction, let me make one appeal to readers that may motivate some to invest more time and effort in reading this book than they already have. Many people (including my wife and son as well as various friends and fellow scholars) have questioned whether the nature-of-nurture ideas have any real bearing on *what we should do* when we discover things about child development we want to change—how our actions might foster the well-being of those (and they are all too many) who grow up under unfortunate circumstances in our society. In several ways, nature-of-nurture ideas deriving from evolutionary considerations will turn out to align with what contemporary developmental and humanitarian thinking already prescribes, although in some important ways they will not.

One might ask more broadly: Why even bother considering the evolutionary nature of nurture? By the time this book reaches its end, it should be clear that the two hypotheses around which this book is organized do carry implications and imply applications that traditional thinking does not. For now, more simply, my answer is that ideas matter not just for their very practical implications but also for the richness and pleasure of enhanced understanding of the world around us. The practical utility of new ideas, and ideas not yet fully understood or embraced, can take time to emerge. Good evidence of this can be found in the application of evolutionary ideas to the field of medicine.[35] This book is thus not a manual advising how to raise children, prevent problems from developing, remediate problems already established, or even promote well-being broadly conceived. It is a book about underappreciated and relatively new ideas about the role of developmental experiences and environmental exposures in shaping who each of us becomes.

My purpose here is to encourage a way of looking at how childhood experiences shape us that is rather different than the traditional thinking about both nurture and nature. I hope to plant a seed—even what some might consider a cognitive virus that might go on to infect other minds—eventually changing how people think about the role of nature and nurture in human development. My own experience convinces me that learning to look at human development through a new lens—viewing it in evolutionary color, rather than traditional black and white—opens up the promise of many more surprising insights.

PART I

# The Puberty Hypothesis

# 1
# A New World Order?

THERE IS A long history behind the thinking, theorizing, and speculating about how early-life experiences and environmental exposures shape who children become. The ancient philosophers Plato, Socrates, and Aristotle all opined on the subject. But the recorded history of ideas about how children should be raised goes back at least to the time of the Old Testament: spare the rod and spoil the child. Not to be neglected are the writings of the English philosopher John Locke, whose metaphor of a *tabula rasa,* or blank slate, carried clear implications for how powerfully nurture affects children's development. We should also recall Jean-Jacques Rousseau, the French philosopher whose book *Emile* advanced a full-blown theory of how children should be raised and about what harms their well-being. Of course, the Old Testament, John Locke, and Rousseau did not see eye to eye to eye.

But it is probably Sigmund Freud we should credit with planting the seeds of modern developmental thinking about the role of nurture in shaping how children develop. His psychoanalytic theory launched, in the hands of others, the empirical study of whether and how early experiences and exposures might shape psychological and behavioral development. There is little embrace of Freudian thinking today among those who study child development, but one of the man's notions plays an important role in the story I am going to tell about the nature of nurture. It was the idea Freud referred to as the Oedipus Complex, describing a preschool-aged developmental phase in a boy's life when he unconsciously harbors a sexual attraction to his mother. Passing through this stage, Freud theorized, was how a boy learned the masculine role—by coming to identify with his father (only after living through some period of fear that his penis would be cut off once the father recognized him as a rival seeking to displace him from the marital relationship).

I call attention to this one idea of Freud's not because it needs to be remembered, but for different reasons. The first, already alluded to, is that it stimulated some of the first, if not the first, empirical research aimed at testing propositions about child development—in this case, propositions implied by Freud's psychoanalytic theorizing. A major implication subjected to systematic research in the 1940s and thereafter was that boys (and perhaps girls as well) who grew up without a father would be psychologically damaged given their lack of opportunity to identify with a man of the house. While one can certainly question the quality of research testing Freudian ideas about father absence (some of it undertaken even before I was born in 1952), the evidence amassed seemed consistent with Freud's conclusions—for both boys and girls, as will be detailed below.

The second reason for highlighting Freud's theorizing about father absence is that it was challenged by evolutionary-minded scholars in a most original way, eventually leading to my own embrace of evo-devo thinking. The two scholars in question were not psychologists but a married team of anthropologists, Pat Draper and Henry Harpending. They published the paper that, in the Preface, I described reading in the mid-1980s almost by accident—a paper that adopted an evolutionary perspective to reinterpret findings from many of the research efforts inspired by Freud's theorizing.[1] It summarized what was then known about the developmental effects of growing up in a father-absent household. In line with psychoanalytic expectations, available evidence indicated that girls growing up without a father, sometimes with a series of men moving in and out of the home in transient relationships with their mothers, tended to experience their first sexual activity (in the language of research, their "sexual debut") at an earlier age than did other girls, and later to have "poor ability to maintain sexual and emotional adjustment with one male." Boys, by contrast, who grew up in such homes proved on average to be more aggressive and, when it came to raising their own children, more neglectful. To be clear, the research behind these findings does not imply that all children raised by single mothers exhibit these tendencies—or that those growing up in two-parent families never do. It shows only that these patterns of development were more likely in circumstances of father absence than father presence.

What proved so striking to me was the anthropologists' claim that the development of both the father-absent and father-present children reflected an *evolved* response to family environments, in the service of the already-mentioned fundamental goal of all living things, *the passing on of genes to future generations*. Draper and Harpending's novel perspective was that humans, just like other species, had evolved to do one thing more than any other: *make copies of themselves!* Most if not all of our bodily parts and processes, as well as much of our psychology and behavior, evolved via Darwinian and Hamiltonian processes of natural selection and inclusive fitness to serve this fundamental goal. It has even been argued that activities like the making of music and art evolved to serve this same purpose.[2] And this is to say nothing of efforts to achieve status, power, and fame.[3]

As a student of nurture I realized what all this implied for development: *Evolution has equipped children to be sensitive to important and informative cues in their environment*—such as the degree of care being provided by parents and the level of danger in the world around them—*because the useful guidance these provide to their development increases their chances of passing on their genes to future generations.* While the observation that children's development is shaped by their experiences and exposures was not new, the assertion that the ability to develop in particular ways in response to childhood conditions has evolved to increase the chances of passing on genes to the next generation most certainly was a novel claim—and to this day, most scholars, policymakers, service providers, and citizens are unfamiliar with it.

So, for example, those children who grow up without protective, caring, and committed men in their lives experience conditions that encourage development along other lines than those who spend their early years with such fathers on the scene, but in either case, the development represents the best pathway to eventually pass on their genes—and those of their parents and kin. This is why their different ways of developing are best referred to not as just environmentally induced *developmental trajectories* (the terminology of developmental scientists) but as *reproductive strategies* shaped by natural selection in the course of human evolution.

Please appreciate that to use the terminology of "strategy" is not to imply any conscious intent. There is no assumption in the preceding analysis that children who lack fathers, or whose mothers are impoverished, or who are subject to any other conditions, understand the underlying biological and psychological dynamics that drive their behavior and development and are making conscious decisions based on that understanding. Not to worry: evolutionary biology and their evolved unconscious minds have their backs. Preparing the developing child for future success in passing on genes is too critical a task for evolution to leave it to children to figure out.

THE EVOLUTIONARY IDEAS advanced by the anthropologists offered a dramatically different perspective because, beyond suggesting alternative answers, they engaged with a fundamentally different question. Child developmentalists focusing on *how* development operates were presuming that psychological explanations would account for it, and investigating processes of imitation, social learning, and familial programming of emotional security, for example. (More recently, with advances in neuroscience, that has been extended to how the brain works.) The evolutionary view was instead principally an account of *why* we develop the way we do in response to particular contextual conditions. From this perspective, neither developmental response—the one to a father-present upbringing or in a father-absent one—is inherently better or worse at promoting reproductive success in passing on genes, any more than wearing short sleeves on a hot summer day is better than wearing a sweater on a cool autumn one.

All too often, we cast alternative ways of developing in moral terms—calling children of different tendencies *good* and *bad*, for example—but evolution by natural selection is not guided by moral considerations. What evolves is whatever *can* evolve to increase inclusive fitness—that is, success in passing on genes to descendants—given the conditions of life experienced by the growing child. Under some conditions this might involve becoming highly discriminating in choosing mates or developing certain ways of treating others, while under other circumstances what increases inclusive fitness could be quite different.

In moral terms, many might consider it the ideal approach to male-female pair bonding and childbearing to carefully choose a mate and maintain a long-term committed relationship with that partner. But from an evolutionary perspective, an alternative approach might be strategically wise for a woman whose development was shaped by growing up in a father-absent household. The same is true of men whose aggressive personality, developed during a father-absent upbringing, contributes to their meager involvement in their children's lives. Humans have evolved to develop in such seemingly problematic ways when growing up without a father, according to Draper and Harpending, because in the environment of evolutionary adaptation—that is, across our evolutionary history—those ways have increased the chances that at least some of their offspring would survive to pass on their genes.

In the evolutionary analysis of father absence and its effects, then, the central claim was that it was simply beyond the capability of many (even if not all) children growing up in father-absent homes to develop in ways more in line with middle-class Western values. Too often in such childhoods, key elements—namely, safety, security, nurturance, and support, especially from a caring and committed father figure—were in short supply. Thus, it was not that girls and boys with absent fathers were making immoral choices—they were only doing what evolution crafted them to do. What we were seeing in the system, then, was not a bug but a feature.

Another important lesson of the preceding evolutionary analysis concerns the judgments many of us render about others' ways of developing and behaviors generally regarded as unwise and problematic—such as a woman having, by different men, many kids who are poorly cared for, or a man becoming aggressive and absent as a father. The lesson is that, to the extent that our generally valued ways of behaving are out of reach for individuals developing under conditions of adversity, it is a mistake to use them as baselines for comparison. Perhaps, as we look upon others, we should gauge their supposed "choices" not against our ideal values and preferences, but against the potentially worse alternatives that their seemingly problematic ways of developing have enabled them to avoid.

Consider the possibility that a girl growing up without a steady, reliable man in her life could refuse to have anything to do with men, thus foregoing childbearing altogether—or could, after realizing she'd made a bad choice of mate, decide to stick with a toxic situation. Or consider the boy whose father-absent upbringing endowed him with heightened aggressiveness. It might have been worse to become weak and helpless; the antisocial alternative might increase (or at least, might in the past have increased) the probability of surviving in an uncaring world, finding a mate, and producing offspring. What should not be lost in such analysis is that different ways of developing do often carry costs for societies (such as criminality or neglected children), as well as costs for the developing individuals (such as peer rejection or poor health).

Perspectives like this can often be interpreted as implying that, even if we don't like how children develop, nothing should be done. People are shaped by the adverse conditions they experience; this is nature's way. But to claim that would be to succumb to what philosophers call the naturalistic fallacy: the assumption that because something *is*—that is, occurs in the natural world—it is what *ought* to be in the modern world. Going analytically from *is* to *ought* is widely recognized as a mistake. If, for example, it is true that evolution has shaped male mating psychology to make a man feel jealous if he suspects his partner is not faithful to him—as part of avoiding care investment in another man's child who carries none of his genes—and some men can therefore tend toward obsessively and aggressively "mate guarding" their partners, this does not serve as license for such behavior, at least not in societies unwilling to countenance domestic violence. Human nature includes various inclinations that once served the evolutionary imperative of passing on one's genes—and in some cases and places still do serve that purpose—but we need not remain slaves to such tendencies. We can choose to go along with nature or not, at least some of the time, though this may require modifying the conditions under which children develop or creating particular laws and regulations. Recall the discussion in the Introduction of engineering around physical gravity when designing a plane, and the analogous possibility of applying our intellect to slip the surly bonds of evolved human tendencies.

WHEN I SHARE the idea with friends and colleagues that evolution has shaped human decision-making in line with the imperative to pass on our genes, I often hear the objection that it can't be true because "people just don't think that way." Maybe that is your response, too. Most of us seem convinced that what we do is based on conscious deliberation—at least most of it—and certainly when it comes to life choices so consequential that they influence, immediately or over the longer term, the passing on of our genes. But like it or not, this is simply not the case. In fact, there is much neuroscientific research to indicate that our deliberate choices are often, perhaps even always, determined by brain processes outside of conscious awareness which *precede* conscious decision making.[4]

Despite what has just been stipulated, there is evidence that individuals sometimes do understand the bio-logic central to evolutionary thinking, even if not in such terms. For example, Arline Geronimus, a University of Michigan anthropologist, found that poor, urban-dwelling African American teenagers who were pregnant were keenly aware that their future health—and even survival—were at risk, and this understanding seemed to influence their early childbearing.[56] I see this finding as a perfect example of evolution's legacy in shaping how children develop in response to their early-life conditions and its effects on eventual childbearing. To my knowledge, Geronimus herself never embraced this perspective but it complements the sociological and public-health ones guiding her work.

Geronimus did clearly understand, however, that early childbearing was reproductively strategic, given the evidence that the condition of growing up in poverty caused Black girls to experience accelerated biological aging, especially when they were also exposed to racism. These conditions made early childbearing the best (reproductive) card that could be played with the (environmental) hand they had been dealt. Nevertheless, Geronimus viewed the phenomenon of teenage pregnancy only through a medical lens, emphasizing how childhood adversity causes wear and tear to the body, rather than recognizing early childbearing to be an evolved, strategic response to that very condition.

BY THE TIME I read the anthropology paper on father absence that so intrigued me, I had been a professor of human development for more than a decade, specializing in infancy, early childhood, and the role of developmental experiences (such as sensitive or harsh parenting) and environmental exposures (such as affluence or poverty) in shaping who we become. When I took my first academic job in 1978, the nature-nurture controversy was in full bloom (though it feels like it has always been) with heated debates about which was the more powerful force shaping us: Mendelian genetics or environmental experiences. Influenced by two factors, I and many fellow development scholars were biased strongly toward the nurture side. One factor was the belief that, the more we understood how experiences and exposures influence the way we develop, the better positioned we would be to improve the lives of those growing up under adverse conditions that compromised their well-being and ultimate life-course potential. The second factor was the pernicious effect we had seen the field of genetics exert on the real lives of all too many. Back in the days of social Darwinism, influential scholars and politicians had gone so far as to argue that allowing certain people to have children would undermine the gene pool and thus our species. This, of course, was not just a theoretical issue. It led to the forced sterilization of more than seventy thousand Americans from the 1920s to the 1970s—and a legacy of suspicion by many that genetic research would again be used for similarly inhumane purposes.

What became clear, however, was that nurture, or how our experiences and exposures shape us, wasn't all about mental health and illness and thus whether we will become healthy, wealthy, and wise as a result of our childhoods. It was not first and foremost, then, about emotional security, self-control, achievement, cognitive competence, and, as a final example, the ability to get along with others. Yet that is what my field of developmental science had long presumed. It's exactly what I cut my teeth on, even what motivated me to become a developmental scholar. Instead, I came to see that nurture is first and foremost about passing on genes to the next generation—and that how we go about that is not necessarily due to choices we freely make. Wow! All this came as quite a surprise to me, as I suspect it does to many readers. But surprises are the point of scientific discovery. As philosopher Karl Popper wrote, "every interesting and powerful statement must have a low probability; and vice versa: a statement with a high probability will be scientifically uninteresting." Thus, "as scientists we do not seek highly probable theories but explanations; that is to say, powerful and highly improbable ones."[7]

None of what I have outlined to this point about evolution and thus the nature of nurture is what I learned as a psychology major in college, in my child development master's and human development PhD programs, or in my first decade as a university professor. How had I—and everyone I worked with and everything that I had read about human development—missed this? This now seems especially surprising, given that Richard Dawkins's worldwide best seller *The Selfish Gene* brought this kind of evolutionary and "genes-eye view" of life to the masses half a century ago, based on the theoretical insights of Darwin and Hamilton highlighted in the Introduction, and so did E. O. Wilson's *Sociobiology*.[8] The perspective was already foundational to most research in the life sciences and certainly all developmental and behavioral research on all other living things on the planet. Multiple subfields of psychology and the behavioral sciences had also been influenced for years by the modern evolutionary viewpoint.

There are reasons, however, that developmental scholars have proven so ignorant of—and even resistant to—the insights afforded by a modern developmental synthesis of Darwinian natural selection, Mendelian genetics, and nurture. The main one, I suspect, is that for all too many developmental scientists (and social scientists, to say nothing of the broader public) the term *evolution* carries the connotation of Mendelian genetics and thus biological determinism, racism, and sexism. To a certain extent, that is understandable. Still, developmental science has been awash with Mendelian-genetic research since at least the 1970s, and this work has made clear, with regard to almost any human development feature of interest, that people's differences substantially result from differences in their DNA. This has been the revelation of "heritability" studies: the extent to which people differ is less when they share more genes than when they share fewer genes (so that identical are more alike than fraternal twins, for example, and siblings are more alike than cousins). Much more will be said about this line of research in Chapter 6, as it poses a major challenge to the ideas developed in this book.

What the anthropologists advanced was a perspective on "nature" fundamentally different than the more traditional, Mendelian approach to the study of genetic influence. According to it, different childhood environments lead to different ways of developing because the nurture side of development has also been shaped by natural selection to increase the chances of an individual passing on genes under different childhood conditions. Thus, children who grow up with present fathers generally develop in certain ways, but Draper and Harpending assert that, had they come from father-absent homes, they would likely have developed differently. In either case it would be for the very same reason—because developing in such a context-dependent manner had, over the course of humanity's evolutionary past, enhanced reproductive success. As a result, genes for adjusting development based on a child's experience growing up would have been incorporated—in biological terms, *selected*—into the human genome. More generally, then, evolution shaped humans to be responsive to developmental experiences and environmental exposures early in life in a manner that once fostered eventual reproductive success—and may still do so today.

IT HAS BEEN four decades since the father-absence paper was published, applying an evolutionary perspective to reframe the developmental effects of father absence. As Chapter 2 will relate, it has been more than three decades since I embraced and extended the anthropologists' foundational ideas. How is it that the evo-devo, nature-of-nurture perspective is still so rarely entertained by parents, journalists, policymakers, and developmental scientists? A critical reason, it seems to me, is that considerations of child and adolescent development are so rooted in the idealized and romanticized view of human nature that remains central to modern Western thought. To browse scientific papers in even the most prestigious developmental journals is to run across repeated references to the notion—or claim—of "optimal" development. Implicit if not explicit in it is the presumption that what is regarded by the author and much of the Western world as the best way to develop—typically, being emotionally secure, empathic, prosocial, cooperative, achievement striving, industrious, and so on—is how nature intended humans to develop. Alternative ways of developing are typically regarded, as noted in the Introduction, as reflecting disturbance, dysfunction, dysregulation, and even diagnosable disorder. Certainly, in my own early career, I thought and wrote this way.

To underscore the point we might revisit various classical psychological and developmental perspectives that I once enthusiastically embraced. Consider Freud, who may never have used the word *optimal,* but who argued that mental health reflected the proclivity "to love and to work." What about having friends, appreciating music, and enjoying nature—or succeeding in raising children to reproductive age? Or think of Abraham Maslow and his theory of human needs, often depicted as a pyramid. At the base of the hierarchy are the biological and physiological essentials for sustaining life, such as food, clothing, and shelter. If these most basic needs are met, higher ones can be addressed, like needs for belongingness and intimacy, further fostering optimal development. Another level higher are esteem needs—the achievement, status, responsibility, and reputation gains that people seek. And at the apex of the pyramid is the need for self-actualization, involving personal growth and fulfillment. This is a theoretical framework clearly based on a belief in the "perfectibility of man."

And it is not just Freud and Maslow, who were not really developmental thinkers in the modern sense, who implicitly or explicitly embraced this view. Erik Erikson, the famous twentieth-century child psychiatrist, advanced an influential theory involving eight stages of development, beginning with basic trust (versus mistrust) in infancy; followed in toddlerhood by autonomy (versus shame and doubt); then in the preschool years by initiative (versus guilt); then in the grade-school years by industry (versus inferiority); then in adolescence by identity (versus role confusion); then in young adulthood by intimacy (versus isolation); then in middle age by generativity (versus stagnation); and, finally, in the aging years, by integrity (versus despair).[9] Attachment theory, which had its origins in John Bowlby's analysis of the infant-mother relationship, has much in common with Erikson. It stipulates how early security lays the foundation for later competence, curiosity, autonomy, emotion regulation, resilience, capacity for intimacy, and sensitive parenting.[10] One is hard-pressed not to regard these "visions" of human development as reflecting views of humans' fundamental nature and thus the presumptions of theorists and theories regarding how development is supposed to proceed and what it is supposed to realize.

The second lesson we can draw from an evolutionary analysis of the nature of nurture is that *optimal* is a word that should be banished from developmental science and from all thinking about child development. We should not be so ready to moralize about how some people develop and behave when we look upon ways that we don't value. This is not only because such moralizing reifies the romanticism I am critiquing. It is also because it attributes much choice and agency to individuals who are often limited on both scores, often through no faults of their own. Much of this book will proceed instead from the presumption that there is no optimal development, at least as far as evolution and human nature are concerned. From an evolutionary perspective, optimal is not about psychological or behavioral health and well-being but about success in passing one's genes on to future generations. And what is optimal depends on the context in which the individual develops—so that virtually nothing is optimal in all contexts.

# 2

# An Uncanny Prediction

W HAT MOST INTRIGUED ME about the reinterpretation of the effects of father absence by the two anthropologists was its focus on what evolutionists refer to as "ultimate" causation, the biological imperative to pass on genes. This contrasts with more proximate causation, which in the case of father absence might include anxiety about the future or a feeling that the world is an uncaring place. No doubt, the fact that this was intriguing to me reflects the limits of my own training as a developmental scholar, a deficient experience that even today remains all too common among students of child development and adolescent development. One has only to look at current college-level developmental psychology textbooks to discover that evolutionary thinking is almost entirely absent. These texts, like the never-ending guides to parenting that are published year in and year out, mostly ignore the *why* of development while emphasizing the *how.* They focus on neuroscience and the brain, physiology, and even these days epigenetics, inflammation, and the microbiome—but, as noted in Chapter 1, ultimate and proximate explanations are not mutually exclusive. Both are central to any complete account of development.

As intriguing as it was to encounter the evolutionary emphasis on *why* development operates the way it does with regard to father absence, there were issues that troubled me about the reinterpretation of evidence offered by the anthropologists. Before addressing these and sharing how I resolved my scientific concerns, three topics need to be addressed. First is the foundational question: Why develop? Second is the nature of early infant-parent attachment, and the need to rethink it. Third is the topic of life history theory. If nothing else, by the end of this chapter it should be clear how the nature-of-nurture view central to this book proves consistent with traditional developmental thinking, yet deviates from and enriches it.

## Why Develop?

Part of the general lack of evolutionary perspectives in considerations of child and adolescent development is a seeming reluctance to ask what should be a fundamental question: Why does development occur at all? Note that it is not a process experienced by every living thing. The axolotl, for example, is a fish-like salamander found in Mexico that remains in the larval stage its entire life. Some other organisms develop during their equivalent of a prenatal period, but past that point only increase in size. Examples include worker bees beyond the pupal stage, aphids which are born pregnant, and the male dwarf perch that can spawn immediately after birth. However ubiquitous development seems to be, at least among mammals, it is important to appreciate that not all living things develop.

So why do we *Homo sapiens* develop at all? The answer is virtually the same as to any question about almost all phenotypes shared by members of a species, be it our two legs and two arms, the gills and fins of fish, or the legless bodies of snakes. The emergence of these and other phenotypes played a causal role over evolutionary history in enhancing, whether directly (as through eating) or indirectly (as through sexual attraction), the survival and reproductive success of the organisms that possessed them. Given that we now know that many species of our *Homo* genus, including Neanderthals and Denisovans, walked the earth before we became the sole surviving member, I cannot but wonder whether it was a particular way of developing that constituted, or at least contributed to, the secret of *Homo sapiens* success. To be clear, our earliest hominin ancestors were more like the great apes in their development than they were like contemporary humans. They nursed for longer periods and matured at a younger age.[1]

The question this raises is whether developmental plasticity (the capacity to modify development in response to lived experiences) has emerged across the course of evolution of our species—and if it has, how does it operate? The central assumption underlying all that is covered in this book is that plasticity did evolve in the service of reproductive success.

## Rethinking Infant-Parent Attachment

Returning to the almost total disregard of evolution in discussions of child development, the sad truth is that, by tradition, the attention devoted to evolution begins and ends with the topic of attachment in infancy. It goes no further than the acknowledgment of John Bowlby's claim that infants form selective and discriminating emotional bonds to a few people, most notably but not exclusively their mothers, because doing so has promoted survival across human evolutionary history. This original explanation earned Bowlby his standing as one of the original evolutionary psychologists, second only to Darwin himself. In ancestral times, the English psychiatrist contended, babies who failed to form attachments to caregivers were prone to wandering too freely, which increased their risk of not surviving, whether by becoming some predator's breakfast, getting lost and not found, or severely injuring themselves by, for example, falling into a fire. Meanwhile, the babies who were more inclined to develop attachments, for genetic reasons way back when, stayed physically and emotionally closer to their caregivers, thus making them more likely to survive; all human infants today are predisposed to form attachments to their caregivers.[2] Note that there is nothing in Bowlby's original theorizing, or in most developmental textbooks today, about survival *in the service of reproduction.*

But here is the interesting issue: We have known for decades that attachments vary in their quality, some reflecting a sense of security and others a sense of insecurity. Why is that? The answers given by developmentalists, myself included, based on decades of research, emphasize only the *how* of development. Specifically, it is the quality of parental care that shapes security and insecurity of attachment, which in turn influences later development.[3] What has been neglected, as a result, is *why* there should be such variation in the quality of parenting, the security of attachment, and the ways children develop. Despite theory and evidence about variation in attachment security, and about the developmental origins and consequences of establishing secure or insecure attachments, the field of child development has almost nothing to say about why development operates as it does. Mainstream development thinking has simply not moved on very much from Bowlby's original emphasis on survival.

## Life History Theory of Reproductive Strategies

What have been characterized above as contrasting reproductive strategies depending on father presence are today discussed in terms of *life histories,* based on evolutionary life history theory. Evolutionary biologists originally developed life history theory as a means of explaining differences *among* species, with respect to numbers of offspring born, for example, and levels of care devoted to offspring. Mosquitoes do not take long to reproduce, they lay thousands of eggs, and, thereafter, they have nothing whatsoever to do with their progeny—who don't live particularly long. By contrast, lions take longer to reproduce, produce relatively small litters, and care intensively for their much longer-lived offspring. These days, the former reproductive strategy is referred to as a *fast life history* and the latter as a *slow life history.* So, the reinterpretation of father-absence effects involved tweaking the notion of the fast and slow life histories of different species to consider the same kind of variation or differences among individuals *within* a species—namely, our own.[4]

Among many other things, life history thinking emphasizes the importance of tradeoffs in allocation of energy.[5] Like so much else in the world, development requires energy, and once energy is expended on one task it cannot be expended on another. When applied to human development, this implies that tradeoffs or reproductive-related choices must be made, though not necessarily with conscious intent. Three tradeoffs are central to differentiating fast and slow life histories and thus of importance to the remainder of this chapter: current versus future reproduction, mating versus parenting, and quantity versus quality of offspring. The first involves whether to bear children sooner or later in one's life. The second is whether to engage in efforts to find and attract additional mates, or to provide care to one's existing children. And the third is whether to bear fewer children—or to have more of them, knowing that this will mean less time, energy, and care can be devoted to each of them. Evolutionary biologists refer to these as matters of *parental investment.*

Looking at the variations in how people make these tradeoffs, what is perhaps especially notable is that some do and others do not map to the dominant, Western middle-class values of affluent societies. In particular, the fast life history "choices" that father-absent girls are disproportionately likely to "make"—to initiate sex at a younger age, to engage in unstable pair bonds or intimate relationships, and to provide limited care to many children—are widely presumed to reflect "problematic development" and are not to be encouraged. Meanwhile, the very opposite is true of slow life history ways of behaving, which are highly prized in the West and many other cultures. The same goes for father-absent boys' tendencies to become aggressive and absent fathers themselves. Critically, a fundamental insight of life history thinking as applied to how and why people develop differently is that, to repeat, one way of developing is not inherently better than another in service of the ultimate purpose of life. Whether the best way to pass genes along to future generations is by adopting a fast life history or a slow life history depends on the context of development.

The clear implication, as previously noted, is that it is mistaken to attribute evolutionary-guided choices we disfavor to moral failings, and just as mistaken to deem choices we prefer as closer to the natural state of human beings. This is not to say we cannot value and prefer certain choices over others, especially given the social costs that fast ways of developing incur.[6] Yet this understanding does suggest that we would all do well to "walk in the other's shoes" and see how limited truly conscious choices may be for people behaving in ways we think ill of, even if for good reasons. For those who understandably point out that plenty of children growing up under conditions of adversity turn out "just fine" and that some who develop under highly supportive ones do not, that reality is a central concern of

Part II, devoted to qualifying some of the observations and claims made in this first part. For now, please be patient.

One last thing to make clear about life history thinking is that everything just outlined is currently up for debate, as will be made clear in pages to come. Thus, even if it has served as a guide to the research shared in the first part of the book, there is much discussion of whether features of life histories "hang together" empirically as tightly as the above summary just implied.[7] Consider, for example, the issue of whether the multiple characteristics of fast and slow life histories are as related to each other as some would assert, with early forces and factors causally influencing subsequent ones. Another significant issue is whether it makes sense to treat life histories categorically—as either fast or slow—or whether it is more valuable in thinking about development to conceptualize a continuum of life histories ranging from the slowest to the less slow, and on to the faster and the fastest. These are questions that should be kept in mind. But to my way of thinking, even if they (along with others highlighted throughout this book) have not yet been resolved, we must not throw the theoretical baby out with the bathwater. If nothing else, it is theory that has stimulated a lot of research and yielded a lot of interesting, and at times surprising, results. This is one reason that an old teacher of mine, quoting an old teacher of his, often reminded students: "There is nothing so practical as a good theory."[8] A theory doesn't have to be perfect—few are—to prove useful.

## Challenges to the Father-Absence Analysis

Now let's turn to the problems I encountered as a scientist intrigued by the evo-devo thinking that emphasized the passing on of genes (the force of biological gravity) rather than mental health and well-being, yet still not ready to embrace it. For me, the risk was that the evolutionary-minded anthropologists might be offering little more than "old wine in a new bottle." Why would I fear that? For several reasons.

To begin with, the reproductive-strategy interpretation of father-absence effects essentially involved an input-output model of development (which is not a bad place to start, theorizing in this case that the input of father absence results in the developmental outputs already described), but by the time I read the father-absence paper in the late 1980s, the field of child development had moved well beyond such models. More than a decade had already been spent on advancing understanding by adding mechanistic or process-oriented thinking to what might be regarded as a first stage of developmental inquiry. Second-stage developmental inquiry sought to illuminate not just *what* effect resulted from a particular experience or exposure, but *how* that effect came about, the question of developmental mechanism. These non–mutually exclusive mechanisms could be cognitive, emotional, and, broadly speaking, physiological.

Why should we care about such mechanisms, which were more or less lacking in the original reproductive strategy analysis? Understanding mechanisms of influence on human development is especially useful for guiding interventions when the objective is to prevent a problem from developing, remediate a problem that has already developed, or even just promote well-being among those not at developmental risk. Consider the example presented in Chapter 1 of maltreated children being hypervigilant to threat and thus being inclined to "hit first and ask questions later." Even if it's too late to prevent maltreatment from occurring—because we can't erase a lived history of adversity—understanding the role of heightened threat vigilance in the developmental "circuitry" of antisocial behavior gives those seeking to remediate aggressive tendencies a target of intervention.

If some treatment reduces these abuse-induced inclinations, then there is a decent chance that the otherwise anticipated antisocial output can be reduced and perhaps even eliminated. This, of course, is exactly how medicine works. Covid vaccinations are based on an understanding of how exposure to the virus, the input, leads to the output of making breathing so difficult for so many. Because research revealed the spike protein to be the linchpin in the infection process, that was what the vaccinations targeted—to great effect, thank goodness.

Thus, my first concern with the evolutionary analysis of father-absence effects was that psychological and behavioral mechanisms of development were lacking in it. How, exactly, did the input of father absence come to yield the output of the sexual and mating behavior associated with it? Was it via attachment insecurity, or feelings of loneliness, or fear of the future . . . ? And my second, perhaps even greater, concern was, again, the impression of old wine in a new bottle. Put another way, was the new evolutionary way of thinking only putting a new frame around an old picture? After all, the evidence about effects of father absence that had provided the basis for its evolutionary reinterpretation had been around for a long time and was widely understood, even if often disputed.[9]

A few things were lacking, in other words, that my training had taught me ought to be present if one were going to discard an old way of thinking for a new one. This was of special concern given that the new one, emphasizing the passing on of genes as the fundamental purpose of all living things, was radically different from the traditional one.[10] First, a new theory or perspective should be able to explain what was already understood—which the evolutionary father-absence story under consideration clearly did. The second reason to embrace a new theory, often referred to as Occam's Razor, is that it is more parsimonious—people can recognize it as simpler, less complicated than the prevailing theory. And, to be honest, an evolutionary appeal to things that happened tens of thousands of years ago via the process of natural selection did not seem clearly more parsimonious to me than just attributing the behavior of father-absent girls and boys to the learning processes of imitation and reinforcement, as well as attachment insecurity. (Before moving on, it must be acknowledged that the Occam's Razor claim that the simplest or most parsimonious scientific explanation is to be preferred over others—when definitive evidence is lacking—has not gone unchallenged.)[11]

The third and perhaps most critical element that allows an established way of thinking to be abandoned for a newer one is that the would-be replacement must yield an *original prediction*—that is, a new hypothesis that no other theory or way of thinking would advance or could even explain should it prove true. Yet the anthropologists offered no original hypothesis. And the final need before jettisoning one perspective for another is for empirical research to test the new prediction and not find it wanting. In other words, the new way of thinking should lead not just to new hypotheses, but to new discoveries. That clearly could not happen, because there was no new prediction.

So, the absence of a critical and theory-distinguishing prediction in the reframing of what already was known about the effects of father absence troubled me. In fact, in forty-plus years as a developmental scientist, I have never struggled with another intellectual problem as I did with this one. I found the reproductive-strategy view of development fascinating, but needed to be convinced on the basis of empirical evidence evaluating a testable hypothesis, not just storytelling. Here was my conundrum: What novel prediction might prove true if this new, evolutionary way of looking at development was on target?

Only by identifying and testing such a novel prediction could I convince myself—and other developmental scholars (or so I presumed or maybe just hoped)—that this new way of viewing human development "had legs." The remainder of this chapter tells the story of how I resolved the intellectual struggle just mentioned—by advancing what I came to regard as an "uncanny" prediction, given its long-shot nature—and in so doing further developed the ideas I found intriguing, but not yet compelling, in the evolutionary analysis of father-absence effects. This story was told in abbreviated form in a previous book, *The Origins of You*, but is so much more central to this volume that it needs a fuller telling here.[12]

## An Uncanny Prediction

The thinking and research of a friend I met in college and went to graduate school with was probably the first source of the insight that would eventually enable me to make a theoretically discriminating prediction based on reproductive strategy thinking. It is what I previously referred to as a eureka experience, the only one I ever had as a developmental scholar. And I say this because, while teaching a graduate course one evening, all of a sudden it dawned on me that *the timing of pubertal development* should be related to the nurture that children experienced while growing up, for reproductive-strategy-related reasons to be explained shortly.

While I was busy specializing in infancy and early childhood during my graduate training and early career, my friend Larry Steinberg, now of Temple University, was busy specializing in adolescence. We spent many hours talking about our respective interests and research, with his focused on whether and how the timing of puberty, as an input, affected the output of family relationships during adolescence. Perhaps the seed of my idea that puberty was important for testing a reproductive-strategy view of development was thus planted that early in my unconscious.

But whereas Larry studied how sexually maturing at a relatively early age affected parent-teen relationships, I more or less flipped his work—without having realized that that's what I was doing until just now, as I write these paragraphs. I hypothesized that pubertal timing should be shaped, at least in part, by the developing child's relationship experiences within the family during the first five-to-seven years of life. This constituted a novel theory that met two of the four requirements already outlined for a new theoretical perspective to trump and thus replace an existing one. With regard to the requirement that a new theory should be able to explain what prior theorizing had asserted, my "evolutionary theory of socialization" (as I initially called it) incorporated much standard developmental thinking. This included drawing on my own and fellow scholars' prior work on factors and forces fostering child abuse and neglect, also affecting parenting more generally, and infant attachment security in particular.

Just like more traditional thinking, my new theory stipulated the following: First, extrafamilial sources of stress and support influence family functioning, including the adult pair bond, parenting, and parent-child relationships. Second, these factors and forces collectively shape the child's social orientation. In time, they influence age of first sex—the third step in this developmental cascade. And still later, they come to affect the stability of intimate adult relationships and the number of children born, as well as the quality of care those children receive and thus how they develop.

To put more meat on the bones of much traditional thinking about how early-life conditions shape development, let's consider first the effects of growing up under adverse developmental conditions, which are in line with the widespread sense that bad things go together when it comes to child, adolescent, and even adult development. Whether childhood adversity involves, for example, problematic employment conditions of parents or living in a dangerous neighborhood, such extrafamilial factors, according to traditional thinking incorporated into the new theory, increase the later risk of troubled marital and parent-child relationships, with the latter featuring harsh, intrusive, insensitive, and neglectful parenting. These ways of parenting induce attachment insecurity in infancy and, along with troubled and conflicted parent-child relationships in childhood, promote an opportunistic, advantage-taking, and exploitative social orientation in the child (such as a predisposition to "hit first and ask questions later"). All this leads to early onset of sexual activity, indiscriminate mating, and eventually problematic parenting, not unlike the parenting the individual experienced while growing up, resulting in many poorly cared-for offspring. It was the latter claim that led me to characterize this reproductive strategy initially as a "quantity" one, in an effort to extend Draper and Harpending's thinking beyond the single condition of father absence. With regard to the requirement that a new theory advance an original prediction that standard thinking could not account for should it prove true, I modified traditional thinking by adding the proposition that, as part of the developmental cascade already outlined, *childhood adversity accelerates pubertal development, resulting in its occurring earlier than would otherwise be the case.*

Now let's consider a contrasting set of contextual conditions in line with the widespread sense that *good* things go together when it comes to human development. How does development operate according to my evolutionary socialization theory under these conditions? When extrafamilial support is sufficient to enable parents to cope with the challenges their family might face, marital relations tend to be reasonably harmonious, and parent-child relations feature warm, stimulating, and sensitive-responsive parenting. In consequence, infants develop secure attachments and go on to develop, in the context of harmonious parent-child relationships, reciprocal and mutually beneficial social orientations (such as tendencies to "go along to get along"). Collectively, these sources of influence lead to a later age of first sex, greater choosiness regarding sexual partners, stable intimate relationships, the bearing of fewer children, and good care of children. The latter claims led me to characterize this reproductive strategy initially as a "quality" one. When it came to the novel prediction, the new theory stipulated that growing up under such supportive conditions *delays pubertal development relative to what would occur under conditions of childhood adversity.*

In so many ways, then, all I really did to standard developmental thinking was recast it in evolutionary, reproductive-strategy perspective. What made it different from standard thinking, of course, was the inclusion of somatic or physical development—pubertal timing—and the idea that it, too, could be influenced or regulated by prior developmental experiences and environmental exposures, especially those occurring in the first five to seven years of life. No one to my knowledge had considered this possibility before—namely, that early-life conditions affect the timing of pubertal development and, thereby, age of sexual debut, sexual behavior, childbearing, and childrearing. Whereas a quantity reproductive strategy—what is now referred to as a fast life history—results from adverse childhood experience and involves trading off current over future reproduction, mating over parenting, and quantity over quality of offspring, a quality reproductive strategy—that is, slow life history—is rather different. It is induced by supportive developmental conditions and yields the opposite tradeoffs: future over current reproduction, parenting over mating, and quality over quantity of offspring.

What consideration of pubertal timing so obviously adds to standard development thinking is what pubertal status implies: the capacity to reproduce. This addition to the prevailing developmental canon of how nurture (broadly conceived) works dramatically transforms how we might think about development—by putting reproduction at center stage. Development becomes not principally about mental health and well-being, as so long assumed, but about passing on genes to future generations. Just to be clear and to avoid any misunderstanding, this does not mean that mental health and well-being are not part of the story. Recall that a mutually beneficial social orientation is central to what is now referred to as a slow life history, just as an advantage-taking and exploitative social orientation is to a fast life history. These are conceptualized as part of the mechanistic process shaping reproductive development. They are means, then, to a reproductive end.

The evolutionary theory of socialization not only extended and enriched standard developmental thinking but did the same for the original evolutionary analysis of father absence that so intrigued me. It did this by focusing on more than father presence or absence, highlighting a multiplicity of contextual conditions that could influence reproductive strategy or life history—including, but not limited to, parents' occupational status (employed versus unemployed), social networks (isolated versus extensive), community safety (dangerous versus safe), marital relations (conflicted versus harmonious), and of course parenting (insensitive versus sensitive). The new theory, then, was about not just father absence or presence but many childhood conditions that create high levels of family stress that challenge the coping capacities of parents.

This is a point often missed, as some scholars continue to treat the theory as focused only on father absence. What is also often missed is that the theory is about much more than puberty. Recall that the puberty prediction was an original hypothesis that distinguished the new theory from prior ones without actually doing injustice to the prior ones. In sum, the new theory was a revised model of development whereby the context of development influenced childhood experiences and in so doing shaped children's psychological-behavioral development, adolescent sexual maturation and behavior, adult pair bonding, childbearing and parenting, and, in turn, the eventual development of the next generation. It was about all the factors and processes that affect the passing on of genes to future generations.

LET ME FURTHER EXPLAIN a few aspects of my theorizing that perhaps would not otherwise be clear. The first is that, just as standard thinking emphasizes, unsupportive family and parent-child relations (themselves stemming from personal, relational, and broader contextual conditions of adversity) pose risks for a child's future well-being. They induce mistrust and tendencies to view the world as an uncaring and even hostile place. Such a psychology, in consequence, fosters an opportunistic, advantage-taking, and exploitative social orientation—toward being a taker, not a giver, and first, foremost and perhaps exclusively looking out for oneself. Such a worldview, or in Bowlby's terminology, such an "internal working model" of the world, makes it more challenging for a developing child to skillfully and harmoniously navigate her future environment, make friends, establish an enduring pair bond, have fewer children, and raise them in a more caring, supportive manner reflective of high parental investment. Not to be ignored are the limits such ways of developing can place on the capacity to be economically productive and thus provide resources for one's offspring.

Where such life adversity and skill limitations prevail, the reproductive best bet becomes to develop fast by maturing quickly, engaging in sex early and often, and siring multiple children, perhaps by multiple partners, who will not be cared for especially well. Such a reproductive strategy or fast life history may not be the most efficient way to pass on genes to future generations, in contrast to the alternative. But another developmental trajectory is simply not available to the developing person in question, due to the psychological and behavioral impact of the care they receive in their early years. In essence, a strategy of fast development and greater quantity of children reflects, again, the best (developmental) card that can be played with the (contextual) hand that has been dealt.

Now imagine better prevailing conditions. If adversity wisely and strategically induces a fast life history by, among other things, accelerating pubertal development and promoting what many would regard as "problematic" behavior, then a supportive and nurturing developmental context can be expected to induce just the opposite: a slow life history and reproductive strategy. Because the latter extends the period of growth and development via delayed pubertal maturation, the child has more time and opportunity to "embody human capital." Developing children are better positioned to incorporate into their own bodies, minds, and behaviors the nutritional, economic, social, educational, and psychological resources that are available and accessible in their developmental environment. This will lead to more robust individuals who should be more attractive to mates, more capable of providing economically for themselves and others, and more devoted to investing time, resources, and effort into the next generation of children. Under such conditions, instead of needing, for example, four children to yield four grandchildren, perhaps only two are required to achieve the same number of offspring. There is no need, in other words, to accelerate development to ensure that one reproduces early if prospects for the future do not appear more adverse than the context surrounding one in advance of sexual maturity.

SOME HAVE WONDERED, not unreasonably, why both traditional developmental thinking and the evolutionary theory of socialization under consideration assign to prepuberty and especially early childhood such influence in shaping who the child will become. To address this issue, neuroscientists point to the nature of the child's (and perhaps especially, the infant's) brain. They highlight how "plastic" it proves to be, how highly "programmable" it is by what it encounters, and how this stands in contrast to later childhood—the claim being that, following the early years, the brain loses much of its plasticity, at least until a now-recognized second phase of heightened plasticity in adolescence.[13] But this analysis, while no doubt true, still leaves the question of *why?* From an evo-devo perspective, the neuroscience explanation addresses how development occurs, not why it operates as it does. This observation raises the following question for neuroscientists and ourselves: What is to be gained when it comes to passing genes on to future generations by regulating development based on early-life experiences?

Consistent with both traditional developmental and life history thinking, the answer is that having future development shaped by childhood experiences and exposures increases children's likelihood of succeeding—however defined—in the future. And this is because it *prepares children to cope with the world they are likely to encounter when they grow up.* As Richard Dawkins writes, "If you want to succeed in the world you have to predict, or behave as if predicting, what will happen next. All sensible prediction must be based on the past, and much sensible prediction is statistical rather than absolute."[14] That means, most significantly, that even if it is tolerably likely that the prediction of the future based on the past will be accurate, there is no guarantee that this will be the case. As Yogi Berra, the New York Yankees catcher of my childhood, is supposed to have said, "It is difficult to make predictions, especially about the future." The basic assumption is that the developmental context of childhood in terms of its stress and support serves as a probabilistic "weather forecast" or harbinger of likely things to come. As such, it serves as a developmental "guidance system."

Given this analysis, it is important to acknowledge that many question whether early life is a major force in shaping later life.[15] This is especially true of Mendelian geneticists who argue that many putative environmental effects are primarily a function of genetic influence, an issue that will be addressed in Chapter 6.[16] I raise it here as assurance that this fundamental issue will not be ignored, just deferred.

Quite some time after advancing the evolutionary theory of socialization, evolutionary-minded pediatricians studying prenatal stress effects on adult physical health—not psychological, social, behavioral, or sexual development—adopted the informative phrase *predictive adaptive response*. Sometimes referred to simply as PAR, it describes how past experience guides an individual's health in adulthood. [17] How this idea differs from the perhaps simpler weather-forecast view is evident from the second word in the phrase, *adaptive*. As in my evolutionary theory of development, the assumption is that natural selection has crafted the development of our bodies and minds to treat information gleaned in childhood about the world as a developmental guide, because doing so not only shapes future functioning but, in so doing, increases the chance of passing genes on to future generations. That, after all, is what *adaptive* in PAR implies. It has always troubled me that the scholars who usefully advanced the PAR terminology never acknowledged that, many years before their work, my own evolutionary theory of socialization had been based on the very same predictive-adaptive-response thinking, even if not so informatively labeled.

IN CLOSING this chapter, let me call attention to intellectual risks associated with advancing a theory based on an uncanny prediction like the one I did about pubertal timing. Years ago, the famous evolutionary biologist and hugely popular writer Stephen Jay Gould criticized those inclined to interpret human psychological and behavioral functioning in evolutionary terms as offering little more than "Just So Stories," cribbing the title of a book by Rudyard Kipling. Just so stories can be defined for our purposes as speculative explanations put forward to account for the origin of something, such as a biological trait.[18]

I recall sharing this critique with a founder of the field of evolutionary psychology, David Buss of the University of Texas at Austin, to see what his reaction was. "Jay," he said, "*all* hypotheses are just so stories"—which made perfect sense, and thus disarmed for me Gould's insightful-sounding criticism of work he was not disposed to embrace. This chapter has explained the evolutionary perspective central to the anthropologists' reinterpretation of father-absence effects, and the opportunity I found to further develop it. In Chapter 2, the focus shifts to research seeking to test my own just so story, hypothesizing on the nature of nurture and, specifically, the pubertal-timing prediction central to it.

# 3

# Testing the Puberty Hypothesis

U P TO THIS POINT we have been considering theory, which might even be regarded as just speculative ideas, about the how and why of human development. But, as implied in Chapter 2, while it is one thing to have a hypothesis, even an essential one (in this case, critical for evaluating the empirical value of a novel theory of the nature of nurture), it is another thing to test it. The work of this chapter is to engage with the empirical discoveries made by investigators seeking to prove or disprove that early-life adversity is predictive of accelerated pubertal development. Appreciate that the focus here is on tests of the puberty hypothesis that is the unique and discriminating prediction of my evolutionary theory of socialization; the research described in coming pages does not represent an evaluation of the entire theory (This is in large part because the other components and their linkages have already been evaluated and documented.)

I was fortunate to have two sets of colleagues prepared to undertake the task of testing my hypothesis about pubertal timing. Presented with a theory centered on gene pass-along as the ultimate goal of life, and my ideas about the influence of early-life experiences on pubertal timing, they did not say (as many did), "that doesn't make any sense; that's not how development works." Instead, these friendly colleagues immediately indicated they had the necessary data to test my puberty hypothesis—data that I did not yet have myself. These fellow researchers, however, were not necessarily embracing the theory underlying the puberty prediction. Their willingness to test my uncanny hypothesis excited me, because there could be empirical support for it, but at the same time made me anxious, because it could be found wanting.

The first indication of a readiness to test the puberty prediction occurred in a far northern town of Finland where I was attending an international conference. As I walked into the hotel bar, I spotted Avshalom Caspi, then of Harvard University, a colleague who at that point was not the very close friend he would eventually become. He was sitting with a woman I did not know, and they were talking about, of all things, puberty—because they themselves were studying pubertal development as part of a long-term study which, to date, has followed a large sample of New Zealand children from birth into their sixth decade of life.[1]

Being the New Yorker that I am (despite having not lived there since college), as soon as I overheard the mention of puberty, I impulsively—and some might say rudely—interrupted their conversation to say, "I have a puberty prediction for you." Once I had shared my ideas about effects of early-life experiences and exposures on pubertal timing, Avshalom's soon-to-be wife, then of the University of Wisconsin, enthusiastically responded, "we can test that." At that moment I knew that Temi Moffitt would become a great friend. Soon, the three of us were collaborating to test the prediction that distinguished my theory from other theories of child development. Their New Zealand data revealed that both father absence and high levels of family conflict within the first seven years of life predicted, just as hypothesized, girls' earlier ages of menarche.[2] Boy, was I excited by that discovery. I should immediately note that boys were not included in this or the next piece of research I will share, not because of any sexist bias but simply because it is easier to measure pubertal timing in females.

Soon after returning from Finland, I also called my old friend Larry Steinberg to share my thinking. He, too, responded by saying, "I can test that," and proceeded to do so. His work only followed a sample of American children from before to after pubertal maturation, but he also documented a link between problematic parent-child relations and earlier age of menarche.[3]

Now that these two pieces of evidence were in place, I was convinced not only that a reproductive-strategy view of development "had legs," but that I could write up the theory for publication. I say this because I knew that without some relevant pubertal evidence to cite, I would have only a rather far-fetched idea which would hold little appeal for most developmental scholars. Because one of the authors of the father-absence paper that had so influenced my thinking, anthropologist Pat Draper, was now my departmental colleague at Penn State University, and Steinberg knew so much more than I did about adolescent development, I invited both to join me as coauthors of the paper. The premier journal of my field not only accepted our submission but invited commentaries from two peer reviewers to be published alongside it—a rarity for that journal.[4]

I share this inside-the-academic-beltway story because it shines a light on peer review at its best. One of the reviewers was Eleanor Maccoby of Stanford University, regarded by many as the grand dame of child development. In all my years publishing numerous scholarly papers, I have never received or even read a review like the one she wrote. Its first line read, all in caps, "THIS IS A REMARKABLE PAPER," and it was followed by a few sentences extolling the paper's original hypothesis, comprehensive theory, and other virtues. But more important was what came next: nearly two full, single-spaced pages of Maccoby finding fault, detailing her concerns and disagreements with our thinking. One notable challenge was that, if ours were a sound theory, it would apply to males, not females, because the adoption of a fast life history would not pay off for females—and this despite our paper heralding the initial New Zealand and US evidence concerning age of menarche.

What made Maccoby's review so memorable was not its flattering opening paragraph. It was her concluding judgment that, despite the issues she raised, the paper merited publication. Here was a scholar that I, after too many years in the academy, can appreciate as quite exceptional. She was open-minded and intellectually secure enough to admire and respect ideas with which she disagreed. Our work had passed muster not because it conformed to Maccoby's own thinking, but on its own merits. Oh, what our scientific world—to say nothing of our political realm—would be like today if there were more Eleanor Maccobys!

In our theory paper, we highlighted a number of issues that still needed sorting out, several of which will be the focus of chapters to come. For now, just two will be highlighted. The first is whether the theory was more applicable to males, as argued by Maccoby, or to females—or both. Truth be told, we hadn't given that issue any thought whatsoever! In the case of Moffitt and Caspi's work, as well as Steinberg's, tests of the puberty hypothesis were restricted to females because it was for that population that both teams had the best pubertal data. Unlike male pubertal development, menarche arrives with obvious evidence, the timing of which can be accurately recalled even decades after its occurrence. The same is not true of when a boy first ejaculates, or grows underarm or genital hair, or deals with a breaking voice.

In addition to not yet being positioned to address the sex-of-child issue empirically, we were also at a loss when it came to the neurobiological and mechanistic *how* of development. Our theorizing had emphasized extrafamilial stress and support, marital quality, parenting and parent-child relations, attachment, and the child's social orientation as developmentally influential in regulating pubertal development and its aftermath. But exactly how environmental effects actually influenced puberty—how they got "under the skin"—remained a mystery, because none of the physiological and hormonal processes implicated in pubertal development had ever been linked to prior childhood experiences and exposures.

IN THE NOW thirty-plus years since our evolutionary theory was published, quite a number of studies have provided additional tests of the ideas advanced. As it

turned out, some scholars jumped at the opportunity to test the puberty prediction, the linchpin in our evo-devo thinking. To be clear, the reason the initial focus
of inquiry stimulated by our work did not concern itself with postpubertal development (such as age of sexual debut, stability of pair bonds, parenting) was because
it was already well established, in line with traditional developmental thinking,
that these phenotypes were related to early-life conditions. This, by the way, is why
pubertal development will figure mostly in my reporting of efforts to test my nature-
of-nurture theory. It is the original prediction that potentially transforms traditional developmental expectations.

To my surprise and even dismay, much of this initial work undertaken to test
the puberty hypothesis was what we developmentalists characterize as retrospective
in research design, as opposed to prospective. What this means is that the work
involved studying individuals well past childhood and puberty and asking them
not only to recall when they sexually matured, but the contextual conditions they
experienced while growing up decades earlier. Unfortunately, what many scholars
were then—and even still—not appreciative of is what has been documented repeatedly in developmental science. Unlike females' reporting of the timing of their first
period, adult recollections of family life and quality of parenting experienced while
growing up are so inaccurate as to be useless in many cases.[5] I am sure that this is
hard for many to believe, just as it was originally for me, given my confidence that
I could recollect childhood experiences accurately when it came to my family of
origin. But I have chosen to live in an empirical world, to believe and embrace what
evidence indicates, even if that doesn't jibe with my own expectations and inclinations. In the world of science, I am not alone in operating this way.

The problem of retrospective data is one that plagues much contemporary work
on so-called ACES—adverse childhood experiences—as so much such work is based
on asking adults about their childhoods.[6] Many investigators doing this work have
not learned the now decades-old lesson of how inaccurate retrospective reports of
childrearing history have proven to be. How has this been demonstrated? Simply
by measuring the experiences children are having while they are growing up and
then querying them about their childhoods when they are followed up in adulthood. Perhaps "simply" is the wrong word, as there is little that is simple about
maintaining contact with and participation of research participants from childhood
to adulthood.

The quality of care in childhood measurements at the two phases of life—when
it actually occurs and many years later—generally do not match up all that well. This
was brought home to me many years ago when I differed with my twin brother—with
whom I shared a very small bedroom for eighteen years—about a childhood event
that I was convinced I recalled with great clarity when we were both in that

bedroom. It turns out that we tend to be good at reporting discrete events retro-spectively, like a parental divorce, a residential move, or the death of a parent, but not whether parents were caring or supportive or harsh or negligent.[7] The same is even true when it comes to child abuse, as documented in a study of studies, known as a meta-analysis, of sixteen investigations collectively involving more than twenty-five thousand individuals.[8] It revealed that over half these persons with documented childhood maltreatment did not report such early-life adversity when queried between the ages of twenty and forty years; critically, the same inconsistency was evident among those who retrospectively reported maltreatment in adulthood for whom there existed no documented evidence of such in childhood.

What this means is that much of the retrospective evidence providing—or failing to provide—early support for the puberty prediction was of questionable value. For that reason, none of it involving retrospective assessments of the quality of childhood experience will be mentioned in this book. Fortunately, there have been any number of prospective studies, like the one involving the New Zealand children, enabling links to be drawn between early-life experiences measured early in life and pubertal development measured later in development.

BECAUSE MY HOPE is not to bore readers of this book by offering an exhaustive review of research on whether and how early-life conditions predict the timing of pubertal development, I will call attention to only a few studies that highlight important themes central to our theorizing. Let me begin acknowledging the con-tributions of Bruce Ellis, now at the University of Utah. I have always wondered if, without him, my evolutionary thinking about development would have died on the vine—at the time it seemed (and even still seems) to interest few students of child and adolescent development. Of those who would judge my ideas to hold promise, I believe Bruce was the first—perhaps because he did not start out as a developmental scholar but as a social psychologist, studying heterosexual dating and mating as part of his graduate work in evolutionary psychology. He was not tied to traditional ways of thinking about the effects of childhood conditions on psychological and behavioral development.

Upon completing his graduate work, Bruce took a postdoctoral position at Vanderbilt University where he chose to test predictions of my theorizing. What he found in his first relevant investigation clearly hooked him when it came to the direc-tion his own career would take—as we will see in the next chapter. Using prospective longitudinal data collected by others before he got to Vanderbilt, Bruce tested the hypothesized link between the quality of the early family environment and girls' ages of menarche. Results revealed that by seventh grade, the less time their fathers spent caring for them, as well as the less father-daughter affection and mother-daughter affection they experienced prior to kindergarten, the earlier they matured sexually.[9] A study conducted in Botswana provides similar results, finding that father absence predicted earlier age of menarche, as did living with a stepfather.[10]

The results of Bruce's first study—and many others—underscore why I have never really been happy with his eventual—and well-intended—relabeling of what I initially conceptualized as an evolutionary theory of socialization as "psychosocial *acceleration* theory."[11] I felt this way because our theorizing was not only about accelerating development under conditions of adversity. It was also about not accelerating development when extrafamilial conditions and family environments are supportive. I would have been happier with calling it "psychosocial regulation theory," implying that developmental experiences could speed up or slow down development depending, respectively, on how unsupportive or supportive they were. This seems even more appropriate to me because Bruce's first effort to test the puberty prediction underscored the importance of greater or lesser psychosocial support (that is, time spent caring for child, parent-child affection), not greater or lesser unsupportive parenting. So as not to confuse future scholars, I have decided not to modify Bruce's label of the theory even if I find it wanting, as it has caught on.

In addition to documenting effects of family context on pubertal timing in girls, the other important contribution of Bruce's work was to make clear that it was not just a father's physical presence that appeared to matter—that is, father presence versus absence, à la Draper and Harpending's theorizing. It was how fathers behaved with regard to their children, the very kind of index of relationship quality that is not accurately recalled in retrospective studies.[12] And this was exactly the point I was making by moving beyond the anthropologists' exclusive focus on a single adverse contextual condition, the social address of father absence, in order to underscore the importance of the quality of relationship experiences children have in their families.

Truth be told, Bruce entertained reframing the theory to exclusively emphasize fathers, just as the anthropologists had, contending that females evolved to be especially sensitive to the male parent in their lives when it came to regulating their life-history strategy. It turns out, though, that there is just too much evidence calling attention to mothers as developmentally influential agents when it comes to regulating pubertal maturation to privilege paternal influence. Indeed, even some other notable work by Bruce, including that mentioned three paragraphs earlier, makes this case.

Upon undertaking a comprehensive review of the evidence related to psychosocial regulation theory's critical puberty hypothesis more than a decade after its publication, Bruce concluded that the existing evidence provided reasonable even if incomplete support for the theory's critical prediction.[13] And this was because the available research principally indicated that it was more and less family cohesion and warmth in the parent-child relationship that were associated, respectively, with girls' later and earlier pubertal development. This led him to conclude that the proposed accelerating effect of troubled family relationships was not yet clearly established. In time, however, subsequent research, including some carried out by Bruce himself, altered the evidentiary landscape.

In one of Bruce's collaborative, prospective studies, for example, authoritarian parenting and negative family relationships predicted girls' advanced development of secondary sex characteristics, such as breasts, in fifth grade.[14] Also predicted by such unsupportive parenting was an earlier age of adrenarche, something another team also documented when the predictor was maternal psychological distress while pregnant.[15] Adrenarche is the first stage of pubertal development, involving the maturation of the adrenal gland around eight years of age, though it has no observable characteristics. Additional prospective research by Bruce showed that family disruption and, especially, father's social deviance—presumed to index problematic father-daughter relationships—predicted girls' earlier ages of menarche.[16] And another team conducting the Great Smoky Mountains Study of Youth in North Carolina discovered that maltreated girls reached sexual maturity earlier than their peers who were not maltreated.[17]

In view of the fact that child maltreatment, like many other problems (such as domestic violence, household chaos, parental drug addiction), are more likely to be found in socioeconomically disadvantaged than advantaged families, let me call attention to another piece of work linking adverse early-life conditions with pubertal development. This involved children born between 1959 and 1963 in New York State who were enrolled in a major longitudinal study known as the Collaborative Perinatal Project and followed from birth to age seven and then re-contacted in adulthood, when women were queried about their age of menarche.[18] After adjusting for a number of potentially confounding factors, results indicated that the more that socioeconomic disadvantage increased across the first seven years of life, the earlier menarche occurred. In consequence, women who resided in lower SES households at age seven reached puberty at younger ages than those who grew up in more advantaged families.

These findings based on individuals studied decades ago have been replicated more recently, in research based on the Adolescent Brain Cognitive Development (ABCD) Cohort. In a sample of 5,645 girls, greater economic deprivation and trauma exposure predicted early puberty (that is, before age twelve).[19] Intriguingly, though, there is reason to wonder whether the effect of adversity on early sexual maturation does not reflect just postnatal influences, as prenatal stress has also been linked to accelerated pubertal development in at least two cohort studies, one of more than fourteen thousand Danes and the other of some fourteen hundred Australians.[20] Recall that we did not advance any hypotheses about effects of prenatal experience.

Evidence like this raises the pressing mechanistic question about *how* psychosocial experience actually "gets under the skin" to affect the physiology of pubertal development. Back in 1991, we could only speculate about what might be involved. Now, more than three decades later, there is most interesting evidence, coming from work with mice subjected to a well-known early-life rodent stressor, namely separation from mother while pups.[21] What the animal work revealed was the importance of the premature and increased expression of two particular genes in the hypothalamus, a small cone-shaped structure located at the base of the brain that regulates hormones by linking the nervous system to the endocrine system via the nearby pituitary gland. Notably, this process proved operative in linking maternal separation with early pubertal development, but only in females, not males. (Much more will be said about gene expression in Chapter 5.) Although we cannot be certain that the same process is operative in humans, it is well appreciated that many biological processes are "conserved" across the mammalian order, meaning that they operate in many species. Perhaps in the not-too-distant future, evidence will confirm that a similar process is operative in accelerated pubertal development in human females.

Let's use this possibility for a thought experiment to underscore a point made in Chapter 1 about using knowledge of mechanisms to inform intervention, especially when the adversity likely to accelerate pubertal development has already occurred and cannot be prevented. Imagine that a means to inhibit or reverse the increased expression of the two genes in the hypothalamus that played a critical role in the study of mice was developed and proved safe for use with humans. Conceivably, it would then be possible to reduce or eliminate the effect of early adversity, be it early separation or something else, in contributing to the development of a fast life history. Now that may seem far-fetched to some, but as we will see when attention turns to epigenetics in Chapter 5, it could actually be within reach in the not-too-distant future.

As ALREADY pointed out and hopefully made clear, psychosocial acceleration theory was not just about puberty. What made pubertal timing central to the theory was, of course, its inevitable influence on reproduction. But when it comes to reproduction, there is also a need to think in terms of sexual behavior, as this is usually essential when it comes to passing on genes to future generations. The only investigation to my knowledge positioned to address the hypothesized three-step developmental cascade from early family experience to pubertal timing to sexual behavior was conducted as part of another prospective study, one in which I was involved. The research in question was originally undertaken to illuminate the effects of day care on children's development, the results of which are also covered in *The Origins of You*; it was carried out by a team of more than twenty developmental psychologists from ten universities who followed over a thousand children from birth to age fifteen.[22] As the children approached adolescence, I encouraged my many collaborators, including Larry Steinberg—who did not need any persuading—that we should collect data on puberty and sexual behavior, which we did.[23] Interrogation of these data revealed that the more harshly mothers of preschoolers treated their children, the earlier the girls had their first periods; and, as a result, the more "sexual risk taking" they engaged in as fifteen-year-olds (including engaging in oral or vaginal sex, and contracting sexually transmitted diseases). Notably, efforts to link early-life conditions to boys' pubertal development, based on physical exams, failed to do so, further undercutting Maccoby's good-faith claim that the theory, if on target, should be applicable to boys, not girls.

Before addressing that issue, a critical point needs to be made about how to think about developmental cascades. In *The Origins of You*, I compared them to dominoes lined up so that when the first one falls it knocks over the next one and, thereby, the next one—and so on and so forth. But the thing about human development is that it is not so rigidly scheduled, a point I will underscore repeatedly, in large part due to the social nature of our species. To be appreciated, then, is that any link between early puberty and subsequent sexual behavior will emerge in a social context. In the absence of particular social contexts, we should not expect to find such links. Consider, in this regard, how in the most conservative Islamic countries, females are often kept out of public settings. I can recall being in the home of a fellow academic in Jedda, Saudi Arabia for dinner. I never saw either his wife or daughter, only his son, as the former only passed food from kitchen to dining room through just a crack in the door connecting these two rooms.

A critical feature of the social context which plays a role in any effects of girls' early puberty on their sexual behavior is boys, especially older boys, and perhaps so-called bad boys. This was beautifully illuminated in research by Caspi and Moffit.[24] They took advantage of an experiment of sorts, in which some New Zealand girls were assigned by the school system to an all-girls school and others to a coed school. It was only in the latter in which early sexual maturation predicted problem behavior, including sexual activity. Clearly, the "evocative" effect of "tits and ass," if you will excuse the expression, contributes to female pubertal development predicting sexual behavior. What this should make clear is that this link is more likely under certain contextual conditions than under others; in other words, it is not inevitable. This is a theme the second part of this book will return to, but for reasons other than those just considered.

Returning to the issue of why the childcare study did not find evidence of the aforementioned three-step developmental cascade central to psychosocial acceleration theory in the case of males, several evolutionary-minded developmental scholars have advanced arguments for why this would or even should be the case.[25] One dramatic—perhaps even sexist—way of conveying their argument involves recognizing that while there is virtually always a man willing to have sex with a woman, the reverse is not true. Men tend to be far less choosy than women when it comes to mating, no doubt because the costs of pregnancy and what follows are so much lower for them. To reproduce, a female, almost whatever her qualities, simply needs to have reached sexual maturity and be fertile; sooner or later sex will almost certainly follow, should she desire it—and, sadly, sometimes when she does not.

Males reside in a different developmental universe. Not only do they need to attract females to reproduce, but they also need to outcompete other males for the opportunity to mate. This is why some evolutionary theorists call attention to the world of peers in shaping male life-history strategy, rather than families, something underappreciated in the original crafting of psychosocial acceleration theory. In the peer group, it is argued, males learn about popularity, power, and status, all of which are so often considered by females when they—or their elders—are choosing their mates. Also to be considered is that early maturation in males can compromise physical growth and strength, which could clearly undermine success with peers due to their influence on power and status in the male peer group and beyond. For these reasons, the family is regarded as less influential than it is for females when it comes to shaping reproductive strategy, at least according to some theorists.

Despite this seemingly compelling argument, it would be wrong to leave the impression that research testing the puberty hypothesis has never linked adverse childhood experiences with boys' pubertal timing. This is because it has.[26] Consider first a study of an Australian birth cohort showing that for both sexes greater socioeconomic disadvantage proved to be associated with earlier pubertal development.[27] Consider as well some longitudinal evidence extending this no-sex-difference result upon finding that the experience of childhood trauma before the age of eight predicted, for both boys and girls, accelerated pubertal development over the next two years and, thereby, greater eventual risk of cardiovascular disease during the third decade of life.[28] Recall that the developmental period in question is the same as that stipulated by psychosocial acceleration theory—the first five to seven years of life—as being especially influential when it comes to regulating reproductive strategy.

All this makes clear that, whatever the state of the data on females, it remains more mixed in the case of males. Hopefully, future investigations will clarify matters, perhaps by emphasizing contextual conditions or personal characteristics that increase or decrease the likelihood of boys' pubertal timing being affected by their childhood experiences and exposures.

IN ADDITION to failing to detect effects of family experiences on boys' pubertal development in the childcare study, the last point I want to make about its findings—and their implications—concerns how early in development it may be possible to predict pubertal timing, at least in females. Recall that in graduate school I studied infancy and, relatedly, was hired for my first academic job (like my final one) to conduct research specifically on infants. Not surprisingly, then, I spent a good deal of effort very early in my career studying factors and forces influencing infant attachment security. The question I became intrigued by, given our initial findings in the childcare study linking harsh parenting during the preschool years with menarcheal age and thus sexual risk-taking, was whether attachment security measured much earlier, at fifteen months of age, would itself predict a girl's age of menarche. It turned out that it did![29] Children judged, based on their observed behavior, to be insecure in their attachments to their mothers very early in life started puberty earlier (at 10.5 years on average) and completed this transformational process sooner (at 13.5 years on average) than those who were secure in their attachments to their mothers.

My strong feeling about this evidence was—and remains—that it should serve as the fulcrum to reintroduce evolutionary ideas to the study of attachment. After all, this was the first attempt to link attachment very early in life to physical development a decade or so later. Recall that Bowlby's thinking about attachment—which stimulated a huge body of theoretical and empirical work—was based on evolutionary thinking. But his untestable (even if most reasonable) claim regarding its origins referred only to a species-general way of developing as a result of natural selection—and one that emphasized only survival, not reproduction. Thus, our research revealed that embracing an evolutionary-developmental perspective could further illuminate the role of attachment early in life in shaping future development.

ONE RISK in books like this is that research can easily be cherry-picked to share evidence in line with a particular point of view, ignoring findings that fail to support it. At the same time, there can be sound arguments for treating at least some negative results differently than positive ones. In my years working at a university in London, I picked up a clever aphorism: "Absence of evidence is not evidence of absence." It's a reminder not to breathe too much meaning into failures to confirm hypotheses. At the same time, as anyone concerned about the "replication crisis" and "file drawer problem" in science today will emphasize, such results should not be ignored. Both phrases refer to problems that arise when authors and journals bring biases and conflicts of interest to their work and make decisions to publish or not publish that run counter to advancing true scientific understanding.

One way to resolve, at least to some degree, the tension between these two points of view about how to think about negative findings is via meta-analyses. These are efforts by scholars to assemble evidence addressing an issue and *quantitatively* rather than just narratively or qualitatively evaluate the overall state of the science in question: Does the existing body of evidence *collectively* support the predicted effect, in this case of early-life adversity forecasting earlier pubertal development, especially in girls? Fortunately, one such meta-analysis that included forty-three studies reliant on forty-six independent data sets evaluated the state of the art. It found that the following adverse childhood experiences were all reliably associated with one or more indices of girls' accelerated pubertal development: sexual abuse, physical abuse, child neglect, low socioeconomic status, father absence, and family dysfunction![30] This does not necessarily imply that we should treat the puberty prediction of psychosocial acceleration theory as confirmed—as an indisputably established fact—and for a variety of reasons to be considered in the next chapter and especially Chapter 6, focused on Mendelian genetics. But it does clearly suggest that something may be going on developmentally that had not been entertained until the theory of psychosocial acceleration was advanced.

Having said that, let me qualify somewhat the point I have been making in closing this chapter. First, not all null results should be treated the same. Second, the same is true of all positive results confirming expectations. Results depend very much on who is being studied and how investigations are conducted. Having more research participants is typically better than fewer, though it also matters who they are and the subpopulations they represent. Greater diversity can be both a strength and weakness, depending on a multiplicity of factors.

In the same way that samples can vary, yielding results in which one might—or might not—have confidence, the same is true of research designs; and this has implications for the meaning that can be breathed into meta-analytic results. Experimental manipulations and intervention studies are generally more strongly positioned to detect true causation than observational studies, a point I will reiterate throughout this volume. I have already made clear that, when it comes to observational work, that which is based on the prospective study of lives over time is typically better than that which relies on retrospective reports of childhood experiences and exposures. Then there is the issue of how measurements are made. The following strategies can be quite different in the quality of information gathered in the case of adversity experiences and exposures: an in-depth interview, a detailed questionnaire asking about a variety of adversities, and a single question asking whether a particular adversity was experienced. There is also the issue of taking into consideration so-called "alternative explanations" of findings. Are effects detected truly a function of children's lived experiences, or do they perhaps have more to do with whether there is a history of mental illness in the family or the family's genetic makeup more generally? Bottom line: Even results of meta-analyses do not always capture the quality-of-research considerations just raised. So, to repeat, even their findings are not entirely dispositive.

# 4

# Not So Fast

The THEORETICAL PERSPECTIVE AND empirical findings discussed in Chapter 3 prompt reflections on a variety of issues. Therefore, this chapter subjects my own theorizing and the research it stimulated to the same treatment Chapter 2 gave to the anthropologists' reinterpretation of effects of father absence. Informed by the thoughtful work of others, I will critique my ideas, addressing concerns that have been or could be raised, and highlighting more recent ideas which can be usefully incorporated into psychosocial acceleration theory to extend it. Thus, sections below are devoted to the following topics: psychological mechanisms not originally included in psychosocial acceleration theory; the fact that adversity accelerates pubertal development by only a few months; the importance of energy when it comes to accelerating development; the significance of physical health; and the need to distinguish different types of early-life adversity and their effects on reproductive strategy.

Some might be surprised at a list that does not include what I called in the Introduction "the elephant in the room"—namely, Mendelian genetics. Recall the concern, already noted several times as a major one, that much of the evidence considered in Part I of this book may reflect genetic effects only masquerading as effects of the environment. This is such a big issue that, rather than giving it the limited consideration that the topics in this chapter receive, I devote a later chapter, Chapter 6, in full to it.

## Psychological Mechanisms and Beyond

As a trained developmental psychologist rather than an evolutionary biologist, I not surprisingly assigned a central role to psychological processes in my revision of standard developmental thinking about effects of early-life experience on child development, even as I drew heavily on it. Recall that my nature-of-nurture thinking is based on the notion that adverse rearing conditions induce a fast life history due to their probabilistic impact on becoming mistrustful, viewing the world as an uncaring place, and developing an opportunistic, advantage-taking and exploitative social orientation.

It would be mistaken to assume that my thinking covered all potentially relevant psychological processes and developmental mechanisms characteristic of a fast life history. Indeed, my brilliant friend and colleague Marco Del Giudice, who is now back in his home country of Italy after several years spent at the University of New Mexico, has called attention to a variety of additional "markers" of fast versus slow life histories that were not explicitly stipulated in psychosocial acceleration theorizing.[1] These include, among others, honesty, humility, impulsivity, self-control, and sensation seeking. Consider in this regard evidence that, for economically disadvantaged children growing up in resource-poor environments, earlier pubertal maturation at age ten predicted poorer cognitive self-control (referred to as *effortful control*) at age fourteen, which itself predicted more sexual activity (such as oral, vaginal, anal sex) with more sex partners by age sixteen, as well as greater use of substances such as cigarettes, alcohol, cannabis, and LSD.[2] Unfortunately, while such evidence might be suggestive of how childhood shapes psychological processing, these findings cannot confirm that, as they link pubertal timing with future psychological makeup.

Other features of life history that I am sure we missed concern future orientation, delay of gratification, and discounting the future. It makes all the sense in the world that children growing up under conditions of adversity, especially ones characterized by promises not kept and hopes and positive expectations not realized, should be inclined to live in the here and now more than in tomorrows. Given the adverse experiences and exposures presumed to foster a fast life history and quantity-oriented reproductive strategy, what would be the developmental basis of expecting that something positively valued, like getting a birthday present or having a friend provide emotional support—something that might happen, is supposed to happen, or even that has been promised to happen—will actually come to pass? Growing up under such conditions should induce the sensibility that "a bird in the hand is worth two in the bush." While I know of no evidence linking such discounting of the future with pubertal timing (the distinguishing feature of psychosocial acceleration theory), there is certainly evidence that childhood adversity fosters a tendency toward it.[3] I think we can presume, then, that it is also a central psychological feature of a fast life history. In contrast, under developmental conditions likely to induce a slow life history and quality-oriented reproductive strategy, children are likely to have discovered that waiting is a wiser strategy, likely yielding bigger payoffs of various kinds.

Another psychological process that we never considered—and which has been only recently highlighted as distinguishing fast and slow life histories—involves the distinction between exploration and exploitation when it comes to searching for something, even just seeking information.[4] These are alternative ways of learning and solving problems, though it is best to think of them as anchoring ends of a continuum rather than completely distinct approaches to learning. Consider a situation in which one must choose between searching widely or within a narrow range of options. Does one choose to exploit a convenient, known solution, or rather explore a variety of possibly better solutions? As individuals grow up, there is a gradual transition from exploration to exploitation and thus movement from random to systematic exploration and from a wide to a narrower search strategy. Metaphorically, children's attention is more like a lantern than a spotlight, having a wider focus than that of adults; this can be efficient when it comes to obtaining information that is irrelevant to whatever one is seeking.

Intriguingly, there is evidence that in response to adversity the normative developmental shift from exploration to exploitation is accelerated, meaning that it emerges earlier than otherwise anticipated, just as pubertal development seems to be. The underlying logic behind such an early shift to exploitation under childhood conditions of adversity is that it facilitates early independence and thus reliance on self more than on others. In response to more favorable conditions, slower development allows for a longer period of exploration.

It is not just with regard to the psychology of a fast life history that I did not get everything completely right. What I also did not appreciate in advancing psychosocial acceleration theory is something Jim Chisholm, an anthropologist at the University of Western Australia, clued me in to, indisputably extending the theory.[5] This was the importance of death, leading some to eventually characterize a fast life history in terms of "live fast and die young."[6] What Chisholm underscored that I did not was that adversity affects survival itself, thus increasing the risk that the developing individual might die before having a chance to reproduce. An even more important reason that adverse early-life experiences and exposures would accelerate development, then, is that sexually maturing earlier than would otherwise be the case increases the chances of passing on one's genes before dying. It's a matter of biological gravity.

From this perspective, accelerated development evolved as a strategic means of limiting the risk of not passing on genes to future generations due to dying before achieving sexual maturity. Although I have not seen evidence linking the risk of death, often indexed by local rates of mortality, with pubertal timing, an increased chance of dying does predict what follows early puberty according to both psychosocial acceleration theory and much standard developmental thinking—namely, a younger age at first birth. It may also be relevant that greater mortality risk is associated with fewer permissive laws and attitudes toward abortion.[7] That is, as risk of dying increases, support for abortion decreases. Of interest is that the work in question was based on data collected in fifty US states and 202 world societies on about three thousand adult individuals in 363 US counties, and more than 147,000 respondents across the globe. Furthermore, results held up even when a host of potentially confounding factors (such as religiosity, political ideology, wealth, education, industrialization) were taken into account (that is, statistically controlled).[8]

## Small Effects

It is important to understand that an adaptation does not need to yield large fitness benefits to be favored by natural selection. For it to shape us, whether via a direct or indirect process, it only has to enhance the passing on of genes to future generations somewhat, relative to what came before it. So even if maturing fast in response to adversity increased fitness by only a small amount, it could still be selected—because over time its benefits would have spread as those who inherited the genes responsible for the adaptation in question would come to bear more children who survived and reproduced than those who had not. In time, then, meaning across many, many generations, such individuals, due to their even small reproductive advantage, would come to comprise ever more of a population.

The issue of small effects is especially applicable to psychosocial acceleration theory in the modern world. This is because the detected effects of adversity on pubertal timing prove to be rather small, even if statistically reliable. These days, early maturing females in the Western world exposed to adversity tend, on average, to experience their first period only two to eight months before other girls. In light of this observation, the question arises of whether the small effects of adversity on girls' menarcheal age has reproductive consequences. Apparently, they can.

To understand why that is the case, the first thing to appreciate is that a female typically is still not fertile when she experiences her first menstruation. The time it takes before just half of menstrual cycles become ovulatory, thereby affording the possibility of conception, is approximately one year for those whose first period occurs before age twelve, but more than four years if it happens at age thirteen or older.[9] Thus, early-maturing girls have the ability to become pregnant sooner following their first menstruation than do those whose first period comes later. In consequence, those maturing earlier would also be able to bear a second—or even a third—child within the four-year period it takes girls who mature at an older age to produce just their first one, clearly affording a fitness advantage.

But there is another issue to consider, as well, when it comes to the small detected effects linking developmental adversity with early puberty. There is a phenomenon in the study of adolescence referred to as "the secular trend;" it captures the change over the past two hundred years or so in the timing of puberty. Back in the mid-1800s it was typical for girls to begin menstruating around fifteen to seventeen years of age in places like Norway, the United States, France, and Great Britain. Yet today it is between twelve and thirteen years of age—we are talking averages here—having steadily moved earlier and earlier in recent history.[10] This is typically attributed to improved health and nutrition.

The idea that developmental stress could accelerate sexual maturation, at least in females, seems to fly in the face of this secular-trend evidence, what with both a good thing, better health and nutrition, and apparently a bad thing, contextual adversity, influencing development in the seemingly same way—by accelerating it. What risks being misunderstood is that in the case of almost anything we are interested in—and I mean anything—there is typically more than a single cause. Most phenomena, be they political, economic, or developmental, are shaped by a myriad of factors and forces and they don't necessarily all fit together in perfect harmony. So even if both developmental stress and enhanced health and nutrition can foster an earlier age of puberty, this does not necessarily mean that something is awry in thinking about the nature of nurture that is central to this book. Development is multiply determined—and complicated.

Returning to the secular trend, whatever its cause, it raises a most interesting question: Is it possible that age of menarche was more developmentally plastic two hundred or more years ago? That is, could it be that the effect of contextual adversity on pubertal timing is far more limited today than it once was, including in ancestral times when our species was made up of hunter-gatherers, and puberty occurred later than it does today? This is what geneticists refer to as a "range of reaction," in this case of pubertal response to contextual conditions. In other words, much of the capacity for pubertal timing to be shaped by developmental experiences may have already been eliminated, "squeezed out," due to the secular trend, resulting in a narrower range of reaction. If so, there would simply be less "room" today, given the secular trend, for developmental adversity to accelerate pubertal development than was once the case, especially in ancestral times. In consequence, perhaps what were once larger effects, in terms of number of months that adversity accelerated pubertal development, have been reduced.

## Energetics

What our paper outlining psychosocial acceleration theory did not make as clear as it should have is that, by the time the theory was advanced, it was widely appreciated that female pubertal development is dependent upon the amount of fat that a prepubescent female carries. This is known as the *critical fat hypothesis*, as also discussed in *The Origins of You*. Undernutrition and low body fat, or an altered ratio of lean mass to body fat, delays the adolescent growth spurt and the onset of menarche.[11] According to some estimates, a minimum level of fatness—17 percent of body weight—is required for menarche to occur.[12] This is why female ballerinas, gymnasts, and other highly skilled athletes, as well as women who diet excessively, experience what is known as secondary or primary amenorrhea, meaning they do not have menstrual periods.[13] Their behavior has simply reduced their fat stores to the point where the critical level of fat needed to initiate pubertal maturation is lacking.

What this analysis should make clear is that the energy available in the body matters when it comes to the dynamic process of pubertal development. In order for puberty to occur, girls must have a certain amount of energetic resources available to support the transformation of their bodies in ways that make fertility possible. What this implies is that, if and when a lack of nutrients characterizes a child's developmental environment, as in the case of famine most obviously, there is no reason to expect that other features of adversity that are also encountered—such as poverty, family violence, or father absence, to cite but three conditions—will accelerate pubertal development.

A nice example of this principle comes from an investigation of the effect of war exposure on, as it turns out, boys' pubertal development.[14] Specifically, exposure to events that risked injury or death, such as bombings or seeing others get beaten or tortured, predicted earlier maturation, but only if the child did not appear to be undernourished, as indexed by a low body mass index (BMI). Having sufficient energy, then, is a necessary condition, even if not a sufficient one, to induce a fast life history in response to adverse childhood experiences and exposures, at least with respect to accelerated pubertal development.

It turns out that, when it comes to the prediction of adversity-linked pubertal timing, it makes a big difference how widespread poverty and insufficient nutritional and health resources are in a society. In countries that qualify as low-income, lower socioeconomic status is associated with later puberty, as children growing up in severe poverty experience substantial energetic deprivation, typically due to food insecurity.[15] Appreciation of this reality led Bruce Ellis and colleagues to argue that "two tiers" of the childhood environment need to be distinguished to understand how early-life conditions shape reproductive development.[16] The first tier is *energetics*, so when nutritional resources are insufficient, the second environmental tier—of non-energetic sources of adversity which threaten childhood survival (such as war or neighborhood violence)—will not accelerate pubertal development. But when energetics are sufficient, this second tier of adversity induces this result.

Perhaps surprisingly, given what has been stipulated about psychosocial acceleration theory up to this point, while pubertal development will not be accelerated when energetic resources are insufficient, other features of a fast life history still can be. (This point is also argued by Ellis and associates.) These other features include early sexual debut, multiple sex partners, and the bearing of many children. Such evidence suggests that physiological and psychological or behavioral features of a fast life history resulting from early-life adversity can be decoupled. This is one reason that, as noted earlier, questions have been raised about the "coupling" of the many features of fast or slow life histories. What would be interesting to know considering the findings just highlighted is whether, as will be made clear in the next subsection, well-documented negative health consequences of early menarche arise in females growing up under conditions of adversity even when puberty is not accelerated due to energetic limitations.

## The Significance of Physical Health

Recall that life-history theorizing presumes that the reason human reproductive strategy evolved to be shaped by early-life conditions is because these function, probabilistically, as a "weather forecast" of what life will be like in the future. If development proceeds in a manner consistent with the anticipated future environment, the chance of passing genes on to future generations should be enhanced. Such predictive-adaptive-response theorizing has not gone unquestioned. The basis of such questioning is that it was no doubt the case in our ancestral past, just like today, that children's early years did not always presage their later-life conditions. Metaphorically, then, a rainy childhood did not always presage a rainy adulthood, with the same being true of a sunny childhood. This indisputable reality will be central to Part II of this book, which challenges some of what is stipulated in this first part.

Considering psychosocial acceleration theory from this "mismatch" perspective, one team of scholars argued that it is not early-life conditions that regulate life-history development. Rather, it is *internal bodily cues to health and well- being* that do so, including things like body size, energetic reserves, immune functioning, and quality of cell-repair mechanisms. And this is because such cues would be better—meaning more accurate—prognosticators of what health and thus life would be like in the future than would the childhood environment.[17] So if childhood health was poor, with increased risk of compromised future health and even premature mortality, then it would be strategic to develop a fast reproductive strategy. By the same logic, good childhood health should presage a slow life history. This analysis presumes, for reasons already highlighted, that bodily energetics are sufficient to get the developmental job done when it comes to accelerating development.

As I reflected on this critique, several concerns came to mind. The first was its failure to appreciate that psychosocial acceleration theory not only emphasized the timing of pubertal development, an obvious internal bodily process, but also failed to recognize that attachment security also involves an internal bodily process, one pertaining to the brain via cognitive development.[18] Central to Bowlby's theorizing was the claim that support and nurturance, as well as lack thereof, influence the child's "*internal* working model" of herself (is she lovable?), her caregivers (are they sensitive or caring?), and thus the world more broadly (is it trustworthy and safe?). In other words, attachment is about affective-cognitive processes that shape not only how the child views the world, but how she relates to it. Recall my proposal that attachment security evolved as an important process in regulating life history—not just in influencing mental health—making it central to psychosocial acceleration theory

The claim that attachment reflects internal bodily processes raises another concern that an emphasis on internal regulators of reproductive strategy fails to take into account: that as children develop, they are active constructors of their own environment, based on what they have already learned about it and, as a result, their expectations of it. In other words, even if life becomes less adverse in adulthood than it was in childhood, children's own behavior could create continuously adverse experiences that continue to influence their development as they become adults. Consider in this regard work showing that the more children aged three to fifteen proved to be negatively emotional, especially with respect to mistrust of others—a basic feature of a fast life history and central to an insecure internal working model— the more likely they were to experience adversity in the form of stressful life events at thirty-two to forty-five years of age.[19] So even if in one respect mismatch and discontinuity might characterize childhood and adult environments, that would not necessarily be experienced by the child exposed to adversity early in life, whose own behavioral development could contribute to the matching of early- and later-life conditions.

My final—and biggest—concern with the idea that it is internal bodily processes that are of critical, if not exclusive, influence in regulating life history has to do with what seemed to be the authors' tendency to cast internal bodily and external environmental influences as mutually exclusive. I could not help but wonder why this interesting and original analysis of what shapes reproductive strategy was cast as an alternative to the predictive-adaptive-response (or weather-forecast) one emphasizing environmental conditions in childhood and later life. Rather, it seemed to be a (welcome) extension to it. To my way of thinking, the two perspectives were complementary—in the same way that Chisholm's thinking emphasizing risk of death complemented a focus on other psychological processes (such as attachment insecurity, distrust of others) emphasized in the original theory.

Truth be told, as I looked at the paper thoughtfully raising the issue of childhood health, it appeared that its authors were actually of two minds. One held the view that the predictive-adaptive-response emphasis on childhood contextual conditions should be replaced by a focus on childhood health; the other held that the two points of emphasis were not necessarily alternative accounts of life history development. It was because of the latter reading that I did three things. First, as one of the paper's reviewers, I encouraged its publication and, second, I willingly contributed an invited commentary about it, emphasizing the point of extending and complementing existing psychosocial acceleration theorizing.[20] Third, because I was so intrigued by the potential theoretical extension of psychosocial acceleration theory, extending it to include physical health, I invited one of the paper's authors whom I knew and admired, Daniel Nettle, then of the University of Newcastle in the UK, to join me and my graduate student, Sarah Hartman, to evaluate theory-extension thinking.

Once again we drew on information collected as part of the large childcare study previously mentioned. What we found was in line with my developmental-cascade expectations.[21] Greater adversity during the preschool years predicted poorer general health in childhood and greater increase in BMI across the first twelve years of life, with both forecasting earlier age of menarche and, thereby, risky sexual behavior by age fifteen. Voila! The early-environment *and* internal-bodily-cue perspectives could be empirically integrated. Subsequent work also focused on pubertal development revealed much the same.[22]

Influenced by our research, another team of investigators, including Larry Steinberg, sought to address roughly the same issue given the availability of data from multiple countries and diverse cultures.[23] The data came from many non-Western nations, including China, Jordan, Kenya, the Philippines, and Thailand. Results proved consistent with what has already been reported, even though this cross-cultural research did not include a focus on pubertal timing. Results, which by this time should come as no surprise, revealed that adverse environments *and* child health problems were each uniquely associated with fast-life-history indicators of an opportunistic, advantage-taking, and exploitative social orientation, reflected in aggressiveness, impulsiveness, and tendency to take risks. Critically, the two sources of influence *collectively* accounted for differences in how children developed better than did either one on its own. These findings certainly suggest that a great deal of sensory information contributes to the calibration of reproductive strategy, underscoring a point made earlier in this book that development is multiply determined.

Before considering the final issue to be addressed in this chapter, one last point needs to be made about modifying psychosocial acceleration theory to include a focus on physical health in adulthood, as well as childhood.[24] It turns out that there is extensive medical research linking early adversity with both disease-related biomarkers (such as inflammation, blood pressure, blood sugar) and poor health later in life (such as heart disease, stroke, diabetes).[25] It is typically discussed in terms of the "developmental origins of health and disease" (aka DOH&D).[26] Perhaps the most appropriate example of DOH&D evidence given psychosocial acceleration theory is that early age of menarche, which we have already found to be associated with early-life adversity, has also been linked to poor health later in life. This is especially true of cancers of the reproductive tract and other bodily organs.[27]

Of special interest, then, is a long-term follow-up of participants in the large-scale childcare study mentioned in the prior chapter. It revealed that by age thirty earlier menarche and earlier onset of breast development each predicted higher cardiometabolic risk (that is, greater waist circumference, systolic and diastolic blood pressure, and blood sugar, and lower good cholesterol). Just as importantly, greater health risk was associated with growing up in a more economically and socially disadvantaged family, findings clearly consistent with psychosocial acceleration theory.[28]

What I want to underscore in calling attention to such DOH&D evidence is a major distinction between evolutionary and medical perspectives. The thinking underlying DOH&D is that adversity generates wear and tear on the body which, eventually, leads to more frequent bodily breakdown and, thereby, ill health, even premature death. But does early-life adversity simply undermine health and well-being or, rather, *strategically regulate it* in the service of reproductive goals? The answer is that Darwinian natural selection favors the passing on of genes and thus privileges inclusive fitness over and above health, wealth, and happiness. Evolution appears to have traded off poor future health and possibly even a shorter life for an increased chance of having descendants. Biological gravity strikes once again.

## Dimensions of the Developmental Environment

In advancing psychosocial acceleration theory, we had not thought deeply enough it turns out, in retrospect, about the many varieties of contextual adversity that might foster a fast life history—and those that might not. Mental health–oriented research at the time typically focused on effects of either just one kind of adverse childhood experience at a time—such as child maltreatment, divorce, or harsh punishment—or the accumulation of multiple and diverse kinds of adversity. The latter reflect "cumulative (contextual) risk." It became central to work by physicians studying the long-term effects of adverse childhood experiences on physical health, more about which will be said below.[29]

Over the past decade or so, developmental scholars have come to be ever more aware of the need to distinguish among different types of adversity, as these might have very different effects on development, including pubertal development. Fortunately, two insightful efforts to reconceptualize the developmental environment have been offered recently which help to get a better handle on such contextual complexity. One by Bruce Ellis and his colleagues is based on evolutionary thinking and a cross-species analysis of the environmental conditions that induce a fast or slow life history.[30] The other by Katie McLaughlin, then of Harvard University, and Margaret Sheridan of the University of North Carolina is, in contrast, based on current understanding of the brain—a neuroscience analysis.[31]

Whereas the evolutionary-minded scholars distinguished the environmental dimensions of *energetics,* already discussed, as well as environmental *unpredictability* and *harshness,* the neuroscientist-minded ones distinguished the experiences of *threat* and *deprivation.* What was central to both theoretical models was the empirically based assertion that different kinds of adversity should not be treated as equivalent when it comes to influencing children's development. It was for this reason that each of the two teams of developmental scientists coincidentally, yet independently, chose the exact same title for one of its early published papers evaluating the empirical utility of its approach: "Beyond Cumulative Risk."[32]

Consideration of the two approaches to conceptualizing underlying, common-denominator dimensions of the developmental environment makes clear that they overlap in some ways. A recent collaboration between the two teams of scholars that developed these frameworks highlights their similarities and differences while seeking to integrate them.[33] In so doing, this work underscores the need to consider both the evolutionists' focus on the *why* of development and the neuroscientists' focus on the *how* when seeking to understand effects of early-life conditions.

The dimensions of harshness highlighted by the evolutionary-minded scholars, and threat by the developmental neuroscientists, are clearly overlapping, even if not the same. For this reason, a graduate student I worked with at UC Davis, Maria Usacheva, combined them to create an index of harshness-threat.[34] *Harshness* refers to experiences and exposures that increase the risk of disability and death and that are relatively unaffected by what a person does, including, for example, war, neighborhood violence, family violence, infectious disease, and famine. In research on current modern societies, indicators of harshness have often included socioeconomic disadvantage, given well-documented associations between it and greater risk of multiple forms of morbidity, as well as premature mortality.[35] *Threat* captures all conditions that are physically harmful or are dangerous, thus inducing fear; it would also include family and neighborhood violence, as well as circumstances like sibling or peer bullying.

Like harshness, environmental *unpredictability* is defined as conditions that increase the risk of morbidity and mortality—but on a *random* basis. In other words, while harsh environments can be predictable—such as when in ancestral times food would be hard to find or when certain animals became especially dangerous (such as male elephants in heat)—they can also occur in an unpredictable fashion. For example, out of nowhere a rare predator attacks a person; a hurricane arises that destroys a settlement; or an earthquake does the same. Measures of childhood unpredictability thus include the comings and goings of different men in the home, episodic residential changes, change over time in family economic conditions, and erratic neighborhood conditions.[36]

*Deprivation* is different from threat-harshness and unpredictability. It refers to conditions that undermine growth and development by providing limited or reduced social and cognitive inputs—stimulation—from the environment, but ones that do not necessarily induce a sense of fear and risk to life and limb. These circumstances often result from insufficient nutrients that reduce children's energetic status, while compromising growth. Deprivation can also deprive the child of opportunities for learning and thus affect cognitive capabilities. Famine, food insecurity, poverty, parental neglect, and under-staffed orphanages with poorly trained staff reflect environmental deprivation. All of these can also increase the probability of death, especially when severe, thus also meeting the criteria of harshness. Not to be missed, then, is that harshness, threat, unpredictability, and even deprivation, while distinct, often co-occur—and can be difficult to disentangle.[37]

Nevertheless, and this is the critical point to be made, there is clear evidence that distinguishing harshness or threat from deprivation is of great importance when considering whether and how different types of adversity affect life-history strategies.[38] Perhaps the most compelling evidence to date is that concerning pubertal development, given its central and theory distinguishing role in psychosocial acceleration thinking. In work conducted by Katie McLaughlin and colleagues, *early-life exposure to threat proved to be associated with girls' accelerated pubertal development, whereas exposure to deprivation was associated with slower pubertal development.*[39] This evidence, of course, is consistent with the aforementioned discussion of energetics when considering adversity effects on pubertal timing. Although it is alone in chronicling the *differential*—and opposite—effects of threat and deprivation on pubertal timing, other threat-related research, along with work focused on contextual harshness and unpredictability, underscores the importance of the dimensional approach when it comes to documenting adversity effects on menarcheal age and other features of life history.[40] Especially notable in regard to the latter point is a review of fifty-one studies which revealed consistent evidence linking exposure to physical abuse and domestic violence in childhood with becoming a bully in adolescence, results clearly in line with the theoretical claim that a fast life history is characterized by opportunistic advantage-taking and exploitative behavior.[41]

A long-standing problem with failing to distinguish among underlying, common-denominator-like dimensions of adversity—when relying on developmentalists' cumulative-risk or physicians' ACE thinking—is that it could end up camouflaging an actual effect of some adverse conditions on reproductive-strategy development. This may be one reason that not every investigation of adversity effects on pubertal timing—or other features of a fast or slow life history—yields the same findings. For example, in the case of pubertal timing, a composite index of diverse adverse childhood experiences could be biased toward deprivation in one inquiry and threat-harshness in another, leading to findings that appear at odds with each other, when actually there is underlying order in the chaos (such as that threat, not deprivation, is predictive of pubertal timing).

WHAT I HOPE I have made clear in this chapter is that our original presentation of psychosocial acceleration theory was not the end of applying an evo-devo perspective to effects of early-life conditions on human development. In the same way that the theory built upon and extended that of the anthropologists who focused exclusively on father absence, others have come along to contribute to the further development of the original ideas we advanced. We now appreciate, as we did not originally, psychological processes like future orientation and mortality risk, the role of energetics, the significance of physical health, and the importance of recognizing and distinguishing underlying dimensions of adversity. All these ideas have enriched and extended understanding of the nature of nurture.

# 5
# Even Faster?

I N  T H E  P R E F A C E  I noted that, back in high school, I never imagined becoming a teacher or a scientist. One reason it happened was that I became enamored with the process of research and discovery in graduate school. Looking back across the decades my career has spanned, one of the things that so impresses me is how much our understanding of human development has advanced. This chapter calls attention to two such advances that, while they occurred well after the advent of psychosocial acceleration theory, did much to extend and enrich it. The first is the field of epigenetics, which burst on the scene in the early 2000s. The second is the science of biological aging, which emerged more recently, and the exploration of how childhood experiences and exposures may influence it.

## Epigenetics

In 2003, as I sat in the audience at a small, invitational conference in Berlin, Germany, waiting for my turn to speak, I suffered multiple moments of confusion. This gathering was focused on the attachment relationships formed by infants with their parents and caregivers, and the presenters made repeated references to apparently brand-new and groundbreaking research by someone called "Meaney." I wasn't familiar with it and, for the life of me, couldn't help picturing the villains in the old Beatles movie *Yellow Submarine,* the green meanies. (Yes, I know, I'm dating myself.) Eventually I gathered that, in fact, it was a developmental biologist from McGill University, Michael Meaney, whose work was being discussed. Here I call attention to his research because it experimentally—and thus causally—documented the effect of early-life experiences on the development of reproductive strategy.[1]

What made the Meaney work so noteworthy, leading multiple speakers to cite it, was that it introduced developmental science to the field of *epigenetics* for the first time. To appreciate why Meaney was being mentioned so often at the conference and why his epigenetic work is highlighted in this chapter, a brief digression is called for here, so please bear with me. In the parlance of science, when we investigate whether and how some factor (like temperament in early childhood) or experience (like being bullied in middle childhood) predicts and perhaps influences an aspect of development (like antisocial behavior or depression), the predictor is called the *independent variable* and the developmental phenotype being predicted is called the *dependent variable*. The assumption is that the predicted outcome *depends* on the independent variable, the predictor. In prior chapters, developmental experiences like harsh parenting and environmental exposures like spousal conflict served as independent variables to predict the dependent variable of pubertal timing.

In Chapter 6, we will return to previously presented evidence linking developmental experiences and environmental exposures early in life to pubertal timing and other aspects of reproductive strategy, and will consider some additional challenges to it. At that point, Mendelian genetics will come to center stage. For now, the point to appreciate is that most genetics studies, and indeed most people's understanding of genetic influence, treat individuals' genetic makeups (their genotypes) not just as independent variables but as *first causes* accounting for why they are as they are. The claim is simply that, because our DNA is set at conception, preceding any developments that will subsequently occur, genetic makeup is the starting point of everything.

While this classical point of view should not be dismissed as entirely misguided, the argument here is that epigenetics forces a reappraisal of it. The fact is that epigenetics is very much about how developmental experiences and environmental exposures, including adverse ones, can affect the functioning of genes—and specifically, whether or not they are *expressed,* due to their being turned on or off. Note, then, what logically follows: It means that environmental effects turn those supposed first causes, the genes people are born with, into dependent variables! Way back at the turn of the millennium this was a rather radical view of how genes operated in shaping development, including perhaps reproductive strategy.

There was a reason Meaney was mentioned so often at the Berlin conference on attachment. It was because of truly groundbreaking research—on rodents—that his investigatory team had reported. They discovered that how a mother rat, or dam, treated her newborn pup affected gene expression in the pup—and thus, how anxious that baby rat grew up to be. When dams licked and groomed their newborn pups a lot, the expression of a particular gene known to play a role in rats' physiological response to stress was "turned off," and the rat was less anxious as it developed than it would otherwise have been. More specifically—and chemically—a stress-related gene was turned off when it had a methyl group attached to the gene, producing a more stress-resistant pup.

While there are other ways of affecting gene expression, DNA *methylation*—which turns genes off so that they are not expressed—is the process that has been most studied, at least in humans. Other mechanisms turn genes *on* so that they *are* expressed.[2] Methylation is not the same as or a synonym for epigenetics or gene expression. Rather, it is one of several epigenetic processes that regulate gene expression. Importantly, the regulation of genes may be influenced by developmental experiences and environmental exposures, including adverse ones and, as a result, affect how the organism develops.

The excitement that the Meaney research generated among students of human development—and the lay public—is hard to exaggerate. Fascination with epigenetics became widespread. In the nature-nurture debate, those of us inclined to emphasize the influence of nurture over (Mendelian) nature when it came to explaining differences in how humans developed celebrated points scored for our side. In one case, it led a distinguished scholar to write in the monthly magazine of the Association for Psychological Science—which was sent to its many thousands of members around the world—about how parenting behavior influences gene expression and, thereby, children's psychological and behavioral development. This was truly earth-shattering news. What the writer failed to acknowledge, though, so excited was he about the possible implications of epigenetic processes for human development, was that the Meaney research had *rats* for study subjects. In another case, the same rodent work and its potential implications resulted in a *Newsweek* article.[3]

Once I returned to my office and tracked down Meaney's work, I, too, became fascinated with epigenetics—but for reasons other than the one just articulated regarding genes as dependent variables. Indeed, it is striking how developmental scholars are forever going on about epigenetic explanations of human development—that contextual conditions can turn genes on and off to affect body, mind, behavior, and development—and yet, even as they herald the discovery of epigenetics and its implications for the nature-nurture debate, they almost universally and routinely (and perhaps purposefully) neglect so much else of what Meaney actually documented about rodent development.

And what was that? It was that the rodent developmental cascade revealed by the Meaney research was strikingly in line with psychosocial acceleration theory and thus the nature-of-nurture view central to this book. It turned out that when licking and grooming by dams of their newborn pups—their developmental experience—was limited, the effect was not only a failure to turn a certain gene off, affecting the pups' physiological stress response. Additionally—and critically from an evolutionary point of view—limited licking also led to earlier pubertal develop-ment, earlier onset of sexual behavior, and the bearing of more offspring than would otherwise have been the case.[4] Sound familiar?

In other words, the experimental work carried out by the Canadian scientists revealed that different developmental experiences early in life causally induced different life histories in the rodents studied. Whereas those not licked and groomed very much ended up following a fast life history, those licked and groomed a great deal followed a much slower one. To my knowledge, Meaney had never linked his work to psychosocial acceleration theory in any of his numerous publications, but when he was invited to address the national meeting of developmental scientists back in the early 2000s, he did just that. He actually began his talk by reproducing a figure from our 1991 theory paper outlining alternative reproductive strategies.[5] As Bruce Ellis was also in the audience listening to Meaney, I walked over to him. Both of us were amazed and excited. Here, in a talk to hundreds of child develop-ment researchers, this renowned scholar was situating his own groundbreaking work within a life-history, reproductive-strategy theoretical framework—based on my thinking! "I could die tomorrow," I excitedly told a friend, "and be satisfied with my (professional) life."

EVER SINCE the reporting of the original epigenetic rodent research, there has been much discussion of the idea of developmental experiences and environmental exposures turning genes on and off and thereby influencing human development. Critically, there is evidence linking variation in development with epigenetic varia-tion, some of it carried out by my son.[6] The truth, though, is that the excitement generated by the idea of epigenetics essentially "turning genes into dependent variables" has far outstripped the human evidence. Like other fields of inquiry, developmental science has its fads, and these often involve getting so excited about something new based on some initial evidence about what *may be* the case that it is transformed into something that *is certainly* the case, a veritably established fact. I have a good friend whom I informed quite some time ago about the new epige-netic science; now, whenever we discuss the possibility of some environmental condition exerting an effect on some aspect of human development, his go-to explanation is—what else?—epigenetics.

In light of this warning against exaggerating what we are learning about epigenetics in the human case, let me just highlight, for illustrative purposes, the results of some recent investigations implicating epigenetic processes in our spe-cies's development. I choose these because they document how fast scientific ad-vances are being made. The first is based on another longitudinal study, not yet mentioned, called the Environmental-Risk Study. Directed by my previously mentioned colleagues Caspi and Moffitt, and carried out in the UK, it addressed contextual determinants of epigenetic methylation. Their results indicated that growing up in socioeconomically advantaged and disadvantaged neighborhoods differentially affected the methylation of genes in young adulthood known to play a role in inflammation.[7] Similar results emerged in another UK Study, the Avon Longitudinal Study, when the focus of inquiry was on whether mothers' financial problems and experience of deprivation during their children's first seven years of life appeared to influence the methylation of a preselected set of their children's genes when seven and even fifteen years of age.[8] What the inquiry did not address, though, was whether this environmental effect on the epigenome cascaded to influence some "downstream" psychological, behavioral, or health phenotype— that is, whether there was a three-step developmental cascade of exposure to epigenome to phenotype.

Fortunately, two other investigations emerged to fill this gap. One focused on the cognitive functioning of children and adolescents, many from marginalized racial and ethnic groups, growing up in socioeconomically disadvantaged families and neighborhoods.[9] Relying on DNA methylation profiles found to be associated in prior research with low cognitive functioning *in adults*, the investigators wondered, first, if the same would be true of *children* with limited cognitive skills and, second, if this would be most likely when children grew up in conditions of adversity. Both suspicions were confirmed: low socioeconomic status contributed to the methylation of a particular set of genes, which themselves influenced children's (limited) intellectual abilities—a now documented three-step developmental cascade.

The third and final illustrative piece of epigenetic research also chronicled such epigenetic "mediation" of effects of contextual adversity on a developmental phenotype.[10] It was conducted as part of the previously mentioned Great Smoky Mountains Study and built on previously established evidence that exposure to trauma in childhood predicts compromised mental health later in life.[11] Thus, the question became whether methylation of select genes might explain how—that is, be the mediational *mechanism* by which—exposure to actual or threatened death, serious injury, or sexual violence in childhood undermines mental health. Findings again provided support for a three-step developmental cascade: trauma predicted the methylation of a select set of genes and these, collectively, predicted psychiatric disorders and other adverse developmental outcomes almost two decades after the trauma had occurred. So here we have data suggesting that trauma exerts at least some of its "black magic" on psychological well-being by turning off the expression of a particular subset of genes. Results such as these make me wonder whether epigenetic processes might mediate the effect of early-life conditions on reproductive-strategy development, including, of course, pubertal timing.

As it turns out, there is yet another way of considering the role that the epigenome might play in shaping life history and regulating reproductive-strategy development. As we turn next to the subject of biological aging and focus on accelerated epigenetic aging, there will be more to say about it.

## Biological Aging

Recall that the evidence consistent with my puberty prediction persuaded me that an evolutionary analysis of the effects of the environment on child development had merit because it involved the development of a phenotype, puberty, to which no other developmental theory, framework, or perspective on the role of nurture in developmental science drew attention. It was thus a theory-discriminating hypothesis. Intriguingly, over the past two decades there has emerged ever more evidence linking contextual adversity with accelerated development, involving not puberty but the chromosome, the epigenome, and the brain, each of which will be discussed below.[12]

With rare exception, the accelerated developments considered in this chapter have not been cast in evolutionary perspective by those carrying out the relevant research—but they are not inconsistent with it. That, of course, is why I am devoting attention to them. The accelerated developments described below are typically viewed through the lens of a medical or mental health model of disease and dysfunction. That is, accelerated development is widely presumed to be stimulated by and thus to reflect the undermining effects of environmental adversity on physical health and well-being, via processes of wear and tear on children's bodies.[13] Recall that this is exactly how early puberty, especially in girls, has long been regarded—and not without reason, as noted in Chapter 4, given its link with cancer in later life.[14]

Such observations return us to a question we have encountered before: *Why* would natural selection have crafted humans to respond to adversity in ways that eventually foster poor adult health and even shortened lifespans? The answer, of course, concerns reproduction and biological gravity—the evolutionary claim that natural selection favors the passing on of genes over and above survival, adult capabilities, and longer-term health and well-being. The evolutionary argument is simply that costs of poor health later in life, especially well after the childbearing and even childrearing years, influenced as it is by childhood adversity and early puberty, are traded off against the potential benefits of increased chances of reproducing when development is accelerated. Better to live fast—and reproduce—and die young than to delay development and risk not passing on genes at all. In other words, the passing on of genes to future generations is privileged by natural selection over health, wealth, and happiness. Never forget: You were never promised a rose garden, and most certainly not by the forces of evolution.

## Telomeres

Perhaps the first evidence to emerge, beyond the study of pubertal timing, that hinted at accelerated biological development in response to early-life adversity involved telomeres, which are caps on the ends of a chromosome. What is critical to understand about them is that, every time a cell divides and duplicates itself, telomeres shorten. Eventually, usually in old age, all telomeres are used up and the result is cellular death. A good way of imagining this process is to think about shoelaces. Imagine that each time someone laced their shoes, the caps at the end of the laces shortened a bit. After some number of lacings, the entire end of the band securing the lace would be gone, resulting in the lace itself unraveling and becoming useless. Metaphorically, that is what happens to telomeres over time.

As already implied, there is good evidence not only that older people have shorter telomeres than younger ones, having experienced far more cell turnover, but that shortened telomeres are themselves associated with poor health.[15] Even more interesting, in a book focused on the nature of nurture, is evidence that early-life adversity accelerates the premature—or accelerated—shortening of telomeres. And some of this evidence—which has been replicated—involves adversity experienced even before a baby is born. Three different investigations reveal that high levels of maternal stress during pregnancy—whether due to general difficulties in such women's lives, depression, or being of low socioeconomic status—predicted shorter telomeres in their newborns.[16]

But it is not just prenatal experiences that are related to telomere length. There is also evidence that poorer quality parent-child relations during the preschool years (that is, less parent-child cohesion, greater disengagement) forecast shorter telomeres among children from low-income backgrounds, as do maltreatment and acute traumatic experiences.[17] Just as notable in light of the work that stimulated the development of psychosocial acceleration theory is research showing that father absence also predicts shorter telomere length.[18] So, too, does the more distal indicator of early life material hardship in infancy and childhood (reflecting a family's economic insufficiency), which is predictive of telomere length at ages nine and fifteen.[19]

Perhaps even more noteworthy is longitudinal evidence that adversity is associated with the actual shortening over time of telomeres. This was first documented by a team led by Terrie Moffitt and Avshalom Caspi, in their long-term study of

New Zealand children mentioned in Chapter 3.[20] Working with their then graduate student, Idan Shalev, now at Penn State University, they observed that greater exposure to violence accelerated the shortening of telomeres over the five-year period from age five to ten. Even more evidence that results of the cited studies are in line with those of many others comes from a meta-analysis of findings from 138 unique investigations involving more than four hundred thousand individuals, linking some type of adversity—including environmental hazard, psychosocial stress, poor parental care, and low socioeconomic status—with shorter telomere length.[21] Notably, a meta-analysis of fifteen studies involving just under 3,600 individuals and focused exclusively on parenting revealed that, whereas negative parenting was associated with telomere erosion, positive parenting forecast delays in this aging process.[22]

What makes this evidence base especially interesting given the life-history thinking central to this book is that there is even a documented link connecting telomere length to pubertal timing in girls. As might be anticipated given all that has been discussed so far, girls who matured early were found to have shorter telomeres—indicating advanced biological age.[23] Such evidence calls attention to the misunderstanding that may arise when only a mental health or medical model is adopted in thinking about adversity effects, rather than a model informed by an evolutionary understanding of development. Consider this: How would traditional health-related thinking account for the fact that girls who mature earlier than others have shorter telomeres?

## Epigenetic Clocks

Returning to the topic of epigenetics, it turns out that it is not just the length of telomeres that normatively changes with age; so, too, does the methylation of particular subsets of genes. Recall that methylation is an epigenetic process that turns off genes so that their potential effects are not expressed. The methylation of such gene subsets are known to increase with age, meaning that the older we get, the more likely it is that the genes in question are turned off. But while this is true in general, there are important differences among individuals. For some, the methylation of relevant genes occurs sooner than would otherwise be expected given their chronological age, whereas for others the turning off of these genes proves less than expected given their chronological age. What this means is that individuals can age biologically faster or slower than expected.

With this knowledge in hand, scientists have developed what are called "epigenetic clocks" that can be used to determine how one is aging biologically: faster than expected, slower than expected, or in line with what is expected. This is accomplished by comparing the expected methylation of the relevant genes given someone's chronological age with the extent to which the person's genes actually are methylated. Having more methylated genes of the identified subset than would be expected given one's chronological age—based on the average number revealed by studying many people of the same age—is regarded as evidence of accelerated biological aging. Conversely, when the number of methylated genes in the subset is lower than would be expected based on normative epigenetic aging patterns, the individual in question is said to be aging slower than would otherwise be expected. Most of us adults would prefer to be among the latter rather than the former.

There are now a number of different epigenetic clocks—based on somewhat different subsets of genes—and, just to make things confusing, they do not always reveal the same thing.[24] A great deal of work is being devoted to understanding why that is so, with an eye toward refining and improving epigenetic clocks to maximize their accuracy in evaluating whether an individual is aging biologically faster or slower than expected, or on time. So, the truth is that there remain many kinks to work out. Nevertheless, let me share some illustrative findings linking adversity with accelerated cellular aging that seem, at the very least, not inconsistent with psychosocial acceleration thinking.

Given evidence highlighted in prior chapters linking lower social-class conditions with earlier puberty, it seems noteworthy that several investigations document links between growing up in conditions of socioeconomic disadvantage, at both the family or neighborhood level, and faster epigenetic aging.[25] Given that such neighborhoods often are plagued with many problems, it should not be surprising that children who proved, epigenetically, to be older than their chronological age had been exposed to twice as much violence as other children.[26] Another inquiry positioned to distinguish effects of early- and later-life adversity revealed that socioeconomic disadvantage during early childhood, not in adolescence, predicted faster biological aging.[27] This, of course, is in line with theoretical expectations of psychosocial acceleration theory given its emphasis on the first five to seven years of life when it comes to early-life conditions shaping reproductive strategy. There is also evidence that child maltreatment accelerates biological aging.[28] To be appreciated, however, is that not all relevant investigations document adversity effects on epigenetic clock measurements.[29]

Nevertheless, work documenting adversity effects such as that highlighted raises the *how*, or mechanism question: How might such adversity get "under the skin" to accelerate biological aging? One relevant investigation of African Americans highlighted the potential influence of stress on glucocorticoid signaling.[30] Other work involving rural African American adolescents called attention to weight gain from age ten to twenty-nine.[31] Initial evidence documented a three-step developmental cascade, such that growing up in poverty predicted increases in weight gain during adolescence and older epigenetic age in adulthood. Further inquiry, focused on the same individuals, also documented an additional four-step cascade, with exposure to community danger predicting problematic parenting, which itself predicted offspring's increased pro-inflammatory tendencies later in life; and these accounted for accelerated epigenetic aging.[32]

By now, it is not just links between adversity and accelerated biological aging as indexed by epigenetic clocks that have been documented. Working in collaboration, my son, Daniel W. Belsky, now a professor of public health at Columbia University, Terrie Moffitt, and Avshalom Caspi developed their own epigenetic clock.[33] Notably, it proved to be related not only to childhood adversity in the previously discussed New Zealand study, just as the prior cited work has shown, but also to evidence of deteriorating physical health from ages twenty-six to twenty-eight to thirty-two.[34]

At least two things still remain to be documented. The first is whether experiences, adverse or otherwise, actually cause biological-age acceleration. One limit of all the work cited through this point is that it is based on observational and correlational, not experimental and thus causal, evidence. Ideally, a randomized control trial in which individuals are assigned randomly to a treatment group or a control group is a means to document causality with confidence. Unfortunately, no such developmental work of that sort is yet available, but I suspect it is being undertaken as I write. The closest we get is a quasi-experimental study which did not randomize children to a treatment but compared those treated for childhood trauma with those not exposed to such adversity. This research found that child-parent psychotherapy slowed epigenetic age acceleration, by comparing epigenetic age before and after the intervention.[35]

What still remains to be documented is whether the aforementioned indices of biological aging themselves predict, perhaps especially when combined together, pubertal timing. Were that the case, it would suggest that prepubertal accelerated aging, itself stemming from early-life adversity, might set the stage for and result in faster sexual maturation. Only one of three published investigations chronicles such a link between the faster "ticking rate" of an epigenetic clock and accelerated pubertal development.[36] That underscores the fact that there remain grounds for uncertainty regarding how much confidence and thus meaning can be placed in this result. Nevertheless, it is an indisputably intriguing finding, despite two failures to replicate.[37] This would seem especially so in light of evidence, from one of the studies that failed to detect such an association, that accelerated epigenetic aging predicted other indicators of a fast life history—namely earlier age at first sex, which itself predicted more lifetime sexual partners.[38]

Returning to the failure to replicate, questions can be raised as to whether the length of time between measurements of accelerated aging and pubertal timing might account for differences in results across the three studies just highlighted, with associations perhaps more likely to emerge when the time between assessments of epigenetic aging and pubertal timing are more closely spaced in time. Clearly, more work addressing this and related issues is needed. Should future inquiry prove in line with the clearly limited evidence that faster epigenetic aging forecasts earlier pubertal development, it, too, would challenge conventional, non-reproductive-strategy thinking that only regards contextual adversity as generating wear and tear on the body and, thereby, poor health later in life rather than an evolved and strategic tradeoff of a long, healthy life in favor of increased chance of reproducing.

One last comment about biological aging, or really question: Does accelerated biological aging in childhood presage the same in adulthood? Life history theory presumes it does, for reasons just mentioned regarding the evolutionary tradeoff involving timing of reproduction and health in later life. What makes such a theoretical claim so interesting is that the previously mentioned one which goes by the name of Developmental Origins of Health and Disease (DOH&D) predicts just the opposite: that later-life biological aging occurs despite non-accelerated development in childhood.[39]

Testing competing theories like these is at the heart of the best science. Once again, my friends Caspi and Moffit, working with their graduate student Kathy Xie, along with myself, my professor son, and many others, were positioned to do so because the New Zealand Study includes repeated measurements of biological aging in childhood, with the same true in adulthood. What does this work reveal? That the data prove consistent with life-history theory rather than DOH&D.[40]

## The Brain

Over the past two decades neuroscientists have developed ever more informative technologies to gain insight into the brain. Initial research on brain-phenotype associations focused on the parts of the brain that implicated particular types of information processing. This involved seeing which parts of the brain appear involved—which, that is, "light up"—when, say, a person is engaged in the processing of spatial or linguistic information while studied in an MRI machine. More recently, advances in MRI technology have afforded the measurement of brain "connectivity"—that is, processes by which the brain communicates with itself. Investigating how brain structures and processes change as children develop has afforded new insights involving effects of early-life conditions. Some of this work documents accelerated brain development in response to diverse conditions of social and economic disadvantage.[41] Thus, there are again grounds for regarding such neuroscientific work as complementary to psychosocial acceleration theorizing.

Let's first consider neuroscience focused on brain structures. The fact that grey-matter volume, a measure of actual neurons in the brain, decreases over time in adolescence, makes the finding that early-life stress before age five accelerates this process particularly notable.[42] It is also established that brain regions involved in emotional processing become thinner with age. So it also is interesting that the more severe is child abuse, the more this thinning process is accelerated in these parts of the adolescent brain.[43] When this occurs in a particular part of the hippocampus, the same work revealed that accelerated brain development also helped account for the degree to which child maltreatment was associated with children's antisocial behavior. In other words, here we again have suggestive evidence of a three-step developmental cascade: from childhood adversity to accelerated change in brain structure to an advantage-taking, opportunistic-exploitative social orientation.

Now let's turn to brain connectivity. In three separate investigations, youths with histories of early caregiving adversity—specifically, institutional care, traumatic experience, or harsh parenting—exhibited more adult-like and thus precocious profiles of amygdala–prefrontal cortex connectivity than agemates who did not have such developmental histories.[44] What makes these findings especially noteworthy is that we now know that brain development continues through the adolescent years and into young adulthood. During this time period, one brain structure, the amygdala, which is involved in emotional processing, becomes more tightly connected to the prefrontal cortex, which plays a major role in self-control, especially perhaps when the amygdala is fostering high levels of emotional arousal and impulsive behavior.[45]

When this neurological process occurs during adolescence, as it does normatively, it is thought to play a role in this developmental epoch becoming a second period of heightened developmental plasticity, following that of the early years. As such, it is now considered a second time in the life course during which experiences and exposures can be especially influential in shaping who we become.[46] Conceivably, then, earlier established developmental trajectories—including reproductive strategy?—could be deflected and redirected by new experiences that prove inconsistent with prior developmental history, a case of early-later developmental context being mismatched.

The fact that childhood adversity accelerates the developmental process that is otherwise expected to take place in the second decade of life, not the first, raises the disconcerting possibility that it could undermine such "second-stage" developmental plasticity—and, thereby, the possibility of trajectory redirection. In so doing, then, it could reduce the likelihood that experiences in adolescence could modify development. For example, a childhood of adversity inducing a fast life history would be less susceptible to being modified should adolescence prove highly supportive, perhaps due to the experiences of a new school and new friends. As a result, the possibility of support in adolescence slowing down development—with consequences for sexual behavior, mating, and even eventual parenting—would be less likely.

It turns out that it is not just childhood adversity that accelerates brain development postnatally and, thereby, undermines developmental plasticity. So does *prenatal* adversity when it takes the form of poor physical and mental health of the mother, especially if she does not have a steady partner and has limited financial resources (that is, cumulative risk).[47] These, of course, are the very contextual conditions presumed to undermine supportive parenting and foster a fast life history. In fact, the evidence just cited revealed that not only did prenatal adversity predict behavior consistent with an opportunistic, advantage-taking and exploitative social orientation, but such psychological and behavioral development proved especially likely when prenatal adversity also forecast a faster ticking of an epigenetic clock during childhood. As noted previously, the possibility of prenatal experiences regulating life history did not occur to us in crafting psychosocial acceleration theory.

There is evidence that epigenetics plays a role in slowing human brain maturation.[48] This raises the possibility that adversity could contribute to the reverse process, accelerating brain development—by affecting the strength of the epigenome's "braking" effect, slowing down development. Whether this proves to be true, there is a need for caution before embracing the research chronicling accelerated brain aging in response to childhood adversity. Whereas a meta-analysis of adversity effects on biological aging yielded results indicating that findings related to telomeres and cellular aging could be embraced with confidence, the same was not so with regard to brain development.[49]

On the basis of four reports published after the meta-analysis, two focused on children, the third to be mentioned on adults, and the last on adolescents, I am inclined to believe that in time and with more research the meta-analytic situation will change. I say this because each inquiry documented an effect of adversity on brain aging.[50] And brain aging is a condition that has itself been found to forecast poorer language development.[51] One child study, carried out in Singapore, indicated that greater (multifactor) adversity (such as maternal smoking during pregnancy, economic disadvantage, poor maternal mental health) was associated with faster right hippocampal growth from 4.5 to 8.5 years of age, which itself predicted greater depressive symptoms in childhood, again highlighting a three-step developmental cascade.[52] Adult work involving more than five thousand individuals from fifteen countries documented links between greater economic inequality and accelerated functional connectivity between brain regions.[53]

The final investigation to be highlighted proves especially interesting because it documents differential effects of deprivation and threat on the pace of brain development by adolescence.[54] Its results are strikingly aligned with the research cited in Chapter 4 showing that, whereas deprivation delayed pubertal development, threat accelerated it: Whereas emotional neglect predicted a slower rate of brain development, threat-related adversity (such as trauma exposure, family aggression, or an unsafe neighborhood) forecast the opposite, accelerated brain development. Such findings raise the possibility that one reason the aforementioned meta-analysis failed to document reliable effects of adversity on brain aging was because some of the included studies did not distinguish among different types of adversity, the contrasting effects of which could cancel each other out.

BASED ON WHAT has been covered in this chapter, what should be clear is that the accelerating development effect of childhood adversity is not limited to the timing of puberty and the age of sexual debut. Perhaps, instead, pubertal timing should be reconceptualized as an earlier index of biological aging, along with others considered above. Dental development might also be included as a biological aging index, as two investigations revealed that more limited family income and more adverse childhood experiences are linked to earlier emergence of a child's first molar.[55] Two other studies found that children who had cavities at age five were less likely than those with none to self-report their health as excellent in their forties.[56] What remains to be determined is whether the indices of biological aging discussed in this chapter involving telomeres, epigenetics, and the brain are themselves linked to the timing of pubertal development. Were that the case, we could conclude that findings linking early-life adversity with these non-pubertal indices of biological aging are not just *not inconsistent* with psychosocial acceleration theory, but critical components of it. This would clearly extend the theory, just as, in Chapter 4, considerations of distinct dimensions of adversity, the importance of energetics, and psychological processes like discounting the future and mortality risk did.

# 6

# A Genetic Illusion?

Whatever environmental effect one might seek to understand and illuminate, investigating it in an empirical manner that can document true causation—proving that an environmental input (such as harsh punishment) doesn't just *look* statistically like it influences a development output (such as accelerated pubertal development) but actually *does* influence it—is challenging. This is especially so in longitudinal studies, such as in the childcare and New Zealand studies repeatedly referenced in earlier chapters. In such non-experimental, *observational* work, investigators only monitor what occurs in the lives and development of those they are studying and do not endeavor to manipulate or affect whatever is their focus of attention. They rely on multivariate statistical methods to determine whether dependent variables (such as age of sexual debut) are a function of independent variables (such as father absence), after statistically discounting effects of other possible sources of influence. Proceeding in even this careful manner does not necessarily allow a strong causal inference to be drawn, concluding that an independent variable was responsible for the dependent variable. It does reduce the chance that the latter was not an artifact of the factors serving as statistical controls—but no study can include all the possible confounding factors both suspected and unknown.

Given this investigatory reality, one of the biggest uncertainties, if not *the* biggest uncertainty, plaguing those of us who study development using longitudinal observational research methods is whether findings linking independent and dependent variables, even using sophisticated mathematical methods, reflect anything more than a statistical mirage. That is, if there is really something more complicated going on, then there is a good chance that the seeming effect of a given environmental input (such as harsh punishment) on a life-history output (such as pubertal development) is nothing more than an illusion, one that obscures the truth that other factors and processes, not considered, are actually responsible for the effect being chronicled.

Obviously, this basic difficulty in drawing confident conclusions about cause and effect in observational research plagues most of the findings about the nature of nurture considered to this point. Ignoring this potentially severe interpretive problem—essentially, refusing to admit there might be alternative explanations of what is going on—would be scientifically indefensible. At the very least, that possibility has to be acknowledged. We must value efforts to overcome such sources of causal uncertainty with respect to statistical associations between predictor and outcome, and pursue them wherever possible. This chapter focuses on such efforts.

Indeed, it is because, in the case of research on development of reproductive strategies, observational evidence might reflect a "genetic masquerade" (specifically, that "it's the DNA, stupid") that I have chosen to devote an entire chapter to the issue. Perhaps I should have done so much earlier in Part I. Another author might have tackled it head on at the outset—but it seemed better to start by presenting the strongest case for psychosocial acceleration thinking. Now, having reviewed so much evidence linking environmental factors to features of life history, we can acknowledge this "elephant in the room."

Thus, this chapter directly confronts the possibility, by no means far-fetched, that genetic similarities and differences among individuals could account for the predictive statistical effects of early-life conditions on child, adolescent, and adult development heralded in earlier chapters. It is now time to delve more deeply into a subject previously highlighted, Mendelian genetics. The aim of this chapter is to determine whether the findings discussed to this point provide reason to believe that development operates in the ways that have been asserted (with, for example, adversity causally contributing to fast life history).

As we shall see, despite the very real (causal-inference) limits of virtually all the observational research findings shared so far, evidence still emerges consistent with the conclusions drawn about the nature of nurture in preceding chapters, even in work that endeavors to take Mendelian genetics into account. Research that is "genetically informed" still yields evidence linking early-life conditions with features of reproductive strategy, including pubertal development. In other words, research findings shared in prior chapters appear not just to conjure a statistical mirage or genetic illusion.

CENTRAL TO THE VIEW that the environmental effects highlighted through this point might be nothing more than an illusion is the claim that they could be masking the actual influence of genes that have gone unmeasured in so much research. More specifically, genes that parents and children have in common could account for why families are poor, chaotic, and unstable and, at the very same time, why children develop the way they do, including perhaps accelerated reproductive development. If that were so, it could account for why the observational evidence appears to chronicle environmental effects when no such environmental effects are actually operative.

In addressing this possibility, it is essential to recall the distinction, discussed in the Introduction, between Mendelian and Darwinian perspectives when it comes to the *nature* of nurture. Whereas a Darwinian perspective on nature is centrally concerned with evolution, adaptation, and reproductive fitness, a Mendelian-genetic focus is concerned with none of these. For Mendelian investigators, the question is simply: Do genetic differences account for differences between humans in how they think, behave, and develop? Thus, the focus is just on the *how* of development, not the *why*. Perhaps the best evidence of this is to be found in an old study of the genetics of television watching—which turned out to be substantially heritable.[1] Hopefully, we can all agree that no genes were ever selected over the course of human history because of the adaptive value of TV watching—which is not to say that genes selected for other purposes, like sitting still and monitoring the environment—could not also affect passively watching television in the modern world.

Before we can consider the fundamental issue of whether research investigating environmental effects on life history that has endeavored to discount potential genetic confounding still yields evidence of environmental effects in accord with psychosocial acceleration thinking, it is critical to consider whether multiple elements of reproductive strategies (including environmental inputs and child outcomes) themselves prove to be heritable—that is, systematically related to differences in the genetic makeup of children and their parents. Only if they do would there be reason to be concerned that the evidence considered up to this point on the nature of nurture—linking environmental experiences and exposures with life-history factors like pubertal timing—could be reasonably regarded as suspect. Once we find that these components of reproductive strategy, including the developmental environment, are heritable to some not insubstantial degree, the question will become whether taking Mendelian genetics into account still yields evidence of environmental effects on life history. If it does, that would be further—and stronger—assurance that claims regarding the nature-of-nurture made throughout the first part of this book are not entirely misleading.

Once the issues of genetic confoundment are addressed, that of gene-by-environment (GxE) interaction will be considered. This is necessary in view of a vital question: Even given the genetic influence documented by many studies of many phenotypes, does this evidence imply, as so much scientific and popular discourse on the topic would seem to suggest, that the same influence would be present, perhaps even to the same extent, across times, places, and populations? That is, is there any variable aspect of the particular people studied or their context of development that affects whether genetic differences influence human development or the degree to which they do? We will see that this does turn out to be the case, raising interpretive questions about what estimates of heritability actually do reflect.

## Ways of Studying Genetic Effects

Before we consider the heritability of reproductive strategies and approaches to addressing genetic confoundment, let me offer a brief primer on ways of measuring genetic influence. This is especially important because it has changed dramatically since the turn of the millennium. More will be said about this matter in Part II, specifically in Chapter 10. For now, a distinction needs to be made between *behavior*-genetic and *molecular*-genetic approaches to studying genetic effects.

In behavior-genetic research, no genes are actually measured. Instead, comparisons of individuals who differ in their degree of genetic relatedness provide an indirect means of detecting genetic effects. Thus, when it proves to be the case that identical twins, who share 100 percent of their genes, are more similar than fraternal twins, who share half that amount, that provides a basis for inferring genetic influence. The same applies when comparing similarity between parents and their biological children, who share 50 percent of their genes, and the same parents and their adopted children who typically share none (unless the adoptee is a relative). Another approach is to determine whether adopted children are more similar to their biological parent than to their adoptive parent.

By the new millennium, technology had advanced which enabled researchers to move beyond the indirect behavior-genetic approach and directly measure actual genes and relate them directly to phenotypes of interest; the stronger the associations, the greater the evidence of genetic effects. Due to the high cost of measuring actual genes, the initial molecular-genetic work focused on very few genes, with genes being examined one at a time to determine whether such "candidate" genes prove to predict variation in the outcome of interest. The particular gene selected to predict a particular phenotype is based in this candidate-gene work on the "biological plausibility" of the gene in question being related to the phenotype in question. This occurs when there is a preexisting biological basis of some kind that a particular gene might play a role in shaping the phenotype of interest. For example, it might be that the gene is known or suspected to influence a neurotransmitter (for example, dopamine, serotonin) that is known or suspected of influencing the phenotype of interest. The candidate genes chosen in such genotype-phenotype research varies depending on the phenotype to be predicted. This is why such work is characterized as "hypothesis testing."

In time, as costs of assaying genes dropped as a result of technological advances, it became possible to measure thousands of genes, if not more, to identify those that proved to be systematically related to a phenotype of interest rather than just one selected because of its "biological plausibility." (I say "many" because, to the surprise of many behavior geneticists, it turned out that very, very few phenotypes proved to be related to a single gene, perhaps having a large effect; rather, numerous ones have quite small individual effects.) Whereas candidate gene work is to some extent theory (of biological plausibility) guided, this numerous-gene approach is "theory free." Identification of genes related to a phenotype becomes simply a matter of statistics, not prior expectations underpinning specific hypotheses.

One of the challenges of this second phase of molecular-genetic research was that one needed huge "discovery" samples to identify so many seemingly reliably influential genes; we are talking thousands and tens of thousands of individuals. Such work is referred to as GWAS, which stands for "genome-wide association studies." Once a set of genes are identified among the huge number considered as potentially being linked to a particular phenotype in discovery research, other investigators could identify them in their own much smaller samples and then create "polygenic" scores by combining the multiple genes, sometimes tens, hundreds and even thousands. These composite indices reflecting the influence of numerous genes could then be associated with a phenotype of interest. They are not unlike the previously highlighted cumulative-risk and ACE approaches to conceptualizing and measuring the developmental environment.

## The Heritability of Fast and Slow Reproductive Strategy

Having distinguished behavior-genetic and molecular-genetic approaches to illuminating genetic effects, as well as the difference between single, candidate-gene and GWAS-related research, the first issue to be addressed is whether genetic influence is evident in the case of those phenotypes of offspring central to life-history thinking. This proves to be the case with respect to pubertal timing, age of first sex, the stability of intimate relationships, and even the number of children born, as well as childlessness.[2] The latter two are, of course, indisputable markers of reproductive fitness. Thus, there is clear evidence that many indicators of life history are heritable, shaped at least in part by DNA. So maybe we should close up the nature-of-nurture shop and presume that all the findings shared in prior chapters turn out just to be genetic illusions.

Just as notable is evidence that even statistical associations linking components of life histories (for example, pubertal timing→age of sexual debut) reflect genetic influence. This is due to the same gene(s) influencing multiple components. Evidence that this is important for understanding the development of reproductive strategies comes first from research indicating that the very same genes play a role in influencing the following phenotypes: menarche, ages of sexual debut and first birth, lifetime number of sexual partners, and number of births.[3] Perhaps even more noteworthy is that the same work further reveals that this shared genetic influence accounts to some extent, meaning not entirely, for why earlier age at menarche is associated with earlier ages at first sexual intercourse and first birth, with the latter leading to greater number of births. In other words, it is not just that individual phenotypes prove heritable but that relations between them are genetically influenced.

Collectively, then, the findings just summarized should make clear that investigations that do not discount genetic influence on reproductive-strategy phenotypes—including virtually all those discussed in earlier chapters—*may* misattribute genetic effects to environmental ones stipulated by psychosocial acceleration theory. The issue which arises, then, is whether we are dealing with only a Mendelian-nature situation or a Darwinian-nature *and* nurture one. The point to be made here is simply that even if Mendelian genetics account to some extent for some of the findings already reviewed, that does not eliminate the possibility that there is still a role for true environmental causation. That is, Mendelian nature and Darwinian nature of nurture are not necessarily mutually exclusive. One of the long-standing weaknesses of public discourse on nature and nurture has been—and even remains—the tendency to see these sources of influence as alternatives, one correct and the other not. Even worse, perhaps, is that such tendencies, whichever is favored, are a function of ideology rather than science for all too many. I should know, if only because I was once one of these biased "choosers."

## The Heritability of the Environment

Whatever tentative conclusion might arise from the genetic evidence just summarized, there remains the issue of the heritability of developmental experiences and environmental exposures, as these are so central to shaping life history according to nature-of-nurture thinking. No doubt surprising to many, just like it was once for me, is evidence that many of the environmental conditions presumed to induce a fast or slow life history have themselves proven to be heritable. This is true of ratings made by children and parents themselves of their family environment. Whether the focus is on the harshness of parenting or the level of chaos in a child's family environment, behavior-genetic evidence indicates that the reason some children experience one kind of childrearing environment rather than another is partly due to their parents' genetic makeup. This was revealed in a groundbreaking paper by Robert Plomin, the father of developmental behavior genetics, and a friend and colleague of mine from our Penn State days.[4] Recall that it was the title of his paper focused on the Mendelian genetics of the environment that I cribbed for the title of this book to emphasize Darwinian nature, while not ignoring DNA.

As it has been more than three decades since Plomin's paper appeared, it becomes of interest that recent molecular-genetic research also documents Mendelian-nature effects on the environments that parents provide for their children. (Molecular-genetic research will be discussed in more detail in Chapter 10.) This proved true in the previously mentioned New Zealand study, the results of which were replicated in a Dutch investigation and also in a study conducted by Caspi and Moffitt in the United Kingdom, along with their graduate student Jasmin Wertz and many others.[5] In fact, similar evidence emerged when this work was extended by including data on four additional large cohort studies from the UK and United States to complement those already mentioned. This resulted in a sample of more than thirty-six thousand parents and their children.[6] Findings indicated that the more gene variants that parents carried which emerged in GWAS discovery research focused on adult educational attainment (that is, number of years of schooling), the more likely parents carrying more of these same genes provided supportive and stimulating parenting to their children and adolescents. The same parents who proved genetically predisposed to parent in this way were even more likely to leave a wealth inheritance to their children! It clearly—and literally—pays to choose the right parents!

## The Heritability of Reproductive Strategy

Given all the genetic research summarized, there is more than sufficient reason to raise doubts about the observational findings discussed in prior chapters putatively documenting environmental effects of childhood conditions on the development of reproductive strategies. So now the critical question becomes, "is there still evidence of environmental influence with genetic influence discounted?" Fortunately, multiple empirical efforts using diverse strategies to discount or control for the effects of genetic inheritance have been carried out when testing central propositions of psychosocial acceleration theory.

Let's first consider three pieces of work that relied on the first approach, that involving statistical controls. One such investigation indirectly discounted some genetic influence by statistically controlling for maternal age of menarche before assessing the effect of harsh parenting experienced by preschool-aged children on timing of daughter's first period.[7] A second did so by controlling for a GWAS-derived polygenic score found to be related to both ages of menarche and first birth. In this work in which my professor son was involved, father presence / absence across the first seven years of life was used to predict ages of menarche, first sex, and even first birth.[8] Finally, a third relevant inquiry focused on predicting girls' ages of menarche also using father-absence as the predictor, after controlling for a GWAS-based polygenic score for menarcheal age.[9] In all cases, evidence of environmental effects consistent with psychosocial acceleration theory emerged even with genetic effects taken into account statistically before evaluating the influence of childhood experience.

Bruce Ellis, while working in New Zealand in his first faculty position after finishing postdoctoral training, implemented a very different approach to test the puberty hypothesis central to psychosocial acceleration theory while taking genetic influence into account.[10] Along with a graduate student, he insightfully predicted that sisters, who share 50 percent of their genes but who spent different amounts of time in single-parent households during their childhoods—due to how old they were when their parents separated—would differ in their ages of menarche more than older and younger sisters whose parents did not separate and also spent different amounts of time with their fathers. The basis of this prediction was that greater time spent without a father in the family, which would be the case for younger sisters—but only those from divorced homes—would accelerate reproductive development. This led the investigatory team to further hypothesize that the younger sister would sexually mature at a younger age than the older sib did. And that is exactly what the evidence indicated: Sisters whose parents separated had bigger differences between them in menarcheal age than did sisters whose parents' relationships remained intact. Even more critically, it was the younger sisters, but only those from single-parent homes, whose first periods occurred at younger ages than those of their older sisters.

Important to consider is that a subsequent and much larger sibling study failed to provide evidence of any early-adversity effects on menarcheal timing (and sexual behavior) when considering sister-differences. At the same time, some limited evidence of such did when the focus was on a larger group of individuals without regard to sibling differences. Also of note is a behavior-genetic analysis presented in the same report that revealed that the non-shared environment, meaning differences in the experiences siblings had, did play a role in reproductive development.[11] While all this certainly sounds confusing and inconsistent, Part II, beginning with the next chapter, will qualify—but not disconfirm—much that has been asserted in Part I, by further considering effects of such environmental influences that are not shared by siblings.

It must be pointed out that, whatever has been revealed by the summary here of relevant work statistically distinguishing genetic from non-genetic effects, all the research cited is clearly limited. In most of the work, this is because genetics are only partially controlled. Consider first that sibling studies discount only the effects of the 50 percent of genes that siblings share, leaving the other 50 percent—and their effects—unaccounted for. Consider next that controlling for mother's age of menarche when predicting the effect of an environmental factor (such as harsh punishment) on pubertal timing does not take into account any unique genes inherited from the father. Even GWAS-based research is severely limited, because polygenic control variables are not all that strongly related to life-history (and many other) phenotypes. Even as behavior-genetic studies tend to show that most phenotypes of interest here are highly heritable, with genetics accounting for 40 to 60 percent of differences between people, polygenic scores tend to predict much, much less—as little as 2 percent of the genetic variance, and sometimes even a smaller portion. Why things turn out this way is a mystery—one often referred to as "the missing heritability problem."

Fortunately, there is another, even more powerful investigatory approach to testing the environmental effects central to psychosocial acceleration theory and distinguishing it from any genetic influence. This is the *natural experiment,* as it is called, even though such experiments aren't always natural.[12] To get a better sense of what a natural experiment involves, consider what mental health researchers did to evaluate the long-term effects of exposure to the terrorist attack on the twin towers in New York City on September 11, 2001. Proceeding on the presumption that, before the attack, children living in the south end of Manhattan near the destroyed buildings would not have differed on average in their well-being from those living further away, in the borough of Queens, a team of investigators compared these two groups fourteen years after the event.[13] The terrorist attack itself served as a kind of randomized control trial (RCT) in that the children, their families, and their locales—which were tolerably similar—had no control over it. This meant that any differences detected in the functioning of "experimental" versus "control" children—such as worse mental health for those near the attack— should truly reflect a causal influence of exposure to 9 / 11.

The first natural experiment to be considered that sought to test psychosocial acceleration thinking compared the development of two groups of Finnish citizens who had been children during World War II when the Nazis invaded their country.[14] Some of them, as children, were evacuated from Finland, sent by their parents to live with temporary foster families in Sweden and Denmark in hopes of keeping them safe. Others continued to remain at home with their parents. The theory-derived hypothesis was that given the stress and fear induced by separation from parents, the former female evacuees would have reached menarche at an earlier age; this proved to be the case. In light of this evidence, I can't but be reminded of the experimental study using rodents discussed in Chapter 3 which found that separation from mother (much earlier in life) caused earlier pubertal development. Perhaps even more important from an evolutionary perspective than the effect of separation on pubertal development is that the Finnish child evacuees, as adults, bore more children than did those individuals who were not relocated to Sweden, just as predicted by psychosocial acceleration theory.

However much this natural experiment appears to provide conclusive evidence of a real causal effect of adversity on reproductive strategy, there is one major limiting factor. What if parents who sent their children away and those who did not differed from each other in important ways, like the former being more prone than the latter to anxiety and fear that the Nazi invasion would harm their children? This unaddressed and potentially confounding *possibility* limits the strength of the causal conclusion that can be drawn about early-life effects on life history in this (semi)natural experiment.

Fortunately, another natural experiment did not involve any decisions that parents had to make or any forced relocations, as it focused on the effects of exposure in childhood to the devastating earthquake in Wenchuan, China, in 2008.[15] With a focus on children who were not yet sexually mature at the time of the quake, some lived where the earth trembled and destroyed many buildings, killing many people, whereas others did not. Comparison of the two groups that were more or less randomly assigned—by geography—to be exposed to devastation or not revealed that earthquake exposure causally, not just correlationally, increased the risk of early puberty—in both girls and boys.

Especially interesting and consistent with psychosocial acceleration theory, the earthquake effect on pubertal development was most pronounced when children were seven years old or younger at the time of the disaster. Indeed, for these young girls, the risk of early puberty was four times as great as for age-mates who did not have direct exposure to the quake. So here we have strong causal evidence that adversity *early* in life can accelerate reproductive development.

Intriguingly, additional evidence of the importance of developmental timing comes from a non-genetically-informed study that, while not positioned to evaluate environmental effects on pubertal timing, was designed to evaluate environmental effects on other aspects of life history.[16] In this work, focused on an at-risk sample of children followed from birth onward by my colleague and sometime collaborator, Jeff Simpson of the University of Minnesota, evidence indicated that environmental unpredictability between birth and age five, but not in ages six to sixteen, most strongly predicted indices of a fast life history. For both males and females, exposure to rapidly changing environments during these infant, toddler, and preschool years proved to be associated with a faster life history. In comparison to age-mates who grew up in more predictable environments, they had more sexual partners, engaged in more aggressive and delinquent behavior, and were more likely to be involved in criminal activity as they grew up.

To summarize all that has been said so far about a potential genetic masquerade regarding the environmental effects on the development of life history, it comes down to two conclusions. *First, it is not just genetic makeup that is responsible for fast and slow life histories; the developmental environment also matters. And second, it is earlier rather than later in childhood that developmental experiences and environmental exposures seem to regulate reproductive strategy development.*

## Gene-by-Environment Interaction (GxE)

Whatever findings have been documented by the research cited here, it is critically important to appreciate that all genetic evidence, like most other evidence pertaining to human development, is specific to the population being studied unless proven otherwise. Thus, just because something—perhaps intelligence or divorce or pubertal timing or age of first sex—is found to be systematically related to genetics (that is, heritable) in one place and time does not mean the same would necessarily be true in another place or at another point in time, or true to the same degree. Evidence that countries differ in the extent to which subjective well-being is heritable nicely underscores this point.[17]

Ever more evidence from research into gene-by-environment (GxE) interaction—that is, the role of the environment in influencing or moderating the strength of genetic effects—indicates that the level of influence of genes on a phenotype, referred to by biologists as *genetic penetrance,* is not fixed in stone.[18] Just because someone inherits the relevant DNA for a particular phenotype does not mean that the phenotype will develop. Consider in this regard the role of epigenetics discussed in Chapter 5, illuminating how developmental experiences and environmental exposures can regulate gene expression, turning it on or off, thus shaping the phenotype. Again, there is a long and winding road, by no means fully understood, linking genotype to phenotype.

Let's consider first GxE evidence related to reproductive strategies, in particular age of both sexual debut and first birth, developments that tend to occur earlier when pubertal maturation occurs earlier. What makes this work so important is that it highlights the utility of thinking in terms of the modern developmental synthesis outlined in the Introduction—that is, simultaneously considering both Darwinian and Mendelian nature along with nurture. Once again, I am referring here to (Darwinian) biological gravity and (Mendelian) genetic influence, along with nurture. Results of two different investigations indicate that genetic influence on these life-history phenotypes proves greater among individuals born more recently—those younger than the older cohort born earlier.[19] Why might this be so? Conceivably, it could be due to the more laissez-faire social climate—and thus sexual permissiveness—experienced by the younger adults and those born more recently, which could have afforded freedom for genetic differences to manifest themselves (and achieve greater penetrance). Perhaps less surprising is additional reproductive-strategy-related research on the age of first consensual intercourse of females who were or were not victims of sexual abuse.[20] The heritability of age of sexual debut turned out to be weaker when girls had been victims. I would be remiss if I did not remind readers that sexual abuse also forecasts earlier pubertal maturation, in line with psychosocial acceleration theory.[21]

But it is not just features of life history whose heritability varies by contextual conditions, making clear that GxE interaction is a general phenomenon.[22] Perhaps the most compelling evidence to this effect is to be found in research on the most controversial topic in the study of genetic influence—the Mendelian genetics of intelligence. The relevant work makes clear that the IQs of toddlers, preschoolers, and adolescents are all more strongly influenced by their genetic makeup when growing up under conditions of socioeconomic advantage than disadvantage.[23] These findings led one team of investigators to predict that such a difference in genetic penetrance would be less likely to materialize in countries in which there exists a greater social safety net than in the United States, because all or most children would be like well-watered and fertilized plants rather than poorly treated ones, thereby enabling only the former to reach their genetic potential. And that is exactly what emerged when the heritability of IQ was evaluated in Sweden, Great Britain, the Netherlands, and Australia.[24] In other words, under more "socialist" regimes, the capability of all children to realize their intellectual potential appears greater than in the good old USA.

Let me make two conceptual points based on the GxE research just considered, the first of which can be stated rather briefly. It is that heritability effects may be widely misunderstood. Certainly, most scholars—and citizens—who embrace estimates of heritability view them as reflecting the degree to which a person's genetic makeup shapes who they become and how they think, behave, and develop. Let's recall the discussion of "first causes" in the prior chapter's consideration of epigenetics. The fact that genetic penetrance can vary depending on the context in which a child resides, would seem to imply something quite different, also challenging the "first-cause" view. It is that *estimates of heritability really reflect—and depend upon—environmental effects!* Why do I say this? Because what they seem, first and foremost, to be all about is *the degree to which the environment affords the penetrance or expression of genetic differences.* Some contexts are thus genetically "enabling," allowing genetic differences to "play out," thus becoming manifest in the phenotype.[25] In contrast, other environments are genetically "disabling," at least to some extent, thus limiting genetic penetrance.[26]

I would be remiss once again if I did not make clear that most genetic research does not focus on GxE interaction, and that even in the case of work that does, it is not always detected. But before the latter observation is embraced too confidently, two points must be made. First, most populations around the world have not been studied, especially those in lower-income countries and societies in which norms and values differ from those in the West (for example, no premarital sex). The question thus becomes: If the same genes and phenotypes were studied across dramatically different cultural contexts, would more evidence of the dependence of genetic penetrance on the environment emerge? The second point is that given the complexity of considering context, genetics, and phenotype at the same time when studying GxE interaction, we lack theoretical guidance as to which contexts and which genes will interact when it comes to predicting which phenotypes. The potential analytic landscape is huge! It is for both reasons highlighted that it would seem premature to draw strong conclusions based on failures to detect GxE interaction to date. Recall the British adage previously quoted: the absence of evidence is not evidence of absence.

The emphasis on the role of the environment in influencing genetic penetrance would seem reminiscent of what we know about evolution more generally. And that is that through the process of natural selection the environment "selects" genes when they afford some kind of eventual—direct or indirect—reproductive advantage (for example, greater hunting skill, better parenting skill). Of course, genetic changes that prove neutral to ultimate fitness can also be environmentally selected. In any event, the preceding discussion of GxE interaction would seem consistent with the claim that when it comes to the role of genes and environment in human development, nurture rules: *Whereas the genome proposes (what could be), it is the environment that disposes (what will be).*

Now let me address the second conceptual point regarding evidence of GxE interaction. Many scholars view the IQ work in similar terms to ones already used, reflecting the realization of *genetic potential,* and thus whether people become "all that they can be."[27] But as an evolutionary-minded developmentalist, one issue, highlighted by thinking in terms of a modern developmental synthesis, has always led me to resist this formulation, advanced by one of my graduate school mentors, Urie Bronfenbrenner, someone I greatly admired (and still do). The problem is that it reflects the idealized and romanticized, optimal-development thinking criticized in Chapter 1. Why do I say this? Because—and completely consistent with the GxE interaction findings involving intelligence—the "all-that-you-can-be" perspective regards adversity as undermining developmental potential rather than adaptively and strategically shaping the way that individuals should develop given their early-life conditions.

What scholars embracing the realization-of-potential view are doing is looking at development through rose-colored glasses, failing to appreciate a core evolutionary insight highlighted in the Introduction—that developing, in mental health parlance, in a "problematic" and fast manner, and thus becoming an opportunistic-exploitive advantage taker, can be advantageous under certain conditions. Now, to see the difficulty with the mental health approach, we need only entertain the possibility that there are also genes for such a social orientation. And in fact there surely is evidence that aggression, criminality, and antisocial behavior more generally are substantially heritable, at least in the Western contexts in which they mostly have been studied.[28]

So here is the challenge: How would romanticized thinking regard evidence that genetics prove more penetrant in the case of such problematic behavior in socioeconomically disadvantaged than advantaged families, perhaps due to the greater freedom to misbehave, especially given the developmental experiences and environmental exposures which can foster a fast life history? Would there still be reference to these developmental contexts affording the realization of genetic "potential" and individuals becoming "all that they can be"? I doubt it. But there is no reason to take my word for it. A Norwegian study of more than 28,000 children made no reference to the idea of "realizing genetic potential" or of "becoming all that you can be" upon discovering that the heritability of behavioral problems— such as aggression, disobedience, and delinquency—proved greater for those from more disadvantaged households than more advantaged ones.[29]

To be appreciated, then, is that for some individuals their genetic potential may reflect ways of developing, thinking, and behaving that society values (for example, fewer problems, higher IQ, later sexual debut), whereas for others it may not (for example, more problems, lower IQ, earlier sexual debut). Idealizing and romanticizing human development by only making reference to "becoming all that one can be" and "realizing one's potential" obscures and distorts this reality and undermines our ability to see development as nature views it. This point underscores the need for the modern developmental synthesis that this book seeks to advance by simultaneously considering Darwinian nature emphasizing the passing on of genes and inclusive fitness, Mendelian genetics, as well as developmental experiences and environmental exposures early in life.

## Conclusion

Given the ample evidence that prior chapters have presented as consistent with psychosocial acceleration theory, the conclusion we can draw about a possible genetic masquerade comes down to three points. First, *both environmental conditions and associated phenotypes that characterize reproductive strategies, whether fast or slow, are heritable,* and this potential challenge to psychosocial acceleration theory's emphasis on environmental influence cannot be ignored. Nevertheless, and this is point two, available *genetically-informed research still indicates that environmental effects detected in many observational studies are not just artifacts of limited research designs that fail to take into account the role of genetics.* Not to be missed either is that behavior-genetic research routinely documents (shared and non-shared) environmental effects even when genetic ones prove rather substantial. The third and final point, just as important, is that *GxE interactions make clear that biology is not destiny,* because the conditions under which a child develops help to orchestrate the relative influences of environment and genetics on life history—and so much more. These points are consistent with the observation shared earlier in this volume that development—like so much else in life—is multiply determined and complicated. It is not, then, a question of nature *or* nurture, but a case of nature *and* nurture, and even nature interacting with nurture (that is, GxE).

This brings to a close Part I of this book. Presumably, a solid even if imperfect case has been made for viewing development, and especially environmental effects, through an evolutionary lens as proceeding in service of reproductive goals. In Part II, the story told in this part will be challenged once more, perhaps in a more compelling way than the challenges considered so far (from genetics, for example, and internal bodily cues). Specifically, the core idea of Part I—that early-life conditions regulate reproductive strategy and life history—will prove to be both right and wrong. Intriguingly, it is additional evolutionary thinking that led me to advance—and test—this prediction. Let's see how.

## PART II

# The Differential Susceptibility Hypothesis

# 7

# For Better and for Worse

As previewed in the opening chapter and just reiterated, what is presented in this book's second part, beginning here, importantly qualifies all that has been stipulated through the first seven chapters about the nature of nurture. Recall the promise made in Chapter 2 to any inclined to object that plenty of children growing up under conditions of adversity turn out fine while many others who develop in highly supportive conditions do not: the pledge there was to devote the second part of the book to qualifying various observations and claims made in the first part.

So let's get on with that task. The first thing to appreciate is that all results shared to this point reflect *average* effects of childhood experiences on life history. Thus, none of the findings reviewed in prior chapters should be read to imply that every single child exposed to adversity develops in the fast way documented, or that all will develop a slow strategy if life proves supportive in childhood. The same truth applies when behavior geneticists discover that 50 percent of some phenotype is heritable, or molecular geneticists find that a GWAS-derived polygenic score accounts for a significant portion of a phenotype.

In all these cases, findings reflect "central tendencies" based on all the individuals included in a study. The figures thus cannot be used to specify how any particular individual in the sample is affected by the source of influence under investigation, be it father absence, child maltreatment, sensitive parenting, or even genetic makeup. This is not a difficult-to-understand idea, even if it is rarely explicitly stated. We all know that when the average test score for a class of thirty children is a B+, that does not mean that every student earned a B+. Some scored higher and some lower; in fact, even if no one in a class earned a B+, that could still be the class average.

Appreciation of this empirical reality has led me to joke about investigators who conduct experiments only to "eat the oyster and throw away the pearl"—because they are satisfied to have found that an experimental group did better *on average* than a control group. The truth is that virtually every experiment, including every intervention targeting children, yields heterogeneous effects. Not every participant is affected to the same degree, if at all, by whatever the treatment may have involved; there is notable variation in treatment response *within* the experimental group. This is so even when there is a statistically significant (average) experimental effect. It is even true of an intervention as radical as gastric bypass surgery, in which the stomachs of obese individuals are surgically made smaller; not every patient experiences the anticipated dramatic weight loss following the procedure.[1]

For me, the oyster is the average effect, and the pearl is the variation—and thus the knowledge of for whom an experience or exposure does and does not exert the anticipated effect. Unlike many, no doubt, I value this variation more highly because it calls attention to the need to understand what caused it. *There* might lie greater understanding than could be gained from documenting only average treatment effects. These are the pearls that are the focus of this chapter and the next three, where effects of rearing environments on development are reconsidered. Critically, the goal of Chapters 7 through 10 is not simply to document variation but to illuminate its causes, identifying why some children are more and others less shaped by their early-life conditions. As it becomes clear that effects of early-life conditions on life history are greater for some than for others, our attention can shift to differences across children in their developmental plasticity and, as a result, in their susceptibility to environmental influences.

A second point that must be underscored in the process of qualifying all that has been stipulated so far about the nature of nurture pertains to the idea of gene-by-environment interaction (GxE). As this idea comes back into focus, especially in Chapter 10, it must also be appreciated that other personal characteristics of individuals, besides their genetic makeup, can interact with the environment to shape human development—features like a child's temperament, physiology, and health. When GxE interactions involving such personal characteristics are the focus of inquiry, they are usually interpreted differently than the way discussed in Chapter 6. Recall that the prior GxE research revealed that genetic penetrance can vary across contexts, just as we saw in the case of the heritability of intelligence among children from socioeconomically advantaged and disadvantaged families.

The way in which person-by-environment interactions that are central to this chapter and especially the next three differ from the ones covered in Chapter 6 involves essentially flipping the role of the environment and the role of genetic makeup and personal characteristics more generally. Thus, instead of the environment moderating, qualifying, or conditioning the effect of a person characteristic like genotype or temperament on some phenotype, the focus from this point forward is whether and how *person characteristics moderate, qualify, and condition effects of the environment.* Let me try to make this a bit clearer before providing a concrete example in the next paragraph. Instead of thinking about some phenotype being more heritable in one developmental context than another, the focus in this second way of thinking about and interpreting person-by-context interactions is on how individuals who differ in some personal characteristic are affected differently even when exposed to the very same developmental experience or exposure.

Imagine, then, two children, one prone to anger (the personal characteristic) and the other not. Whereas the first child could become highly aggressive or highly co-operative depending on the rearing context—as when exposed, for example, to harsh or sensitive parenting, respectively—the second child is far less likely to be similarly affected. In other words, there can be differences in the extent to which developmental experiences and environmental exposures influence how children develop and function due to differences in their personal attributes. Rarely is it the case that every child is affected in the same way or to the same degree, even by the same early-life conditions. This is why an average effect masks as much as it illuminates.

A situation like the one described, where one individual succumbs to some adversity whereas another does not, is often described in terms of *diathesis stress* or *dual risk.* Diathesis is a fancy term for a predisposition in an individual—usually one, like being prone to anger, that is a vulnerability and increases the likelihood of the person's developing a psychological or health problem if exposed to some adversity, like harsh parenting. This points to why some of us prefer the alternate term, dual risk, as more descriptive. It implies that difficulties are most likely to arise when two contributors are present: having a personal vulnerability of some sort, risk number one, *and* finding oneself in a stressful and challenging context, risk number two. The latter could be a situation of growing up in poverty, being a victim of child abuse, or having an alcoholic parent.

What a person-by-environment interaction of the dual-risk sort indicates is that, among those exposed to such adverse conditions, those individuals carrying the personal vulnerability are most likely to succumb to the negative contextual effect. Individuals carrying a "risky" personal attribute are therefore considered *vulnerable* to adversity, whereas those not carrying that attribute are, by definition, *resilient,* as they remain mostly unaffected in the face of conditions that undermine the well-being of others. Consider the examples of one person prone to sadness who loses a loved one, and another person who has the same sad experience but is not predisposed to be sad. The vulnerable individual is at increased risk of becoming clinically depressed, while the resilient person is not.

WITH REGARD to mental health, thinking in terms of diathesis stress or dual risk has generated a wealth of theoretically insightful and practically useful research over several decades. Yet something I find strange is that for a long time—until the work reported in Part II emerged—there wasn't much consideration of the possibility of a person-by-environment interaction that is the mirror image of the dual-risk one—that is, the possibility of *dual benefit*. Posed as a question, this observation becomes: Are there also individuals who, relative to others, are especially likely to *benefit* when exposed to a *supportive or enriching* environment as a result of their genetic makeup, temperament, physiology, or some other personal characteristic?

There may be several reasons scholars took so long to address this question of dual benefit. First, mental health research is really about psychological and behavioral dysfunction, for obvious and understandable humanitarian reasons. The guiding concerns involve identifying those most at risk of developing problems and providing services to prevent or remediate those problems. Second and relatedly, the omission might be a function of thinking only, or principally, in medical and disease terms and not in evolutionary ones.

Another explanation for why the focus on dual risk has never seemed to suggest the possibility of dual benefit may involve, of all things, language. According to a very old idea referred to as the Whorfian hypothesis, our perception of reality is shaped by our thought processes, which are themselves influenced by the language we use.[2] In this way, language influences our reality and informs how we think about and respond to that reality. While the word *vulnerable* comes easily to mind to describe a person disproportionately likely to be adversely affected by negative experiences and exposures, what word conveys the opposite idea, being the antonym of vulnerable, characterizing a person disproportionately likely to benefit from support and enrichment?

I have posed this question to audiences around the world as part of talks on the subject of this chapter and the next three, including in Germany, the Netherlands, Italy, China, Japan, Portugal, Sweden, Norway, and the United States. And never has a clear word for the idea—the opposite of vulnerable—been proposed, one that can be used as an adjective to characterize a person. *Flourish* has often been suggested, but it does not work as an adjective to characterize a person in the way that vulnerable does. "Tom is vulnerable to harsh parenting" is simple and straightforward, but "Barbara is [what?] to sensitive parenting." This inability of speakers of English, German, Dutch, Italian, Chinese, Japanese, Portuguese, Swedish and Norwegian to identify a word that is the opposite of vulnerable, and that can be used as an adjective to characterize an individual disproportionately likely to benefit from support and enrichment, has amazed me. This would seem consistent with the Whorfian hypothesis—that, because we lack language to describe individuals who benefit more than others, we have not gone looking for the phenomenon.

The only word I have been able to come up with to capture being disproportionately likely to be positively affected by supportive experiences is *lucky*. So, whereas John is vulnerable, Peter is lucky.

In contrast to the many productive decades of work on dual-risk, vulnerability, and resilience, consideration of dual benefit has captured the imagination of psychological and behavioral scientists only since the turn of the millennium. Intriguingly, four different yet related ideas have been advanced regarding the possibility of dual benefit, including one by me. Three were independently arrived at, meaning that those advancing them had no awareness of the others' thinking, and of these, two were based on evolutionary considerations. The fourth was also evolutionary in character but emerged only after the other three had been disseminated. All four will be discussed in turn in this chapter. Then, in the next three chapters, the research stimulated by these perspectives will be considered to see, again, if the theoretical ideas shared in this chapter have empirical "legs." As we will see, the perspectives considered here call attention to different personal attributes considered important when it comes to individual differences in developmental plasticity—that is, susceptibility to environmental influences. Along the way, I will start referring to these characteristics of individuality as *plasticity factors*.

## The Differential Susceptibility Hypothesis

Evolutionary reasoning led me to consider both dual-risk and dual-benefit possibilities simultaneously.[3] Why? The reason was that I recognized that even if the kind of predictive adaptive responses central to psychosocial acceleration and life history thinking evolved to better fit the developing person to the probabilistically likely environment he would encounter in adulthood, thus fostering reproductive success, again probabilistically, it was certainly the case that "mismatches" must have occurred throughout human history between early- and later-life contexts, just as they surely do today.[4] Recall that the prospect of early-life / later-life mismatch was the very reason one group of thinkers, as highlighted in Chapter 5, contended that it was more likely that natural selection shaped development to be guided by internal bodily cues pertaining to present and future health than to be guided by environmental experiences and exposures in childhood, as stipulated by psychosocial acceleration theorizing.

Surely some children who grow up in the face of adversity find themselves in much better circumstances later in life, with the reverse being true, as well. Recall the claim made earlier that those shaped by life in such childhood contexts could end up with their reproductive success compromised as a result of such early-late contextual mismatch, as they would fit more poorly than others the future environment.

My favorite—or really, least favorite—example of a reproductively costly early-life / later-life mismatch in modern times involves the late 1970s genocide in Cambodia, a man-made tragedy depicted in the award-winning film *The Killing Fields*. It was after the United States withdrew its troops from Vietnam in 1973 that the communist Khmer Rouge party came to power in Cambodia. This radical political sect forcibly emptied the country's cities, pushing urban populations out to the countryside where, under a harsh regime of forced labor, violence, and food scarcity, millions died.

What is most relevant to consideration of early-life / later-life mismatch is whom the Khmer Rouge murdered first. It turned out to be people like you and me, individuals who were known to be educated—Cambodia was very much a peasant society—or who were sometimes just thought to be educated because they wore spectacles or had uncalloused hands. Now let's think back fifteen or more years prior to Cambodia's capture by the Khmer Rouge, to a time when many uneducated parents, just like my own—my father never graduated from high school and my mother never got the chance to go to college—encouraged their children to be good students, study hard, and respect their teachers. By doing so, these parents likely believed, just as my parents did, that being educated would enable their children to get a better job than their parents had and, for example, not have to stand on their feet all day—my father ran a restaurant—or bend and stoop planting and harvesting rice or lifting heavy things.

Yet those Cambodian children who "got with the program," proving susceptible to parental entreaties to be dedicated students, ended up most at risk of an early death—and not passing on their genes—because of the disconnect between the world in which they grew up and the one they came to inhabit later in life under the Khmer Rouge. In contrast, their friends, neighbors, and even siblings who disregarded education-promoting adult counsel, skipped school, did not do their homework, and did not respect their teachers were more likely to live to breed another day, thus retaining their chance to pass on their genes. In other words, when Cambodian children's early lives led them to be focused on education, this proved to be out of sync with their later ones. It resulted in disaster for some and greater possibility for those others less likely to have had their development shaped by their childhood experiences.

The moral of this story, of course, is that the future is inherently uncertain. In consequence, early-life / later-life mismatches have always occurred, just as they continue to do to this day. Given that reality, one can wonder whether notions of predictive adaptive response central to psychosocial acceleration thinking are bankrupt, misguided, and thus simply wrong and best discarded. I don't think so. And this is because the differential susceptibility hypothesis I advanced upon appreciating the potentially severe fitness costs of mismatch—in light of the reality of the future being inherently uncertain—was very much in line with what virtually every financial advisor would recommend: Diversify your investments. Don't put all your money in the bank; it could fail. Don't put all your money in the stock market; it could crash. Don't put all your money under the mattress; the house could burn down. Sure, put some money in these places, as well as possibly in real estate, gold, even cryptocurrency, should you have enough to go around. This is the time-tested strategy for insuring that, *on average and over the long run,* you will get the best financial return on your money.

Differential susceptibility thinking simply replaces one currency, money, with another: genes to be passed down to descendants. Its central assumption is that, because the future is uncertain, natural selection has hedged its bets with respect to reproductive strategies being shaped by early-life experiences and exposures (as discussed in Part I). In other words, *whereas some children's life histories should be shaped by childhood conditions just as psychosocial acceleration theory stipulates, for others that should be much less the case, if at all. Children should vary in their developmental plasticity—that is, their susceptibility to being influenced by their developmental experiences and environmental exposures while growing up.* Such variation I further surmised would be inborn; thus, children would come into the world being more or less susceptible to the effects of the developmental context in which they grow up.

While I didn't initially add the following proviso to my thinking, eventually I did so and will share it now. There are at least two ways of thinking about the variation in susceptibility to environmental influences just articulated. On the one hand, we can imagine, typologically, two types of individuals. One is, in the main, quite susceptible to effects of early and perhaps even later-life conditions when it comes to the development of reproductive strategies (or any other phenotypes of interest, such as athletic skill). The other, in contrast, is quite unsusceptible to the effects of the very same developmental experiences and environmental exposures. I will make reference to such types as we proceed through Part II as, respectively, developmentally "plastic" and "fixed" strategists. Most initial research testing my differential susceptibility hypothesis adopted this way of conceptualizing individual differences in susceptibility to environmental influences—that is, two types of children.

But there is another approach, which might more accurately "carve nature at its joints." Instead of thinking typologically, it involves thinking dimensionally. Some children are highly susceptible; some are modestly susceptible; some are only a little susceptible; and some are not at all susceptible. In other words, susceptibility is a "gradient" just like temperament or height, perhaps even reflecting a traditional bell curve. Even though we might say that it is a hot or cold day, temperature can be measured much more finely than that. By the same token, we can characterize someone as tall or short even though we can measure height much more precisely than that.

Surprisingly, most developmental scholars, especially those who emphasized nurture over (Mendelian) nature, never seemed to have asked themselves whether there might be variation in developmental plasticity. Like many of my intellectual brethren, that certainly was true of me early in my career. For so many, then, the capacity for development to be shaped by early-life conditions is simply assumed to be a universal trait, like being born with two eyes, two legs, and so on. But for reasons of mismatch, it should be clear that being highly developmentally plastic could be as much a liability, as in the Cambodian example, as the benefit it has long been assumed to be.

IN DEVELOPING the differential susceptibility hypothesis before there was any evidence for it, at least of which I was aware, I reasoned, based on evolutionary understanding of kin selection and inclusive fitness, that having children who vary in their developmental plasticity would be in the reproductive best interests of not only the children themselves, but also their parents and siblings. In fact, this is why I theorized that variation in susceptibility to environmental influences should have evolved—and thus why I originally proposed that we should see variation in developmental plasticity among siblings *within* the same family. That is, in households with more than one child, one or more should be prove highly developmentally plastic and others much less so.[5] Let's return to the killing fields of Cambodia to illustrate this point.

Imagine that some of the children in a family were highly developmentally plastic and so followed their parents' directives to study hard and be good students, whereas some of their siblings were less susceptible to such parental admonitions. In light of what has already been stipulated about inclusive fitness and kin selection, the former children's early demise—and thus failure to pass on their (and other family members' genes)—would have been "insured" to some extent in terms of being passed (that is, biological gravity). This is due to their surviving siblings, the one-time bad students, sharing—and thus carrying—50 percent of their good-student siblings' genes. Thus, even if dead, 25 percent of the good-student's genes would be passed on to the surviving siblings' offspring, the deceased individual's nieces and nephews. This figure derives from the fact that siblings carry 50 percent of each other's genes. So, the 25 percent figure for nieces / nephews is based on multiplying $.5 \times .5$. By the same token, in an environment in which being developmentally plastic paid off reproductively, those siblings who were not so plastic yet share

50 percent of their own genes with their more contextually susceptible siblings would also have 25 percent of their own genes present in their siblings' offspring.

Parents, too, would benefit from such variation in developmental plasticity across their offspring. If all children were, for example, highly susceptible to parental educational aspirations and the future turned out substantially different than expected, just as it did in the Cambodian case, then all that genetic investment would be at risk of loss, of leaving no descendants, metaphorically going over the reproductive waterfall.

In sum, having a family of "mixed strategists" when it comes to offspring developmental plasticity—with some siblings being highly susceptible and others much less so when it comes to their reproductive strategies being shaped by childhood experiences—serves as an inclusive-fitness insurance policy for all family members. To fully understand this, do not lose sight of the fact that the future is uncertain, so it would be impossible to know whether it will favor more or less developmentally plastic offspring. That, of course, is the reason for the theoretical proposal that evolution should have varied developmental plasticity across siblings within in a family. This is what evolutionary theorists refer to as "bet hedging."

What the preceding discussion of developmental plasticity implies is that being highly susceptible to environmental influences should not be regarded as an unmitigated good for the developing individual and, thus, as something that should be pronounced in all individuals. In some cases, it would appear wiser not to be plastic or to be less developmentally malleable than others, manifesting a more fixed rather than plastic pattern of development. What this analysis led me to realize was that there should be *individual differences in developmental plasticity*—that is, variation across individuals, perhaps especially within families.

Moreover—and critically—those most and least likely to benefit from a childhood marked by support and enrichment should also be similarly likely to succumb to the effects of adversity. It occurred to me that upon viewing development through evolutionary lenses, we should do more than just expect children to vary in their susceptibility to adverse environmental influence, à la dual risk and diathesis stress. Nature should instead have crafted individuals to vary in developmental plasticity more generally, "for better and for worse." Those most vulnerable to adversity should also be most likely to benefit from environmental support and enrichment. And, perhaps even more intriguingly, those most resilient in the face of adversity, so as not to be negatively affected by it, should, being less developmentally plastic, also be less likely to benefit, if at all, from environmental support and enrichment. In sum, developmental plasticity should be conceptualized as a trait and thus a phenotype in its own right, something that will vary across individuals for a variety of reasons, just like weight, height, running speed, intelligence, and so much more.

Based on their mental health worldview, then, dual-risk scholars who have long sought to identify only personal characteristics that predispose particular individuals to succumbing to adversity might have missed half the story. They only considered what my Dutch friends and colleagues Marinus van IJzendoorn and Marian Bakermans-Kranenburg labeled the "dark side" of plasticity—what happens in response to adversity, and not what happens when support and enrichment are encountered, the "bright side."[6]

To make this point is not by any means to imply that dual-risk thinking is inherently misguided. It remains possible, when it comes to some contextual inputs and phenotypic outputs, that there are true experiences and exposures that do not reflect both the dark and bright sides of differential susceptibility thinking. This would seem especially likely in the case of certain early-life conditions of adversity to which no children would be entirely immune. So, even children who prove resilient to many adversities, such as growing up in a chaotic home or even a dangerous neighborhood, are unlikely to be impervious to enduring effects of extreme stressors such as torture and famine. Nevertheless, it remains theoretically possible that some might be less adversely affected than their more developmentally plastic counterparts, perhaps especially over the longer term, or at least take longer to succumb.

The integration of the two core evolutionary ideas central to this book, psychosocial acceleration theory and the differential susceptibility hypothesis, led me to wonder whether there might be "fixed" and "plastic" reproductive strategies and thus strategists. Might some children be born to develop a faster or a slower life history as a result of their Mendelian-genetic makeup (or some other personal characteristic), whereas others, also due to their (different) genetic makeup (or other personal characteristic) have life histories shaped by their childhood experiences and exposures? The former children could be thought of as "alternative" reproductive strategists who are "born" to be faster or slower developers, whereas the latter could be "conditional" ones who are "made" in the course of their early-life conditions to develop one way or the other.[7] The latter, of course, is what the first part of this book was about, given its focus on how early-life experiences and exposures shape life history.

By entertaining the prospect that, for some individuals, reproductive strategy could be "born" as a result of genetic makeup or other personal characteristics, yet for others it could be "made" due to their early-life conditions, *differential susceptibility thinking requires a radical revision of psychosocial acceleration ideas advanced in the first part of the book. That revision is simply that the theory applies to some children more than it does to others.* Reproductive strategies and life histories are not always or entirely orchestrated and calibrated by what early life is like, even if they often are. For some the Mendelian nature of nurture is to be susceptible; but for others it is to be unsusceptible or much less so. Evidence bearing on this possibility will be the focus of the next three chapters.


BEFORE SAYING ANYTHING MORE about my differential susceptibility hypothesis, I must warn readers of its potential disconcerting implication. I do this because of the way many respond to conversations I have had and talks that I have given on the subject over the years. For some, the differential susceptibility hypothesis would seem to imply that nothing should be done to better the life conditions of children who are less rather than more developmentally plastic because it would be a waste of time, money, and effort. They would not benefit at all or not very much. So at the very least it would be more efficient, as well as productive, to focus more on one set of children than the other, presuming we could differentiate them.

While that may not be an illogical deduction, especially given evidence to be discussed in the next three chapters consistent with the hypothesis, I do not think it is the only inference to be drawn and I most certainly do not find it acceptable. To begin with, it is based on the naturalistic fallacy, discussed in Chapter 1—that is, the misguided view that what "is" (in nature) is what "ought" to be (in society). In not succumbing to this error of reasoning, we should, in our extremely affluent society, recognize that every child, no matter whether highly developmentally plastic or not, deserves a decent quality of life, affording them a sense of safety and security. Why? Because they never asked to be here—and we can afford it!

Returning to the issue of "return on investment" when it comes to how we should respond to children who may prove mostly unsusceptible to their childhood experiences and exposures, I have come to believe that those interested in child development, especially in children growing up under conditions of adversity, have treated children, all too often, as commodities. I say this because the arguments for providing better developmental conditions for less advantaged children are almost always grounded in terms of economic payoffs—believing, that is, that interventions that enhance the development of disadvantaged children, increasing their chances of becoming productive taxpayers rather than tax consumers, should be supported if and only if economically evaluated payoffs exceed the costs of the service or program. Thus, cost-benefit analysis should be applied to any and all interventions and policy prescriptions. What seems to have been lost, or at least regarded as of secondary importance, are moral and ethical considerations— namely, what all children deserve in rich society, which is to have a decent quality of life. To me, that is a real scandal.

This future-consequences approach to thinking about development was on full display when the first Trump administration implemented a policy of apprehending all illegal border crossers from Mexico, even if they were traveling with babies, toddlers, or young children. Confronted with the horrifying images of crying families being forcibly separated, the developmental scientists, physicians, psychologists, and others I saw reacting all focused on how the trauma of so young a child's being separated from parents could have long-term adverse effects on the brain and give rise to problematic and costly psychological and behavioral development further down the road.

Without taking anything away from that well-founded concern, where was the moral outrage at these very young children's being *tortured* via forced separation? I purposely use this loaded term because there is little that is more painful and threatening to an infant, toddler, or young child than being forcibly separated from a parent who is actively resisting that separation. This is why the president of the American Academy of Pediatrics called it "government-sanctioned child abuse."[8] Why, then, was the immediacy of the pain of separation itself not the first and foremost reason to stop this inhumane policy? Fundamentally, why do we seem to discount the quality of everyday life, a child's lived experience, at least relative to the importance we assign to long-term consequences? Put another way, why do we often ask what the consequences of some experience will be, and rarely wonder what it actually feels like as it occurs?

Sometimes I am even led to wonder why we developmentalists have spent so much time and taxpayer money documenting the ill effects of child abuse, though I certainly have no concerns about efforts spent remediating any such effects. To what extent do we need to keep "discovering" that child abuse is not good for children's brains, behavior, and health? Shouldn't most money go to preventing abuse rather than chronicling that it is bad for children?

RETURNING TO the differential susceptibility hypothesis, consider these words of Johann Wolfgang von Goethe that my graduate-school mentor Urie Bronfenbrenner was fond of quoting: "What is hardest of all? That which seems most simple: to see with your eyes what is before your eyes." I share them because, upon reflection, I find it rather astonishing that the fields of child and human development never entertained the idea of differential susceptibility, for better and for worse, to any real degree until the twenty-first century. Why, when so much time and effort has been spent investigating dual-risk phenomena, has there not been more curiosity about whether it is not just adversity that some individuals prove more susceptible to, but also positive experiences and exposures? As the next several chapters will make clear, it is not as if differential susceptibility–like variation in environmental responsiveness to adverse and supportive developmental contexts—was not there waiting to be discovered, once we went looking for it.

Well after I developed the differential susceptibility hypothesis, a scholarly experience occurred that brought home the truth of Goethe's observation. It involved reading a GxE study about how prenatal smoking interacts with a particular gene to predict ADHD.[9] While the authors interpreted their findings as providing evidence of dual risk, as I studied the data presented in one of their tables, it seemed like something was amiss—not presumably because of any intention to hide anything, but perhaps because data points were omitted to simplify the presentation. It made me wonder whether the missing information might reveal the results to be more consistent with differential susceptibility than dual risk. So I suggested that my graduate student, Michael Pluess, who will figure importantly in subsequent chapters, email the senior author. In the best spirit of science, she supplied the data and, just as I suspected, dual risk was not what was going on—the children carrying a putative "vulnerability gene" seemed to be carrying, instead, a "plasticity gene."

Why do I say this? Because the children carrying the particular gene variant in question and who were thus most likely, relative to all other children, to develop ADHD when exposed to prenatal smoking (that is, susceptibility "for worse") proved to be least likely to develop the disorder when not exposed to that prenatal condition (that is, susceptibility "for better"). Just as critical was that the children carrying other variants of the same gene were far less affected by their prenatal experiences, for either good or ill. In other words, the data were consistent with some children being more susceptible than others to an environmental influence due to their genetic makeup—and in a for-better-and-for-worse manner. More Mendelian-genetic evidence like this will be the focus of Chapter 10.

As we did not want to embarrass the research team that published the original article, I suggested to Michael that we invite its senior author to join us in writing a short communication revising—and reinterpreting—the findings of her team's published paper. She was happy to join us, so we published the revised, differential susceptibility–related results in the same journal in which the original paper appeared.[10] The original problem, of course, was that the investigatory team missed something, differential susceptibility, because it was busy looking for something else, dual risk. "What is hardest of all? That which seems most simple: to see with your eyes what is before your eyes." Having outlined the underlining evolutionary logic of the differential susceptibility hypothesis, I now turn to the work of the three other teams of developmental thinkers who came to the same general idea, but for different reasons and via different routes.

## Biological Sensitivity to Context

Upon reading about differential susceptibility to environmental influences, many readers will likely be reminded, as they should be, of another developmental perspective, one that characterizes some children, typologically, as orchids and others as dandelions. For those not familiar with this catchy terminology—which I wish I had coined (just like "predictive adaptive response")—orchid refers to children highly responsive to their developmental environment. Thus, like orchids they thrive under good conditions but wilt under poor ones; in other words, they, too, are highly developmentally plastic, for better and for worse. In contrast, dandelions are sturdy little buggers that are pretty much unaffected by the environment, more or less thriving under both positive and negative growing conditions—unless, of course, circumstances are so severe that survival is not possible.

Whereas the differential susceptibility hypothesis started out as a prediction based on evolutionary reasoning well before any data in support of it had materialized, just as in the case of the puberty prediction central to psychosocial acceleration theory, that was not so with what would become the evolutionary-inspired theory of "biological sensitivity to context" (BSC).[11] And this is because BSC was a creative post-hoc attempt to account for a surprising finding by the pediatrician Thomas Boyce, of the University of British Columbia, and his colleagues. They discovered that the children who were most physiologically reactive—in terms of increased heart rate and blood pressure when subject to a series of stressful laboratory procedures—proved to be most *and* least at risk of developing respiratory illness, depending on whether their families were, respectively, high in support or low in support. Thus, high physiological reactivity in the face of high support was associated with the least illness, and the same physiology, in the face of low support, was linked to the most illness. Just as notably, the children who were not so physiologically reactive proved to be unaffected by family support, be it high or low, when it came to experiencing respiratory illness.[12] In other words, these investigator stumbled upon what I have labeled "fixed and plastic developmental strategists" and "differential susceptibility."

One of the most interesting contrasts between my differential susceptibility hypothesis and BSC theorizing is in how each regards Mendelian-genetic nature, as well as nurture—a difference of theory despite the fact that both are anchored in evolutionary analysis of why it makes reproductive sense for individuals to develop differently depending on their context of development. My differential susceptibility thinking presumed that whether life history was "born" or "made" depended on the genetic makeup of the individual, having nothing to say about the role of nurture in determining whether a child was more or less developmentally plastic. By contrast, what became BSC theory in the hands of Tom Boyce and

Bruce Ellis attributed different degrees of developmental plasticity to whether the child's developmental environment induced high or low physiological reactivity. In other words, whereas I attributed susceptibility to genetic makeup or some other inborn personal attribute, they attributed it to the childhood environment via its influence on physiological reactivity.

As we made clear in a collaborative paper highlighting similarities and differences between our two theoretical frameworks, there was nothing in either theory that precluded what the other heralded about the origins of variation in susceptibility to environmental influences, Mendelian-genetic nature on the one hand and nurture on the other. Indeed, we collectively came to the conclusion that in different children such variation could be a function of genetic makeup or the developmental environment. Thus, whereas some children would be born high or low in developmental plasticity as a result of their genotype or some other personal characteristics, others would be made that way by what they experienced early in life.[13] Once again, development is complicated.

THREE THINGS were fundamentally original about BSC. The first concerned how the stress-response systems involving autonomic, adrenocortical, or immune reactivity to psychosocial stressors function. The standard psychological and biological view was that these systems prepare the individual to cope with challenge and threats, as in the familiar fight-or-flight response. But what Boyce and Ellis added to this was the claim that these well-studied stress response systems served to amplify susceptibility to environmental influences in a for-better-and-for-worse manner—or to dampen it.

In addition to explaining the original and surprising Boyce findings, this physiologically centered focus led to the second original proposition: that, in response to the developmental environment, whether supportive or adverse, children highly reactive to stress would develop, respectively, best or worst not just in mental health terms, but also in terms of biomedical health. The fact that Boyce is a pediatrician no doubt led him to entertain possibilities that I never considered.

The third original idea was based on two sets of evidence. The first was research indicating that trauma early in life can increase reactivity to stress. The second was that being highly physiologically reactive fosters, in settings high in nurturance, developmental health and competence. When combined, these empirical observations led to the intriguing proposal that a curvilinear or U-shaped relation should exist between the degree of support or adversity the child experiences and the consequent degree of stress reactivity that support or adversity induces and, thereby, susceptibility to environmental influences.

Whereas growing up under very stressful circumstances fosters heightened physiological reactivity and, in consequence, heightened susceptibility to adverse environmental influences, being exposed to an especially nurturing environment has the same enhancing effect on reactivity but, as a result, heightened susceptibility to the benefits of a supportive developmental environment. In other words, these children become orchids. Derivatively, those children exposed to neither very bad nor very good rearing environments, according to BSC theorizing, but just average ones, do not become highly reactive and thus are not particularly affected by their developmental experiences and environmental exposures, be they good, bad, or indifferent. In terms of differential susceptibility, then, they become fixed rather than plastic strategists—that is, dandelions.

Marco Del Giudice and Bruce Ellis have further developed these ideas, applying them to the developmental origins of psychopathology in what they call the "adaptive calibration model" of stress responsivity. This extension of BSC has much in common with psychosocial acceleration theory in that it is also about how experiences in childhood *calibrate* the way children should develop as a result of their early developmental experiences and exposures.[14]

The last comment to be made at this point about BSC, which emerged from a different set of evolutionary observations and ideas than did my differential susceptibility theorizing, is that it also stipulates that developmental variation in biological sensitivity to context has been maintained via Darwinian natural selection. And this is because the way of responding to stress reflected in a U-shaped function yielded distinctive fitness benefits in different environments over the course of human evolutionary history. Developing high physiological reactivity in response to an especially supportive developmental environment increased the chances of passing on genes, just as did the development of high physiological reactivity in response to an especially harsh and unpredictable developmental context. Whereas developing a socially-reciprocal and mutually beneficial social orientation in the former context promoted reproductive fitness, in the latter context the same was true of an opportunistic, advantage-taking, and exploitative social orientation.

## Sensory-Processing Sensitivity

The third perspective on variation in susceptibility to environmental influences has neither strong evolutionary nor developmental roots. Nor was it originally based on systematic empirical research. All this is not to imply that it lacks value, just to distinguish its origins from the more "academic" frameworks already outlined, with still another to come. Sensory-processing sensitivity theory was advanced by Elaine Aron, associated with the State University of New York at Stony

Brook. As a clinical psychologist seeing patients, she developed her ideas in response to her experience providing therapy.

Most of Aron's work has appeared not in peer reviewed, scholarly journal articles but in books, which is quite different from how the other frameworks considered in this chapter were disseminated. I share this only because in recent years Aron's books have become best sellers and her ideas have penetrated the mainstream media far more than any other perspectives addressing variation in susceptibility to environmental influences. At the same time, her work is also far more founded on mental health thinking, especially concerns for the life challenges faced by so-called "highly sensitive persons" (HSPs), rather than evolutionary and developmental analysis.

Aron's thinking about highly sensitive individuals stipulates that they have a heightened sensitivity to sensory information available in their environment (SPS: sensory-processing sensitivity). She further hypothesizes that the nervous systems of HSPs are more responsive to stimuli than those of non-HSPs, leading to a greater awareness and deep processing of sensory information. HSPs tend to be more easily overwhelmed by sensory stimuli, such as loud noises, strong smells, or bright lights, and may require more time and space to recover from these experiences. HSPs are also more likely to pick up on subtleties in their environment, such as changes in facial expressions or tone of voice, and may have a greater capacity for empathy and emotional awareness. In consequence, Aron's most relevant claim insofar as this chapter is concerned is that persons endorsing such self-characterizations are highly susceptible to the effects of the environment, also for better or for worse, though that is not phrasing she uses.[15]

Perhaps the best way to get a sense of sensory-processing sensitivity and a feel for the so-called HSP trait is to consider a self-assessment questionnaire Aron developed. It queries respondents about a range of psychological attributes, covering topics like sensitivity to stimuli, emotional reactivity, and depth of processing. Specific items ask respondents to register agreements, from weak to strong, with statements such as the following: I am easily overwhelmed by strong sensory input like bright lights, strong smells, coarse fabrics, or sirens close by. Other people's moods affect me deeply. I tend to be very sensitive to pain. I am conscientious and detail oriented. I am easily startled. I avoid violent movies and TV shows.[16]

Aron theorizes that heightened sensitivity to the subtleties in the environment in the case of HSPs is innate. Further—and despite the claim about her views not being strongly anchored to evolutionary considerations—she contends that SPS evolved as a survival mechanism, thereby enabling HSPs to be more attuned to potential threats and opportunities in their environment. Note that no claims are made about reproduction, fitness, and related ideas central to modern evolutionary understanding, as was the case for the previous two perspectives already considered.

Despite such possible survival benefits, Aron acknowledges that in today's world, so different from so much of the evolutionary past, HSPs may struggle to function. This is because so many modern environments are overstimulating or lack opportunities for quiet reflection.

Let me raise one concern about terminology with respect to notions of highly sensitive persons. I believe there is a need to distinguish susceptibility and sensitivity because, in terms of this book, they should not be treated as synonyms. I have no problem with the use of the term sensitivity by Aron and her collaborators when they refer to how individuals process and respond to their *immediate* experiences, be they loud noises or other people's moods. But in my mind—and use—susceptibility refers to *enduring effects* of developmental experiences and environmental exposures. So, for example, a hungry man can be sated after a meal, his immediate response, but that is different than whether the ingested food will make him fatter or build muscle, more enduring effects.

The reason I think this distinction is important from a developmental point of view is that two people can be affected in exactly the same way at time of exposure, but only for one of them will that experience contribute to shaping the individual's longer-term development. Consider, for example, that many people lose weight when on a diet, proving their sensitivity to the change in their eating habits, but only some actually keep the lost weight off, proving their susceptibility to the diet. So, for the purposes of this book, the focus is not just on the immediate response to an experience or exposure (except when considering the quality of children's everyday lives) but, critically, on the potential enduring effects of it—that is, susceptibility not sensitivity. Just to be clear, Aron's view is that differential sensitivity to immediate experiences and exposures can and often does result in developmental downstream effects on well-being, implying that, in the case of HSPs, sensitivity can foster susceptibility.

## Hawks and Doves

The three ways of thinking about differential susceptibility considered through this point were all advanced without knowledge of the others. But that was not the case when it comes to the final one to be considered. In fact, while addressing the same differential susceptibility issue, the fourth framework is based on evolutionary-biological ideas advanced long before any discussion of individual differences in developmental plasticity emerged in developmental science.

The hawk-dove theory was first proposed fifty or so years ago. It sought to account for systematic and within-species differences in the temperaments and behavior of many animals. Research on more than a hundred species has identified a correlated suite of characteristics that distinguish animals judged to qualify as hawks and doves based on their temperaments and patterns of behavior. Overall, studies suggest that the behavioral and survival differences between animals within a species that are classified as hawks and doves can have important implications for reproductive success.[17]

Hawks are aggressive, competitive, and willing to take risks to obtain resources such as food, mates, and territory. Doves, on the other hand, are more cautious and passive, one consequence of which is the tendency to avoid conflict whenever possible. In some bird species, males that exhibit hawklike aggressive and territorial behavior are more successful in securing and defending mating partners. By contrast, males that exhibit dovelike behavior, such as being more cooperative and sharing resources, may be less successful in securing mates but may have higher survival rates due to avoiding conflicts and conserving resources.

In other animal species, such as fish and rodents, hawks and doves may exhibit different strategies for foraging for food and avoiding predators. Hawks may be more likely to take risks to obtain food or territory, which can increase their chances of becoming a predator's lunch. Doves, on the other hand, may be more cautious and avoid taking risks, which can reduce their chances of predation, but may also limit their access to resources.[18]

The hawk-dove theory has recently been applied to children by colleagues from the University of Rochester, Patrick Davies and Melissa Sturge-Apple, based on the inference that there are also two basic types of individuals. Hawk children tend to be more assertive, aggressive, and risk-taking, whereas children who exhibit dovelike behavior tend to be more cautious, passive, and risk-averse. As in Aron's HSP theory, the cautious and restrained proclivities of dove children allow them to pause to register, process, and deliberate on how they manage their encounters with the world around them. In benign contexts that invite exploration, dove children evince greater calmness, persistence, and intrinsic engagement with stimuli than their hawk counterparts. In contexts of rewarding environmental stimuli, doves exhibit enduring expressions of temperate appreciation and contentment rather than brief bouts of exuberance or intense anticipatory excitement. Finally, in social contexts, a dove temperament is reflected initially in aloofness and reticence to engage others that, with time and greater familiarity to their surroundings, is increasingly superseded by peaceful and cooperative behavior with others.[19]

Hawk-dove theorizing suggests that the different temperaments and behavioral styles of the two types of children are influenced by a variety of factors, including both genetics, like differential susceptibility theorizing, and early-life experiences, like BSC thinking. For example, individuals who grow up in environments that are characterized by competition and aggression may be more likely to develop hawk tendencies, whereas those who grow up in cooperative and nurturing environments may be more likely to develop dove tendencies.

These temperamental characteristics are theorized to have important implications for children's susceptibility to environmental influences. Given that hawk children tend to be more impulsive, reactive, aggressive, and prone to taking risks, they are thought to be less responsive to social cues or feedback from their environment. Dove children, on the other hand, being more cautious, reserved, and risk-averse, tend to be more sensitive to social cues and feedback from their environment.

In consequence, dove children are presumed to be more susceptible to environmental influences than hawk children. Dove children may be more vulnerable to negative experiences in their environment, such as harsh or inconsistent parenting, because they are less likely to assert themselves or challenge authority. Conversely, they may be more responsive to positive experiences in their environment, such as warm and supportive parenting, because they are more attuned to social cues and feedback. Once again, then, we see a for-better-and-for-worse theoretical analysis of variation in how children are shaped by their developmental environments.

## Conclusion

It seems rather remarkable that the first three sets of thinkers discussed gave birth to the same basic idea—differential susceptibility to environmental influences, for better and for worse—without knowledge of each other's ideas. Two etiological explanations come to mind. It may be simply a case of good minds thinking alike. And, not unrelatedly, it could also be that the field of child development was ripe for extending dual-risk thinking by entertaining the possibility that some children also benefit disproportionately from supportive developmental contexts, thus eventually leading to the view of individual differences in developmental plasticity.

Irrespective of the cause, what is also intriguing is how the four sets of theorists came to their ideas from different starting points. In my case, it was via reasoning from first principles about the uncertainty of the future. In Boyce and Ellis's case, it was after the (empirical) fact, based on a desire to understand why the same surprising findings emerged in two different studies. For Aron, it was clinical experience with clients in therapy that prove informative. And finally, in the hawk-dove research, it was a result of considering what evolutionary biologists knew about differences in the temperaments and behavior of animals.

Even if similar ideas about variation in developmental plasticity emerged from different starting points, that does not ensure that differential susceptibility thinking is "on target." Multiple scholars could simply have gotten things wrong for different reasons. If so, it wouldn't be the first time. This is why we turn in the next three chapters to, respectively, the subjects of temperament, physiological reactivity and being a highly sensitive person, and Mendelian genetics. This will enable us to determine whether they operate as "plasticity factors," as the theoretical perspectives considered in this chapter suggest.

# 8

# The Difficult Infant

W ITH REGARD to the claim that some children are more susceptible, for better and for worse, than others when it comes to having their development shaped by environmental forces, at least one of the perspectives considered in Chapter 7 advanced this view before there was human evidence substantiating it. That, of course, was my differential susceptibility hypothesis. So, the challenge I faced once I had this idea in mind, based as it was on reasoning from first principles about the fundamental goal of life and the fact that the future is inherently uncertain, was to determine whether there was any existing evidence consistent with it that might have been overlooked.

As I have made clear repeatedly in this book, theory is one thing—a guiding light, perhaps—but evidence is another. Without the latter, the former is little more than an interesting possibility, still a just so story, or hypothesis. As I was looking around to find any evidence in line with my thinking, I attended a lecture by a visiting primatologist at my then university, Penn State, about temperamental variation in a species of monkeys, rhesus macaques. Some, it turned out, were like doves, though that term was not used to refer to them. When very young they tended to be very shy, nervous, and inhibited, thus hesitant when confronting new things. "Uptight" was the colloquial term used to characterize these animals. Others were described as "laid back" because they did not show the fearfulness that the uptight ones did and were interested, comfortable, and curious when exposed to new things. What was so interesting about these two groups was the discovery that they were differentially affected by their rearing experiences, for better and for worse.

Such differential susceptibility in the case of the monkeys was revealed in an experiment in which the uptight and laid-back animals were randomly assigned to foster mothers known from prior observation to be highly skilled parents or maltreating ones. The animals with the dovelike temperament became more or less incompetent "basket cases" when they were raised by mothers who had a history of mistreating their offspring, yet they rose to the top of the dominance hierarchy—with all its mating and thus fitness advantages—when placed in the care of highly skilled mothers. In contrast, such differences in the quality of care that the laid-back monkeys received had little detectable effect on them.[1]

So, this animal work led me to go searching for evidence that *temperamental* variation in human infants might help identify those more and less developmentally plastic—that is, susceptible to environmental influences. What caught my eye first was not so much evidence of the for-better-and-for-worse pattern of susceptibility central to differential susceptibility thinking. Rather it was evidence that seemed to challenge the still prevailing view of highly negatively emotional infants with "difficult" temperaments who tend to become easily upset in many situations and hard to comfort once they are distressed. Other characteristics of these babies often include irregular sleep and feeding schedules, as well as heightened sensitivity to stimuli in their environment, such as changes in temperature or texture. I myself had one of these infants, my previously mentioned professor son, who was so challenging to care for as an infant that it made me wonder, honestly, why there wasn't more child abuse, especially given evidence of predictive links between infant negative emotionality and childhood maltreatment.[2] It also made me glad that we had him rather than a family less able to cope with such a difficult baby.

What I discovered in searching the research literature was that there was some limited evidence that it was not only the case, as long documented in studies testing dual-risk thinking, that difficult infants were more likely to develop problems than other children when growing up in challenging circumstances. There existed some limited research indicating that these difficult babies were also especially susceptible to the benefits of supportive care.

Consider in this regard the following underappreciated findings. In research published more than four decades ago, evidence emerged that highly irritable infants were most likely to develop secure attachments to their mothers when their parents experienced high levels of social support.[3] Some ten or so years later, another investigation, this one conducted by my friend and colleague of the University of Iowa, Grazyna Kochanska, focused on the development of conscience in children. It revealed that the effects of skilled parenting proved most influential—and beneficial—in the case of highly fearful infants.[4] Collectively, these results—and another set to be shared toward the end of this chapter—raised the question, at least in my mind, whether so-called difficult temperament early in life is not so much a "risk factor" making children vulnerable to adversity, but a "plasticity factor," making them highly susceptible to the effects of both supportive and unsupportive care.

The results of the two infant studies just highlighted—which had never been interpreted in the terms just suggested—stimulated me to undertake my own research testing this proposition, while keeping an eye out for related work, especially efforts stimulated by my differential susceptibility theorizing. By now it is striking how much evidence there is underscoring the importance of early temperament when it comes to individual differences in developmental plasticity. It is to such work that I now turn.

MY FIRST ATTEMPT to empirically address the issue of differential susceptibility only partly accomplished this task, because it evaluated only whether observed mothering and fathering would predict problems with aggression and disobedience ("externalizing" problems) more strongly in the case of children aged thirty-six months who had been highly negatively emotional as one-year-olds. It turned out that it did. In fact, the size of the parenting effect was three times greater for this more susceptible subgroup than for the less susceptible one.[5] For some reason that I simply cannot explain, I failed to address the critical issue of susceptibility for better and for worse. Was it the case for these children, then, that if they had experienced sensitive and supportive parenting they would have proved less likely to engage in problem behavior?

The mistake I made in my first empirical study was not repeated in my subsequent work, this time supervising Michael Pluess's doctoral dissertation. What made this next differential susceptibility study so interesting was that, when the childcare-study team tested the prevailing hypothesis that higher versus lower quality childcare would predict, respectively, fewer and more behavior problems, no evidence of that highly anticipated effect emerged. Yet when we distinguished these same children on the basis of their temperaments as infants, voila! It was like the biblical story of the Red Sea parting so that the Hebrews could escape the pharaoh's legions in ancient Egypt. Now it became clear that quality of childcare across the first 4.5 years of life did matter as an influence on children's problem behavior at kindergarten age, but only if they were highly negative as infants, and in the very for-better-and-for-worse manner that had been neglected in my earlier work. Clearly, the original childcare research that yielded null results when it came to the question at hand was due to the failure to entertain the possibility that children vary in their susceptibility to environmental influences.[6] This again reminds us of the wisdom of the previously mentioned English aphorism regarding null results: "the absence of evidence is not evidence of absence."

LET'S CONTINUE to consider how early temperamental difficulty moderates or conditions the effect of parenting and other family processes on children's development. One noteworthy piece of work showed that the negative reactivity of newborns influences whether the stress their mothers experienced during pregnancy, as indexed by the levels of cortisol circulating in their blood, affected how capable the infants were of self-quieting at age six months when distressed, considered an index of emotion regulation. Critically, it was only highly negatively reactive newborns whose emotional regulation was affected by their mothers' prenatal stress—and, again, in a for-better-and-for-worse manner: less self-quieting if mother was highly stressed during pregnancy but more such emotion regulation if she had not been.[7] Similar results emerged in an investigation that evaluated whether mothers' level of empathy predicted their eight-year-olds' externalizing problems. Once more, results showed that this was so—in a for-better-and-for-worse manner—but only for those boys scoring, at ages two months and two years, high on a measure of difficult temperament.[8] Recall that the phrase "for better and for worse" is shorthand for evidence showing that the susceptible children do better, on average, than all other children when exposed to supportive early-life conditions, but worse developmentally when they experience unsupportive care.

My students and I realized that almost all research focused on variation in developmental plasticity guided by the differential susceptibility hypothesis, whether or not discussed in this or the following chapters, relied on rather small samples of children that were not necessarily representative of the larger populations from which they were drawn. This is a common and now widely recognized limitation of many developmental inquiries. In response and working with Xiaoya Zhang and Kristina Sayler, both PhD students of mine at UC Davis, we decided to secure data from a large project being carried out in the United Kingdom, involving over fourteen thousand families. When we tested whether difficult infant temperament moderated the effect of parenting in early childhood on the externalizing problems, emotional problems, and peer problems of children aged eight through eleven, we found evidence for what we came to call "weak" differential susceptibility, but only in the case of externalizing problems. This is the terminology we developed when evidence indicated that while all children proved tolerably susceptible, some did so more than others. The terminology of "strong" differential susceptibility, in contrast, refers to findings in which some children emerge as unsusceptible and the others as highly so. So what we observed using data from the Avon Longitudinal Study was that while all children proved, on average, to be susceptible to the parenting effect under investigation, this was more so the case with those who evinced greater temperamental difficulty than those who were characterized as being less difficult at six months of age.[9]

Another approach to addressing the issue of whether being highly negative as an infant and having a difficult temperament demarcates children especially likely to be influenced by their early-life experiences involves using a marker of difficult temperament rather than a direct index of this phenotype. Such markers include being born prematurely, having "mild perinatal adversities," and being "small for gestational age." The latter refers to being born smaller than expected given the time of premature birth (such as thirty or thirty-five weeks rather than the normal forty-week gestation). Notably, all these conditions, which are themselves associated with heightened negative emotionality, have been linked to increased susceptibility to environmental influences, for better and for worse.[10]

With the exception of the "weak" differential susceptibility evidence cited, all the work considered through this point has followed the orchid-dandelion strategy of creating two groups of children based on their temperaments or newborn health status, thus making them biased toward the stronger version of differential susceptibility, even if not guaranteeing it. The risk here involves reifying the idea of two types of children rather than children who range across a full spectrum of susceptibility, from very high to very low. Recall that the former approach to testing the differential susceptibility hypothesis is not the only way to go. In fact, it may not be the best way to conduct such work because, like so many other personal characteristics (such as height, IQ, and athletic ability), negative emotionality and difficult temperament are continuous in character, ranging by degree from low to high, rather than reflecting two distinct groups—those who are highly negative and those who are not particularly negative at all.

What makes this distinction important, as we will also see in Chapter 9, is that susceptibility often operates as a gradient, such that the more an infant or toddler is, in the current case, negatively emotional, the more susceptible she proves to be. Instead of thinking in terms of orchid and dandelion children, then, it may be better to think in terms of degree of negativity and thus susceptibility. Whereas some children are highly susceptible based on their very high levels of negative emotionality, and some rather unsusceptible due to their low levels, still others are moderately susceptible because they have intermediate levels of negativity. It turns out that when you conceptualize—and measure—negativity in terms of a gradient, the more negative a young child is, the more susceptible she is, with the reverse being true, as well.[11]

IN SEEKING to understand effects of developmental context on child development, one question that merits consideration is whether it is only the quality of parenting or childcare providers, or prenatal stress—the foci of all work considered to this point—that influences children's development in a differential susceptibility manner due to early temperament. Too address this issue, let me call attention to two more investigations, one focused on parents' mental health and the other on their marital relationship. One team of researchers tested a hypothesis outlining a three-step developmental cascade: they predicted that greater or lesser levels of *maternal depression* across the child's first two years of life would predict, respectively, less or more *supportive parenting,* and in turn, greater or less *separation distress* at age three. This turned out to be the case, for better and for worse, but only for children who scored high in *negative emotionality* at age six months.[12]

Turning to the marital relationship, a long-appreciated influence on children's development, another team of investigators led by Dante Cicchetti discovered that the relationship between marital conflict and the development of behavior problems from two to three years of age proved stronger for children aged twenty-four months who were highly irritable than it did for less irritable ones. [13] To be honest, these results were somewhat of a surprise to me; when *infants* were highly negatively emotional, I was (and I remain) most prepared to consider that characteristic inborn, attributing it to genetics or perhaps prenatal stress. But by the time a child is two years of age—and certainly older—the risk is that we are no longer witnessing such an inborn and temperamental source of negativity, but rather one induced by adverse experiences within and beyond the family.

I say this for two reasons. First, years ago, I conducted research which remains surprisingly rare in the field of developmental psychology, at least in the infant years, which found that increases and decreases in infant negative emotionality within the first year of life appeared to be influenced by family factors like parent personality and marital quality, as well as the parenting of mothers and fathers.[14] So consider how these factors and processes might affect the development of negativity across even longer stretches of time, especially at older ages. The important point to appreciate here is that heightened negative emotionality in infancy, while somewhat predictive of later negativity, is not fixed in stone. As my work made clear, some children increase and others decrease in their negativity as they develop.

The other reason I was somewhat surprised by this team's findings was that I had seen the results of a meta-analysis of numerous investigations focused on how children's temperaments, interact with parenting to influence their well-being. It turned out that the age at which temperament is measured matters a lot. Consistent with my thinking about early temperament, negative emotionality in the first year emerged in the meta-analysis as a plasticity factor consistent with differential susceptibility thinking, for better and for worse—but when measured at older ages, it operated more as a risk factor, consistent with dual-risk thinking.[15] Evidently, measurements of negativity at very early ages versus at substantially later ages do not reflect the same things, with regard to either the origins of negativity (such as prenatal stress, genetics, or early-life adversity) or susceptibility to environmental influences.

INTEREST IN the influence of sensitive parenting in much developmental research derives from the role it is theorized to play in the development of infant-parent attachment security early in life. There is no shortage of work (some of it conducted by me) consistent with the claim that, whereas high levels of sensitivity foster security, low levels promote insecurity. In fact, many years ago now, a meta-analysis was carried out that showed the effect of more sensitive care versus less sensitive care on infant-mother attachment to be real, but perhaps not as strong a predictor—in observational studies—as many devotees of the theory (myself included) had presumed. A much larger meta-analysis carried out three decades later—focused on attachment both to mothers and to fathers, and of course including many more studies—documented more or less the same anticipated effects, linking greater sensitivity with greater likelihood of security in relation to both parents.[16]

Back in 1997, having been invited to write a commentary on the first meta-analysis, I raised the possibility that its findings reflected a failure in virtually all the relevant research (including my own) to take differential susceptibility into account. Perhaps, I reasoned, the security or insecurity of attachment that some infants developed was due to the quality of care they received, whereas for others this was not the case. The failure to entertain this possibility, I suspected, could be the reason for the very modest overall effect detected in the meta-analysis, and its main result may have masked as much as it illuminated. In other words, the meta-analysis, like the research it was based on, had averaged sensitivity effects that were both high and low depending on children's susceptibility. I went further, based on the very early evidence cited at the beginning of this chapter, hypothesizing that more negatively emotional infants might be much more susceptible to the effects of maternal sensitivity on the development of attachment security than were infants with less difficult temperaments. [17]

I share this as a lead into an observational study that revealed, *many years later,* that my suspicion was on target. I do this not to highlight my insight but to set the stage for differential susceptibility–related intervention research involving the purposeful manipulation of parenting so that true causal—and not just statistical— effects of nurture could be evaluated. In a now three-decade-old investigation, a Dutch PhD student evaluated effects of an intensive home-visiting program designed to foster sensitive-responsive parenting and thereby promote infant attachment security, while studying a carefully selected sample of *highly irritable* newborns. The fact that the economically disadvantaged mothers of these infants who had been randomly assigned to the experimental group raised more children who developed secure attachments than those randomly assigned to the control group was, at least for me, not the most significant finding. Rather, it was that the rate of secure attachment in this carefully selected sample of very irritable newborns was *three times* as great in the experimental group as in the control group! That was a much bigger difference than there was really any reason to expect based on prior observational research and the previously mentioned meta-analysis. In fact, it was so different from other studies that it was not even included in the first meta-analysis of effects of parenting on attachment security because the findings seemed questionable, outside of a reasonable range.[18]

Yet it would later be supported. More than fifteen years later, Jude Cassidy, a friend and colleague from our Penn State days and now of the University of Maryland, extended the Dutch intervention research in an attempt to directly test the differential susceptibility hypothesis. Cassidy distinguished more and less irritable newborns within a sample of highly irritable ones, then randomly assigned them to experimental and control groups. This experimental intervention, also designed to foster sensitive mothering and, as a result, infant attachment security, was briefer and less intense than the previous one—but it produced the same basic result. It was only among *the most irritable* of these highly irritable newborns that the intervention succeeded in increasing the likelihood that children would develop secure attachments in response to increases in their mothers' sensitive parenting.[19] My speculation decades earlier in commenting on the first meta-analysis thus appeared to be right.

These findings regarding children who do and do not benefit from various interventions carry important and all-too-unrecognized implications for the traditional risk-and-resilience thinking that is so widespread in the developmental sciences and beyond. While much of the observational evidence indicates that infants and children who are not highly negatively emotional are resilient in the face of adversity, the intervention work indicates that the same is true when efforts to enhance development and well-being are instituted. That is, these children are less likely to benefit from intervention efforts in the same way they are less likely to be influenced by early-life adversity. More evidence to this effect will be shared in Chapter 10, where consideration turns to the Mendelian genetics of plasticity.

What all this implies, no doubt surprisingly, is that resilience, at least when based on personal characteristics, may be a double-edged sword, something of great value in the face of adversity, but potentially costly when developmental "nutrients" are available. Whether resilience based on personal characteristics is a blessing or a curse may depend on the quality of the environment under consideration: it could be a blessing in the face of adversity but a curse in the face of environmental enrichment.


BEFORE MOVING on to Chapter 9 and considering evidence evaluating the biological-sensitivity-to-context framework of differential susceptibility, we can engage with some issues raised by this chapter's content. Let's consider first the fact that developmental-plasticity-related investigations of both negative emotionality and difficult temperament typically fail to distinguish different negative emotions. It has thus remained unclear whether it might be proneness to anger or instead to fear that accounts for the differential susceptibility effects highlighted in this chapter. To my knowledge, only a single investigation, conducted by Grazyna Kochanska, has sought to address this question by measuring separately these types of negative emotion. Notably, results revealed that anger and fear, measured at age sixteen months, each functioned as a plasticity factor when it came to predicting preschoolers' violations of conduct rules—after being told what not to do in a university laboratory setting—when effects of both supportive and unsupportive parenting by mothers were the focus of inquiry.[20]

Results such as these raise the question of *why* infants (and perhaps toddlers) who are highly negatively emotional should prove so developmentally plastic, for better and for worse. To frame this critical issue, I can share an anecdote about my firstborn, who was five weeks premature and had a very difficult temperament, as already noted. When he was just a few weeks old, I was holding him with the front of his body touching the front of mine in an attempt to soothe him, but this was not working at all. When his mother noticed this, she, having figured out something that I had not, suggested turning him around, so his back was touching my front. Amazingly, that did the trick.

Reflecting on this memory and all the evidence considered in this chapter makes me wonder if what makes some infants so negatively emotional is that they have extremely sensitive nervous systems, ones on which everything registers extremely powerfully, overwhelming their capacity to cope and self-regulate. This idea is central to Elaine Aron's thinking about highly sensitive people. When parents are attuned to their infants' sensitive nervous systems, as my son's mother was, then accommodations can be made, eventually reducing the negativity and opening up many more pleasant experiences. But when parents lack that ability—as I initially did—the consequences can be anything but developmentally enhancing.

In light of this, it becomes noteworthy that some developmental evidence indicates that, whereas high levels of irritability and negativity provoke aversive responses from parents overwhelmed by many things in their lives, the very same stimuli have the exact opposite—and comforting—effect on well-resourced parents. Perhaps not surprising is that this differential response to the very same infant emotional stimulus results in notable differences in how children develop—and in a manner consistent with psychosocial acceleration theory.[21]

Given all that has been documented in this chapter, it is important not to lose sight of the fact that the dual-risk way of thinking remains the dominant developmental perspective when considering infant negative emotionality and difficult temperament, as well as prematurity and perinatal adversities. Indeed, these conditions are routinely regarded as "risk factors" for healthy development.[22] Perhaps the best evidence of this can be found in the cottage industry of developmental scholars investigating direct links between heightened negative emotionality and other characteristics of difficult infants when it comes to accounting for psychological problems down the developmental road.[23] Clearly, my view is that these early temperamental characteristics should be considered "opportunity factors," at least when contextual conditions are supportive.

To me, it is most disconcerting that, while the often-burdened parents of highly negatively emotional infants are often alerted by pediatricians, nurses, and psychologists to the future challenges they might face, they are rarely if ever informed that they have children who appear to be especially susceptible to the quality of care they experience, for better and for worse. By the way, given that my professor son is now in his forties, it was only long after his infancy that I became aware of his heightened developmental plasticity. This is why I always share this new understanding with parents as soon as I discover that they have infants who are temperamentally like he was.

The last point is that it would be a mistake to assume that only negative emotionality operates like a plasticity factor. One reason I was drawn to evidence pertaining to negativity was that so much empirical attention has been paid to it, given the long-standing dual-risk bias in developmental science. When I went looking for evidence that might prove in line with the differential susceptibility hypothesis, there was no shortage of pertinent studies to consider. This is in sharp contrast to, say, developmental studies of positive emotionality.

These observations call to mind two important facts that should not be missed. First, positive and negative emotionality should not be regarded at opposite ends of a single dimension of temperament (such that high negativity simply equals low positivity), as there is evidence that they are "separable" and thus to some extent independent of each other early in life. Knowing that an infant, or even older child or adult, is prone to negative emotionality does not necessarily imply that she is low in positive emotionality—or vice versa.[24] Second, it is still early days when it comes to identifying characteristics of children that operate as plasticity factors. In that regard, we need to be alert to the drunk's mistake of looking for dropped car keys under a nearby streetlight, because "that's where the light is better." If we hope to identify other potential plasticity factors, we are going to have to rummage around in the dark, at least for a while, and not just focus on the personal factors central to dual-risk thinking that have long been the focus of developmental inquiry.

# 9

# Physiological Reactivity
# and Sensory-Processing Sensitivity

MORE EMPIRICAL WORK has been based on the differential susceptibility perspectives of biological sensitivity to context (BSC) and sensory-processing sensitivity (SPS) than on the hawk-dove perspective. Still, in both cases, the research is far more limited than the work on negative emotionality and difficult temperament, the focus of Chapter 8, and the work on genetics, the focus of Chapter 10. Therefore, this single chapter will suffice to cover research bearing on both BSC and SPS. The core issue addressed is the empirical one: Do heightened physiological reactivity and being a highly sensitive person operate, as theorized, as plasticity factors, to make some children more and others less susceptible to environmental influences?

## Physiological Reactivity as a Plasticity Factor

Tom Boyce and Bruce Ellis's BSC theory of differential susceptibility to environmental influences makes two predictions. The first is based on their view that especially supportive and especially unsupportive rearing milieus induce elevated physiological reactivity in children, the U-shaped curve hypothesis. The second prediction, building on the first, is that such heightened reactivity increases susceptibility to environmental influences, for better and for worse. These two predictions are considered in turn below, but to clarify the various kinds of physiological reactivity about to be discussed, it makes sense to start with a primer on the stress response system.

### The Stress Response System

The human physiological stress response system involves a complex cascade of physiological changes that occurs in response to a perceived threat or a stressor.

These responses are mediated by the autonomic nervous system that is a part of the peripheral nervous system controlling involuntary actions in the body, such as heart rate, digestion, and breathing. It has two main branches: the sympathetic nervous system and the parasympathetic nervous system. Together, these systems work to regulate the body's response to stress and help maintain the steady state of homeostasis.

The sympathetic nervous system is responsible for the activation of the "fight or flight" response, which prepares the body for action in response to a perceived threat. When activated, the sympathetic nervous system releases the hormone adrenaline, also known as epinephrine, into the bloodstream, including cortisol. This triggers a series of physiological responses, including increased heart rate and blood pressure, dilation of the pupils, increased blood flow to the muscles, and increased respiration rate. These changes are designed to help the body respond quickly by increasing its physical abilities and readiness to take action to defend or protect itself.

The parasympathetic nervous system, on the other hand, is responsible for the relaxation response, which counters the effects of the sympathetic nervous system and helps to restore the body to a state of rest and recovery. When activated, the "rest-and-restore" parasympathetic nervous system triggers a series of physiological responses, including decreased heart rate and blood pressure, constriction of the pupils, decreased respiration rate, and increased digestive activity. These changes are designed to conserve energy and promote the rest and recovery already mentioned.

One convenient way to think about these two interrelated systems is that the former serves as an accelerator, upregulating the stress response, and the latter as a brake, downregulating it. The balance between these two systems is crucial for overall health and well-being. While the sympathetic response is critical for safety and survival in the face of a perceived threat, its chronic activation—due to ever present threats of one kind or another, such as child abuse or bullying—can lead to negative health outcomes over time.

## Hypothesis 1: Environmental Inducement of Physiological Reactivity

Recall that especially supportive *and* unsupportive developmental conditions are expected to induce elevated physiological reactivity in the child and, thereby, heightened developmental plasticity. These are the *orchid* children, in the terminology of BSC, and *plastic strategists* in the terminology of differential susceptibility. The related claim is that children exposed to neither of these more extreme environmental circumstances would be much less physiologically reactive and, in consequence, not particularly susceptible to the effects of nurture on development.

These are the *dandelion* children in BSC, also referred to as *fixed strategists* in differential susceptibility theorizing.

Working with both Marilyn Essex of the University of Michigan and Tom Boyce, Bruce Ellis reported two studies testing BSC claims regarding the contextual determinants of high physiological reactivity. One focused on five-year-olds and the other on children studied longitudinally. In the initial inquiry, the focus was on the quality of the home and preschool environments and cardiovascular reactivity in response to challenges presented in a university laboratory, like having to remember and recall a series of numbers, identify an object by touch alone while blindfolded, and verbally describe an emotional event. In the second study, family stress was monitored in infancy and later at preschool age, and autonomic and adrenocortical reactivity was assessed, again in a university laboratory, at age seven. At the later age, one of the challenging tasks administered to evoke physiological reactivity involved placing a few drops of lemon juice on the child's tongue, and another had the child view videotapes designed to evoke fear and sadness.

In both investigations a disproportionate number of children in highly supportive, low-stress environments evinced high automatic reactivity, in line with BSC theorizing. Additionally, in the second study, a relatively high proportion of children growing up in very stressful environments manifested heightened sympathetic and adrenocortical reactivity, also consistent with BSC claims. Critically, further analysis indicated, in both inquiries, that children from moderately or intermediate stressful environments evinced the lowest levels of reactivity, in line with the BSC expectation regarding effects of developmental conditions on physiological reactivity.[1]

Similar results emerged in a third piece of research conducted by Boyce and Ellis. This time the focus was on kindergarten children, aged four to six. Across both sympathetic and adrenocortical systems, a disproportionate number of children growing up under conditions characterized by either low or high adversity—as indexed by restrictive parenting, high levels of family stress, and limited family economic resources—displayed heightened stress reactivity, compared with peers growing up under conditions of moderate adversity.[2] In sum, the findings across all inquiries testing the first BSC proposition provided clear support for it. I find this impressive because, when the U-shaped curve ideas were first advanced, I had my doubts.

## Hypothesis 2: Variation in Susceptibility to Environmental Influences

Turning to the second hypothesis central to BSC thinking, the question is whether the most physiologically reactive children prove to be the most susceptible of all children when it comes to their experiences shaping their development—for better and for worse. Given our Part I focus on reproductive strategy and the puberty hypothesis, the first pertinent research to be considered evaluates BSC theorizing with respect to pubertal development. Perhaps not surprisingly, the study in question was carried out by Bruce Ellis. Results revealed, for highly stress-reactive children, that lower quality parent-child relationships forecast not only earlier pubertal development but also a faster rate of such development. In the case of higher quality parent-child relationships, the opposite pattern emerged: later and slower pubertal development. Critically, no such family effects emerged among less stress-reactive children. Here, then, is evidence integrating and documenting empirical support for both of the evolutionary ideas central to this book—the development of reproductive strategy and differential susceptibility.[3]

These findings pertaining to the rate or tempo of pubertal development remind me of an observation once shared by David Geary of the University of Missouri. Thinking about how the complex process of pubertal development reflects the role of evolution in shaping life history, he ventured that it might show up not so much in *when it begins* as in *how fast it is completed,* perhaps especially in the case of males (who were also participants in the work just cited). Because maturing males were regarded as potential competitors to more mature males, he hypothesized, achieving adult pubertal status as quickly as possible would reduce their chances of being "picked on" by males two, three, or more years older. Wouldn't it be interesting if early onset of puberty matters mostly for females, as perhaps implied by all the work considered in Part I, but that it is rate (or speed) of sexual maturation that is central to males' developing fast life histories? Indeed, might this be the reason why the available evidence is less consistent in the case of males than females? It is my fervent hope that future work will directly address Geary's proposal, which, if supported, would clearly extend and refine psychosocial acceleration theory.

It is not just pubertal development that yields evidence consistent with BSC theorizing. Work focused on one feature of an opportunistic, advantage-taking, and exploitative social orientation of a fast life history—antisocial behavior in adolescence—revealed that its level depended on a history of family aggression in a manner consistent with differential susceptibility. This proved so, however, only for teens who evinced heightened cortisol reactivity in response to a lab-based conflict discussion with their parents—just as predicted by BSC.[4]

Three additional investigations focused on different relationships also yielded results in line with evidence already considered about family influence, though I will not go into them in detail. Two of the studies focused on the effects of marital conflict and a third on teacher-child conflict. There is also evidence consistent with BSC theorizing that two distal factors, kindergarten classroom climate and family income, differentially predict children's development, in line with BSC theoretical expectations.[5]

But even more compelling than the results of these diverse *observational* studies, which, again, can only document statistical associations from which true causation cannot be inferred, are the findings of the only randomized control trial I know to have included physiological reactivity as a plasticity factor. Notably, this work was carried out before the BSC theory was advanced. It involved an attempt to remediate the behavior problems of Dutch children diagnosed with disruptive behavior disorder. Consistent with BSC theorizing, the intervention succeeded in reducing both oppositional behavior and overt aggression, but only for children who scored high on cortisol reactivity in response to a laboratory-based experimental challenge.[6]

To summarize, both observational and experimental studies provide evidence consistent with the two core theoretical propositions of BSC thinking. This research clearly indicates that developmental plasticity can be influenced by early-life conditions of both adversity and support. And this certainly supports the claim advanced in Chapter 7 that greater and lesser susceptibility to environmental influences is not just born, but can also be made.

## Sensory-Processing Sensitivity and Developmental Plasticity

Recall that Aron's differential susceptibility theory of sensory-processing sensitivity highlighted personality differences among individuals of varying susceptibility to environmental influences, with the more susceptible being labeled as HSPs—highly sensitive persons. Recall as well that such individuals are characterized, in comparison to others, as people who process experiences more deeply, are more aware of subtleties in their surroundings, and are more easily overwhelmed in highly stimulating environments.[7]

The first piece of HSP work evaluated whether changes in negative and positive parenting over a one-year period predicted changes in the externalizing behavior problems of Dutch kindergarten children as rated by teachers over the same period of time.[8] It turned out that they did. Externalizing problems, it should not be forgotten, are features of a fast life history. Increases in negative parenting (such as power assertion, ignoring, inconsistent discipline) predicted increases in children's problems. And increases in positive parenting (such as sensitive-responsive, autonomy granting, provision of explanations for disciplinary actions) exerted the opposite effect—decreases in children's problems. But this was most true for children scoring high in sensory-processing sensitivity. The finding that other children changed in similar ways *but to a lesser extent* than the highly sensitive provided evidence of weak differential susceptibility. Not inconsistent with this was a related finding that a psychologically embedded consequence of parent-child relationships—a child's internalized representation of maternal warmth—served as a predictor of emotion regulation, but again most strongly for children scoring high on HSP.[9]

Turning now to environmental exposures, or more distal sources of influence, let's consider the stress parents themselves experience in raising children and its potential effects on the capacity of five- to eight-year-olds to manage or regulate their emotions. The research in question also documented weak differential susceptibility. While both higher- and lower-sensitivity children evinced less emotion regulation when their mothers experienced a great deal of stress, and greater regulation when mothers experienced limited stress, this was more so the case for children who qualified as more sensitive based on an index of sensory-processing sensitivity.[10]

This might be a result, at least in part, of how marital quality impacts parental depression. As a basis for this conjecture, consider work showing that parents scoring high on HSP are more likely to exhibit high levels of depression when dissatisfied with their marriages, and low levels when satisfied.[11] Such similar results in the case of children and parents, even if derived from different investigations, should remind us that sensory-processing sensitivity is, to a degree, heritable, so that highly sensitive adults are more likely than their counterparts low in sensitivity to have highly sensitive children.[12] (Implications for what might be expected when both parent and child are highly susceptible to environmental influences will be addressed in Chapter 10.)

This likelihood of heritability raises the question of how accurate and reliable the measurement of sensory-processing sensitivity is in the above-mentioned studies of children. It is a fair question given that all preceding research has relied on parental reports of children's sensory-processing sensitivity. Might it be that parental reporting of children's psychological characteristics is somewhat biased by their own sensory processing? To avoid this possible problem, two teams of investigators sought to assess children's sensitivity more objectively in their evaluations of strong differential susceptibility. One team of Italian investigators, collaborating with Elaine Aron and my one-time PhD and postdoctoral student Michael Pluess, accomplished this by bringing three-year-olds into the university lab and exposing them to a variety of well-established situations typically used to assess temperament. One such situation was a "risk room" in which children encountered a variety of objects, some obviously attractive, some less so, and some clearly off-putting. The scoring of the children's levels of sensory sensitivity and depth of processing of the environment were based on their observed behavior across twelve different situations.

With such detailed measurements in hand, the question became whether, as expected, children scoring high and low on observed environmental sensitivity appeared differentially susceptible to effects of parenting on externalizing problems, internalizing problems, and social competence. While not every test result supported the hypothesis that children scoring highly sensitive would prove more susceptible to parenting effects, there were repeated indications that this was the case. For example, in tests of whether permissive parenting predicted externalizing problems and whether authoritative parenting predicted social competence, the signature of differential susceptibility—the for-better-and-for-worse pattern of input-output statistical associations—emerged for the high- but not low-sensitivity children. In both cases, the evidence proved consistent with strong differential susceptibility.[13]

The second effort to measure sensory-processing sensitivity based on observed child behavior was led by my former PhD student Zhi Li, by this time a postdoctoral researcher. Here the predictor variable was based on Bruce Ellis's evolutionary analysis of underlying dimensions of the environment, harshness and unpredictability, as discussed in Chapter 4. Li's work also relied on laboratory procedures to assess sensitivity by measuring children's fearful distress (vigilance, anxiety, fear, worry), persistence, focused attention, careful exploration, and emotion regulation. Just as in the prior investigation, evidence of strong differential susceptibility emerged: environmental unpredictability predicted externalizing problems in a for-better-and-for-worse manner, but only in the case of children judged high on sensory-processing sensitivity.[14]

IT MUST be acknowledged that all the preceding HSP work, whether based on parental reports or observational measurements of sensory-processing sensitivity, has been observational in character—again meaning that caution should be taken in drawing causal influences that the environmental conditions under investigation actually influenced the developmental phenotypes of interest. So let's now turn to HSP-related *intervention* studies, which are much better positioned to determine whether a contextual condition in question actually does causally influence an aspect of child development, and do so more for high-HSP children. In contrast to the huge literature on documented effects of early intervention, a good deal of which chronicles eventual fade-out of effects when participants are followed well past the time of the intervention, the unfortunate fact is that most relevant differential susceptibility intervention work has simply not followed participants over more than short periods of time to determine whether such fade-out characterizes this area of inquiry, as well. (In Chapter 10, where the focus shifts to genes as plasticity factors, at least one study will be highlighted in which the evidence of differential susceptibility showed up only in follow-up assessments of children two years post-intervention.)[15]

The first (quasi-experimental) HSP-related intervention to be considered involved a school-based preventative mental health program available to some students in a public high school in East London. The program was administered to all children in sixth grade in one year, and for purposes of evaluating intervention effects, children a year older (who did not receive the program) served as the comparison group. This was not, then, a randomized control trial. The intervention was designed to foster resilience, and its evaluation was initiated by Michael Pluess while he was working on his doctoral research under my supervision at Birkbeck University of London. Results revealed that, in the case of symptoms of depression, only female students scoring high on an HSP questionnaire benefited from the intervention. Whereas the other girls' depression remained unchanged across a twelve-month period, it steadily declined for those scoring high on HSP. The study provided more evidence of strong differential susceptibility.[16]

Interestingly, one of Michael's collaborators on this research helped implement and evaluate—with HSP in mind—the same program, using the same quasi-experimental research design, after it was culturally modified for Japanese high-school students aged fifteen to sixteen. This work, too, chronicled differential effects for adolescents scoring higher and lower on a questionnaire assessing sensory-processing sensitivity. Only in the case of depression and self-esteem, however, and not self-efficacy, did students scoring high on sensory-processing sensitivity benefit more than students scoring lower. In other words, both groups benefited, but one did so more than the other, thus providing evidence of weak differential susceptibility.[17]

The final intervention, unlike the previous two, was a true randomized control trial, thus positioned to draw strong causal conclusions about, in this case, the efficacy of a program targeting bullying. This work was also school-based, involving fourth through sixth graders, and was carried out by one of Michael's graduate students. Although the intervention significantly reduced average bullying behaviors and mental health outcomes in the experimental group in comparison to controls, the highly sensitive youth in the experimental group were the ones to benefit most when it came to not being victims of bullying and not manifesting internalizing problems (such as depression and anxiety). The fact that children scoring lower on HSP also benefited, but not to the extent that those scoring high did, serves as evidence, once again, of weak differential susceptibility.[18] In sum, HSP-related observational and experimental research yields evidence consistent with the claim that children who are highly sensitive prove more susceptible to a variety of environmental influences than do those less sensitive, just as Elaine Aron would expect.

Before drawing some chapter-wide conclusions, there is one more point about differential susceptibility that has not yet been addressed but that applies to all the chapters in Part II (and was raised by at least one of the anonymous reviewers of this book in manuscript). It has to do with whether the evidence documenting variation in developmental plasticity presented here is also evident beyond the early- or even middle-childhood years. The answer: It is! In the case of HSP, work by a team of Hong Kong investigators found that low levels of socioeconomic resources and social support predict increased risk of maltreatment by parents, but this affected only children who scored high on HSP—making them susceptible to such adversity. As we will see in Chapter 10, there is also evidence of differential susceptibility when the focus is on adolescent experience and its effect on adolescent development. Perhaps even more striking is evidence of differential susceptibility in research on adults caring for spouses with dementia and thus at greater or lesser risk of becoming depressed. [19]

IF THE SECOND PART of this chapter makes nothing else clear, it shows that there is much to learn from an insightful, veteran clinician's years of clinical experience. I say that as someone who has taken himself to therapy on more than one occasion and found it wanting. I should have gone to see Elaine Aron! What is especially impressive about Elaine, whom I only met once, is that she took the risk of participating in efforts to evaluate her theory of sensory-processing sensitivity (several of them mentioned in this chapter) knowing full well that her ideas, when subjected to rigorous empirical scrutiny, could crash and burn. Perhaps she just had so much confidence in them that this felt not like jumping off a high diving board into very cold water but like wading into a warm pond. Her faith turned out to be justified since, while not every test provides empirical support for her ideas, quite a number indisputably do. As I have said before in this situation, it would be great to have a meta-analysis of results from all the available work to better know how much confidence we can place in its findings.

## Conclusion

Having considered much evidence documenting the utility of BSC and HSP thinking, what is perhaps an obvious question arises: Could we be dealing with the blind-men-and-the-elephant problem—the one in which each man, touching a different part of the animal, concludes rather differently what elephants are like?

Applied to the topic at hand, might the BSC emphasis on physiological reactivity and Aron's emphasis on HSPs be identifying the very same individuals as highly susceptible to environmental influences for better and for worse, but by different means? Simply put, do the most developmentally plastic individuals score high on both physiological reactivity and sensory-processing sensitivity? That has yet to be tested, but to me it seems likely.

# 10

# The Genetics of
# Developmental Plasticity

Obviously, in advancing the differential susceptibility hypothesis, I was claiming that some individuals would prove more developmentally plastic than others. This prediction was, after all, based on appreciation that the future is inherently uncertain; that it would be in the reproductive interests of parents, siblings, and individuals themselves for nature to have hedged its bets by varying plasticity within the family; and thus, that the evolutionary process of natural selection should have fostered variation in susceptibility to environmental influences, including via our genome. I was further claiming that the nature-of-nurture argument outlined in Part I, concerning how childhood experiences and environmental exposures shape reproductive strategy, applied to a greater degree to children who were more genetically susceptible than their peers.

This final chapter, pertaining to the evidentiary basis of the differential susceptibility hypothesis, addresses whether individuals who vary in their developmental plasticity, especially in childhood and adolescence, differ in their genetic makeup, as I hypothesized. To the extent that this proves to be the case, it will further underscore the need for a modern developmental synthesis of Darwinian and Mendelian natures, the former emphasizing the passing on of genes and the latter individual differences in the genetic makeup of individuals, while considering whether and how early-life conditions influence development.

Consideration of evidence pertaining to this hypothesis is organized so as to underscore how the use of genes in molecular-genetic research has changed since the turn of the century, a topic briefly covered in Chapter 6. Recall that, initially, investigators were restricted to considering one gene at a time due to the huge expense of just assaying such "candidate" genes. But as costs dropped rapidly as the technology developed, it became reasonable to assay a few genes, so as to construct what I will refer to as "a poor man's" polygenic score. But as costs continued to drop, it became possible to assay thousands, even millions, of genetic variants using whole-genome assays, the ones that made it possible to do genome-wide association studies (GWAS). Polygenic scores based on GWAS thus relied on very large numbers of genes to create composite indices, like the ones referred to in Chapter 6, reflecting educational attainment, menarche, and age of first birth. By relying on molecular-genetic evidence to test a proposition based in Darwinian adaptation—that more and less developmentally plastic individuals should differ in their genetic makeup—this chapter integrates the two perspectives on genetics distinguished in the opening chapter of the book, ones capturing Darwinian and Mendelian nature. Candidate-gene research pertaining to differential susceptibility is considered first, after which the discussion will turn to multi-gene polygenic approaches.

## Candidate Genes

The first wave of molecular-genetic research on human psychological and behavioral phenotypes was, for the most part, based on arguments of biological plausibility. Recall that this involved hypothesizing that a particular gene was related to a particular phenotype (such as antisocial behavior, intelligence) because there was some plausible biological reason for that expectation. As made clear in Chapter 6, in time serious questions arose about almost all candidate-gene research for two reasons. First, the magnitude of the effect of single genes proved to be extremely small, especially in research directly linking genotype with some phenotype. Second, even when such genotype-phenotype evidence emerged, it proved very hard to replicate. This led to the abandonment of the approach by many researchers.

This mini-history obviously raises the question of why this book should spend space and thus reader's time on any candidate-gene evidence pertaining to the differential susceptibility hypothesis. There are two answers to this question. The first is that an abundance of certainly suggestive candidate-gene research was published that proved consistent with the claim that variation in developmental plasticity—and not just susceptibility to adversity—is at least partly due to the molecular-genetic makeup of individuals. The second reason is that there has been much less work investigating developmental plasticity using GWAS-derived polygenic scores—and as we will eventually see, even reasons for questioning whether they are well positioned to evaluate the differential susceptibility hypothesis. Truth be told, most relevant polygenic work involving more than a single gene has "simply" combined from two to eight candidate genes, what I refer to as the "poor man's approach" to creating polygenic plasticity scores.

My goal in this first section of the chapter is not so much to specify with great certainty that this or that candidate gene reliably accounts for variation in susceptibility to environmental influences. Rather it is to contend that the existing—and limited—evidence to that effect makes a strong case for entertaining the prospect that some of the variation in developmental plasticity is in our genes. One reason for this is because most of the early work that provided at least suggestive evidence of differential susceptibility, for better and for worse, was not undertaken to address this particular issue. Because most such research was carried out by investigators in the fields of psychiatry and psychology, it focused on genes presumed to influence a particular dysfunction or disorder, like antisocial behavior and depression. In consequence, the relevant GxE investigations were undertaken to test dual-risk thinking. The working hypothesis was that it was particularly under conditions of adversity (such as family violence, poverty) that "risk" or "vulnerability" genes—of either the candidate-gene or polygenic-score variety—would predict the psychological and behavioral disturbances of interest. Nothing was stipulated about effects of benign or enriching environments. It was not until my colleagues and I pointed out that much of the published evidence being interpreted in this risk-and-resilience manner suggested something else—namely, differential susceptibility—that the question became whether even the psychiatric evidence pointed in that alternative direction.

The real conceptual limitation of even seeking to determine whether evidence of for-better-and-for-worse susceptibility was being misinterpreted as documenting dual-risk thinking was that the candidate genes or polygenic scores used in GxE research were virtually never selected based on a view that they influenced developmental plasticity. It was, rather, that for biologically plausible reasons they were presumed to causally contribute to the mental health problem under investigation, thus making them part of a dual-risk process. It turned out, though, that reliance on many of these supposed "risk" genes in initial GxE investigations yielded evidence in support of the for-better-and-for-worse proposition central to differential susceptibility theorizing, which is not to say that this was recognized at the time. Indeed, it was really not noticed until my colleagues and I pointed this out. This, then, is another reason why I have chosen to present candidate-gene evidence, but characterize many of these putative "genes for mental health problems" as "plasticity genes" throughout this chapter.[1]

From my perspective—and I am by no means a disinterested observer—the fact that genes selected for mental health purposes seem to highlight genetic differences in developmental plasticity is kind of like succeeding in not getting knocked out of the boxing ring while fighting with one arm tied behind your back. That is because the strongest evidence for genes functioning as plasticity genes would most likely come from targeted efforts to find such genes—rather than stumbling across intriguing evidence of such a possibility in research designed to test dual-risk and thus vulnerability-gene thinking. In some ways the initial dual-risk GxE research was like trying to understand the cosmos when looking through a first-generation telescope. While clarity and distance will be limited, it is a promising start. After all, every journey begins with a first step.

Given the size of the genome, even when considering that only a small portion of it includes genes that vary across individuals and thus could contribute to differences in the way people develop, think, and behave, many candidate genes have been studied in tests of GxE interaction. This is true of work originally designed to test dual-risk thinking that subsequently "repurposed" putative vulnerability or dual-risk genes in order to test the differential susceptibility hypothesis.[2] In the interest of efficiency and illustration, I will focus principally on two candidate genes to underscore the possibility that variation in developmental plasticity is in our genes. One is referred to as serotonin transporter gene, labeled *5-HTTPLR* by geneticists, and the other the dopamine receptor gene 4, labeled *DRD4*. To repeat, my goal is not to reify these candidate genes as plasticity genes, but to make the case that there likely exist genes for plasticity by considering the candidate-gene work that first indicated this could be so.

Before turning to relevant evidence involving the two candidate genes in question, let me share the results of two GxE studies that are probably most relevant to this book, but rely on yet a different candidate gene than those just mentioned, while focusing upon pubertal timing. Both investigations address the very qualification that Part II of the book poses with respect to Part I. That is, they pertain to the hypothesis that psychosocial acceleration theory applies to some but not to all individuals, at least not to the same extent. In so doing, both inquiries nicely illustrate the utility of integrating biological gravity, genetic influence and nurture—in a modern developmental synthesis—in order to illuminate whether and how early-life conditions shape development.

The first inquiry was carried out by Stephen Manuck of the University of Pittsburgh. He hypothesized and found evidence that a variant of an estrogen receptor gene moderated the effect of childhood family environment on age of menarche in a manner consistent with differential susceptibility.[3] But this work had one serious limitation: Information about the family environment in childhood was based on the recollections of adults, because the data under investigation came from a study of breast cancer in adult females. We have already seen that, whereas the timing of puberty in females (at least with respect to age of menarche) can be recalled with great accuracy decades later, the same is not so when it comes to the quality of relationship experiences in the family while growing up.

Concerns, then, about the aforementioned work led my doctoral student, Sarah Hartman, along with myself and another UC Davis colleague, Keith Widaman, to see if we could replicate Manuck's results using data from the repeatedly mentioned childcare study. Given concerns about the lack of replication in GxE research involving candidate genes, the fact that we did replicate Manuck's differential susceptibility results when the environmental predictor, measured prospectively in early childhood, was maternal sensitivity seems to me quite significant.[4] In both researches, then, one retrospective and the other prospective, evidence emerged that variants of at least one candidate gene can reliably distinguish females more and less likely to have an important feature of their reproductive strategy, age of menarche, regulated by their childhood experiences.

## Serotonin Transporter Gene 5-HTTLPR

The serotonin transporter gene is responsible for encoding the serotonin transporter protein that regulates the reuptake of serotonin in the synaptic cleft. Thus, it is thought to play a role in modulating serotonin neurotransmission and behavior. 5-HTTPLR has two variants, referred to as the long (L) and the short (S) allele. The L allele is associated with increased transcriptional activity and higher serotonin transporter expression, whereas the S allele is linked to reduced transcriptional activity and lower transporter expression. Genotype-phenotype research has implicated the 5-HTTPLR gene in several psychiatric disorders, including depression, anxiety, and obsessive-compulsive disorder.[5]

As with all genes that vary across humans, one gene variant is inherited from mother and one from father. Whenever an individual inherits the same variant from both parents, be they (in the current case) short or long, the individual is said to be "homozygous" for that genetic variant, making the individual a short or long "homozygote." And when this is not the case, because the person has inherited a different variant from each parent, one short and one long, their genetic makeup is "heterozygous" and the person is considered a "heterozygote."

To provide evidence that the serotonin transporter gene appears to function as a plasticity factor, I will, as I have done repeatedly, first call attention to results of observational research before moving on to consider more causally compelling experimental interventions that also tested the proposition that 5-HTTLPR is a plasticity factor. Presuming that, by this point in the book, readers know what to expect in the work I am going to share—that it is carriers of one or two short alleles of 5-HTTLPR who prove most susceptible to their developmental experiences and environmental exposures in the for-better-and-for-worse manner of differential susceptibility—I will provide fewer details when it comes to observational research. I do this in the interest of maintaining reader interest.

The first observational study considered infants' and toddlers' ability to calm themselves when emotionally upset (that is, emotion regulation) as a result of whether and the degree to which their mothers were depressed while pregnant. Evidence proved in line with strong differential susceptibility in the case of children carrying at least one short allele (L-S, L-L). That is, only they proved susceptible to effects of their mothers' degree of depression, being more likely to be emotionally regulated when depression was low and more likely to be dysregulated when depression was high.[6]

The three remaining investigations to be considered focused on adolescents. In one, the effect of parenting on change over time in teens' alcohol consumption was the focus of inquiry. The second adolescent study, by my friend and colleague Gene Brody of the University of Georgia, evaluated the effect of perceived racial discrimination on the conduct problems of rural African American youth growing up in the deep south. The final illustrative observational research involving 5-HTTLPR examined the effects of two distal factors—school-level smoking and school-level drinking—on each of these risk behaviors by individual teenagers in the schools. In the first two investigations, evidence emerged that was consistent with strong differential susceptibility; the third investigation documented weak susceptibility.[7]

To be sure, not every relevant GxE investigation involving 5-HTTLPR yielded results like those just summarized. To gain some purchase on what the collective evidence indicated, I joined Marinus van IJzendoorn and Marian Bakermans-Kranenburg in a meta-analysis of relevant work. This drew on findings from thirty studies, collectively involving more than nine thousand children—and revealed that children and adolescents carrying at least one short allele (L-S, S-S) were more adversely affected by negative environments, and benefited more from positive ones, than their peers who were homozygous for long alleles (L-L). For reasons that remain unclear, this for-better-and-for-worse pattern of results was more pronounced when the investigations included in the meta-analysis focused only on Caucasian children, rather than children of other races and ethnicities.[8] This finding may underscore a point suggested by other work—namely, that the polygenic character and strength of genetic effects might not be the same across racial or ethnically defined groups.[9] Whether this is more true or less so likely depends on the phenotype under consideration, such as IQ or athletic ability, and on the context of development, such as whether an individual lives in conditions of poverty or affluence, or in one location or another, whether America, Sweden, or Malaysia. (Recall that development context was a focus of Chapter 6, with its account of heritability differences among children from poor and affluent families.)

MOVING ON from observational studies to consider what intervention research has revealed, a personal story comes to mind. When I was living in London, I got a call from someone (whose name now eludes me) asking if I might join a project to evaluate the success of a large-scale intervention planned for young children in Ireland. Given my thinking on differential susceptibility, the possibility that intrigued me was that the research might include an examination of whether the program's efficacy varied as a function of children's genetic makeup. Indeed, I was so excited by the prospect of conducting what I considered cutting-edge research that I phoned Avshalom Caspi, also working in London at the time, to see if he knew of any ongoing work dealing with the genetics of intervention efficacy. Note that this was early days for GxE inquiry using measured genes—so it should not be surprising that he had none to tell me about.

It turned out, though, that even if the proposed research had gone forward (which it hadn't, for lack of sufficient funding), we would not have been at the cutting edge. Already, gene-by-intervention (GxI) research was underway, led by those astute Dutch colleagues mentioned above.[10] They were way ahead of me—and everyone else in the field—and not for the first time. (More will be said about their research when this narrative turns to the second candidate gene to be considered.)

Returning to consideration of 5-HTTLPR, the first relevant randomized control trial to be highlighted sought to foster the sensitive parenting—and, thereby, the attachment security—of the infants of poor African women living in an impoverished South African township. As hoped, the parent-training intervention proved effective in increasing the number of infants who developed secure attachments to their mothers, but the effect was significant only in dyads where mothers carried one or more 5-HTTLPR short alleles (meaning they had strong differential susceptibility).[11] Presumably, that genotype helped to make these women more susceptible to the intervention to promote sensitive parenting than the genetically different mothers also assigned to the experimental group. This is work alluded to in Chapter 9, where it was suggested that differential susceptibility might not be restricted to children.

A second randomized control trial was designed to test the hypothesis that the development of young children living in an understaffed orphanage would be enhanced if they were relocated to homes of foster parents who had received special training to care for them. The children in question were growing up in Romanian institutions that were well known to employ poorly trained and underpaid staff and to provide very negligent care. The intervention proved quite successful in reducing levels of externalizing problem behavior and another tendency regarded as a signature behavior of institutionalized children: indiscriminate friendliness. This refers to a readiness, likely due to emotional neediness, to approach almost any adult, including perfect strangers, without the wariness that most young children would typically display in such encounters.

Critically, both developmental benefits of the intervention (reduced externalizing behavior and indiscriminate friendliness) were restricted to children carrying
two short alleles (S-S), thereby again providing evidence of strong differential
susceptibility. In fact, genetically similar (S-S) children who remained in the orphanage up through 4.5 years of age manifest the most externalizing problems and
indiscriminate social behavior of all the children studied. Thus, it was those
children who were short-allele homozygotes who developed best when randomized
to high-quality foster care, yet worst when remaining in the orphanage. In fact,
when the single-gene index of genetic susceptibility was revised to include another
suspected plasticity gene, thus making it a two-gene (poor man's) polygenic score,
it turned out that the same pattern of results emerged, but even more strongly. In
sum, then, there is both observational and experimental intervention work that
would seem to underscore the potential role of the short-allele variant of the serotonin transporter gene operating as a plasticity factor.[12]

## Dopamine Receptor Gene, DRD4

The dopamine D4 receptor gene (DRD4) has been extensively studied in relation
to personality, behavior, and psychopathology. The DRD4 gene codes for the D4
dopamine receptor, which plays a role in modulating dopamine neurotransmission
in the brain. The most well studied variant and the primary focus of this subsection
of the chapter is the DRD4 7-repeat (7R) allele, which has been associated with
novelty seeking, impulsivity, and ADHD.[13] One interesting observation of this
gene is that the DRD4-7R allele, associated as it is with novelty seeking, becomes
more frequent in populations the farther they are from the African homeland of
the first humans. This raises the possibility that it may have been this genetically
influenced psychological attribute that led some Homo sapiens to keep moving
beyond wherever they originally came from and eventually populating the world.[14]

The first DRD4 observational investigation to be highlighted, as discussed in
a previous chapter, involved the effect of prenatal smoking on ADHD, and its
results were initially interpreted in terms of dual risk. But, due to efforts of Michael
Pluess and myself, this conclusion was modified because the evidence reflected
differential susceptibility. There is also strong differential susceptibility evidence
from a related study showing that the sensitive responsiveness of mothers in parenting their children across the first six years of a child's life predicts children's
levels of inattention in fifth grade—but again, only for children carrying the 7R
allele.[15]

Given the fact that boundaries between psychological disorders are not crisp
and clean but often overlapping, at least with regard to certain symptoms, it is not

surprising that findings very similar to those pertaining to ADHD and inattention emerged when the developmental phenotype was antisocial behavior and mothers' prenatal stress was the predictor. But in this case, a weak-susceptibility plasticity gradient characterized the findings, as stress effects were estimated separately for children carrying zero, one, or two DRD4-7R alleles. As the number of 7R alleles increased—from zero to one to two—so did the extent to which low levels of stress predicted little antisocial behavior and high levels forecast more such behavior. Somewhat similar results emerged in research examining effect of parenting on teen's aggressiveness, a feature of a fast life history, and on children's prosocial behavior, a feature of a slow life history.[16]

To my knowledge there is no meta-analysis of observational studies focused exclusively on the 7-repeat variant of the dopamine receptor gene in order to evaluate whether it operates, as it would seem to, as a plasticity factor. But there does exist a meta-analysis of published GxE investigations that included research that relied on three different dopamine genes, one of which was DRD4. Analysis of nine different investigations that collectively included more than 1,200 children yielded evidence that these dopamine genes operated like plasticity genes, fostering strong differential susceptibility.[17]

GIVEN REPEATEDLY highlighted limits of causal conclusions drawn from observational research, it is fortunate that there are several informative intervention studies that provide stronger grounds for inferring causation in the case of children or their parents carrying the DRD4-7R plasticity allele. My previously mentioned Dutch collaborators, Marinus and Marian, documented this in the very first gene-by-environment (GxI) intervention study, the groundbreaking one alluded to earlier. This work involved implementing a parenting intervention to promote responsive parenting and, thereby, reduce children's externalizing problems. What was most interesting about this randomized control trial was that it was mothers carrying the 7R variant whose quality of parenting improved the most as a result of the intervention; and probably this was why their children's problem behavior was reduced the most.[18] Even though these results might have also depended on these children inheriting from their mothers the same 7R plasticity variant, thereby making them especially susceptible to effects of changes in their mothers' parenting, this could not be evaluated because children were not genotyped. Hypothetically, it could nevertheless be that a dual-genetic benefit accounted for the results, with one benefit involving the mother being genetically predisposed to change her parenting in response to the intervention and the other benefit being her child's genetic predisposition to be influenced by that change.

Could it be the case, then, that interventions designed to foster supportive parenting and, thereby enhance children's development, prove most beneficial to children when both parent and child are especially susceptible to environmental influences for shared genetic reasons? If so, this raises another possibility. When parenting interventions are administered and only the average treatment effect is evaluated, any resulting evidence of the treatment's efficacy could be due principally to a potentially rather small subgroup of parent-child dyads within the experimental group in which both mother and child are highly developmentally plastic due to their genetic makeup. It would be like a five-person basketball team winning a game not because *all* its players were better than the other team's, but thanks to two or three exceptionally good players. This recalls my admonition about eating the oyster, focusing on the average effect of an intervention, while ignoring the pearl, the variation of response within the treatment group—and the determinants of such variation. Until investigators assay the genotypes of both parent and child in the same study, it will not be possible to empirically address the intervention-efficacy issue just considered.

Given this situation, the same issue arises when considering the results of an intervention program designed to prevent problems and enhance the development of African American youth growing up mostly poor in the rural south of the United States. This is because the program targeted both parents and their teens, but this time only the genetic makeup of the teens was measured. Of importance, though, is that the Strong African American Families Program, developed by Gene Brody and his colleagues, was found to have quite beneficial effects—in two separate randomized control trials—on the development of substance use in the case of teens carrying the *DRD4-7R* allele. This was most clearly demonstrated by the fact that genetically similar teens in the control group used substances the most of all youth, so together the findings document, experimentally, the for-better-and-for-worse signature of differential susceptibility.[19] Once again, then, there is both observational and intervention evidence highlighting the role that particular candidate genes may play in fostering developmental plasticity, in this case the *DRD4-7R* variant.

What remains unclear, to repeat, is that we do not know whether such results are also a function of the parents participating in the intervention being highly susceptible, whether due to their genetic makeup or some other factor. This certainly seems possible in light of evidence that it is not just children whose susceptibility to environmental influences varies across individuals, but adults as well. This has now been shown in several studies of mothers, including at least one not previously mentioned and also in another focused on teacher burnout.[20]

## Polygenic Approaches

Given previously mentioned concerns regarding the size and reliability of findings involving candidate genes, attention will now turn to evidence from two different sets of studies reliant on multiple genes when testing the differential susceptibility hypothesis. Studies in the first set rely on the "poor man's approach" based on investigators combining a few (candidate) genes selected for reasons of biological plausibility. Studies in the second set rely on the results of GWAS discovery-study findings, in which the computer identified the gene variants most strongly, even if still rather weakly, associated with the phenotype of interest.

### The Poor Man's Approach

I believe I was the first to composite multiple genes when testing GxE interaction—in the course of further evaluating the differential susceptibility hypothesis. This work was stimulated by a long history of creating composite environmental indices presumed to reflect "cumulative risk". Recall that the idea guiding such work, which long preceded doing the same under the banner of ACES, was simply that the more contextual risks children faced—like being poor, living in a violent neighborhood, having a depressed mother, and being socially isolated—the more problematic would be their development. It thus occurred to me that it might be worth combining the plasticity variants of genes that candidate-gene research had identified—like $DRD4$-$7R$ and short alleles of $5$-$HTTLPR$—as a means of testing the differential susceptibility hypothesis.

My challenge was to find a data set that afforded this possibility. This led me to contact my friend, Terrie Moffitt, to ask her about this strategy. In response, she directed me to Kevin Beaver of the University of Florida, whom I did not know. Yet when I called Kevin from London and explained to him what I wanted to do, he was all in, in principle. I told him I had a set of candidate-gene "suspects" based on prior GxE research documenting differential susceptibility that were worth combining if available in his data set to create a polygenic plasticity score; he indicated that he had five of the plasticity "suspects" I shared with him. Then I told him we needed a good predictor variable and a good outcome. That also proved easy for him to identify. So, he put the relevant data in the computer to test the proposition that there would be a "dose response" relation such that the more of the five plasticity-gene variants an individual carried, the more that childrearing experienced in the family would predict adolescent self-control in a for-better-and-for-worse manner. In other words, our goal was to test whether there existed a gradient of plasticity.

When Kevin sent me the results, depicted in a graph, I looked at them and thought, "yeah, that's what I expected." It was only a few days later that I realized how amazing this was. All I had was a simple idea and yet the data conformed to it so closely that I actually worried that someone might accuse us of "cooking the books." The results showed that as you proceeded from children carrying no plasticity alleles or just one of the five, to those carrying two, to those carrying three, and finally to those carrying four or five, the stronger became the association between the way teens were parented and their degree of self-control—and, of course, in a for-better-and-for-worse manner.[21] More than anything, this convinced me that whatever the merits of thinking in terms of two types of children, orchids and dandelions, that was not how development did its business. What we had uncovered, for the first time, was an indisputable genetic plasticity gradient. I was not surprised that getting the work published was a breeze.

Since that research appeared, ever more investigators have done as we did, taking advantage of whatever suspected plasticity genes they had in their data sets. In several cases it was just *DRD4* and *5-HTTLPR*. Given what has already been covered, it will not be surprising that two studies found that the more plasticity alleles of these two genes that children carried, the more strongly the environmental index being used to predict the child outcome of interest did so, and in a for-better-and-for-worse differential susceptibility manner. In one case the work evaluated the extent to which prenatal maternal depression predicted the negative emotionality of young infants. In another it was the extent to which living in a favorable versus adverse social environment predicted aggression. Similar results obtained when yet another investigative team added a third presumed plasticity gene to the two just considered. Perhaps even more impressive is that a similar genetic plasticity gradient emerged when eight different candidate genes were composited and used to link parenting in adolescence with both positive and hostile romantic relations in young adulthood.[22]

For me, the most important polygenic-plasticity study focused on children growing up in the same family. Recall that my original differential susceptibility theorizing outlined in Chapter 7 stipulated that siblings would vary in their developmental plasticity because then each would genetically "insure" the other, with parents benefiting, too, when it came to passing on genes to the next generation—a case of not putting all your eggs in one basket. The work in question focused on sibling genetic differences in terms of the number of plasticity alleles that each sibling carried; because siblings only share 50 percent of their genes, there is much ground for them to differ from one another genetically. Results revealed that family economic status while growing up, presumably the same or at least quite similar across siblings, predicted children's own economic status in adulthood—in a for-better-and-for-worse manner. But this was more so the case when siblings within the same family proved more rather than less genetically plastic.[23] Is it any wonder, then, that children who grow up in the same family end up so turning out so different from one another?

The final research I will share reflective of the poor man's approach to compositing plasticity genes was carried out as part of a gene-by-intervention (GxI) study in collaboration with a young Dutch PhD student who came to work with me at the University of California, Davis, for a few months. She had data from a Dutch randomized control trial of the *Incredible Years* parenting intervention—an approach that has been positively evaluated and widely disseminated around the world.[24] Like the original version of the program, the Dutch trial targeted children aged four to eight with serious behavior problems in an attempt to reduce or eliminate them by fostering skilled mothering.

To determine whether the program's efficacy might vary as a function of genetic plasticity, we composited five presumed dopaminergic plasticity genes available in the Dutch data set, one of which was *DRD4*. Just as we suspected, the parenting-education program varied in its efficacy as a function of children's genetic makeup, proving most effective in decreasing externalizing behavior in boys (but not girls) who carried more rather than fewer dopaminergic plasticity alleles. This was the study previously alluded to in which the genetically moderated effects of the intervention emerged not immediately after the end of intervention, but over the following two years. It remains unknown whether, over a longer stretch of time, these GxI effects endured or faded out.[25]

Raising again the issue of the role of mothers' own genetic plasticity in accounting for variation in the efficacy of parent-education programs was an additional finding from the same GxI investigation. The data showed that the boys who benefited most from the intervention tended to be the ones whose mothers' parenting had changed the most in response to the program. Could it be that a boy was equipped to benefit the most from the intervention when not just he but also his mother carried more plasticity genes than the other mother-child pairs? Unfortunately, that question could not be answered as, once again, no genetic data was collected on the mothers.

## The GWAS Approach

Many fewer investigations of GxE interaction revealing differential susceptibility-like effects using GWAS-derived polygenic scores have been reported than is the case with the poor man's approach. As stipulated earlier, there is good reason to question whether the GWAS approach is even appropriate for testing differential susceptibility. This claim was outlined in a paper written in collaboration with my graduate student, Ziaoya Zhang, based on the fact that most GWAS discovery research involves identifying genes associated with some kind of problem, such as antisocial behavior, depression, or ADHD. When problem-related GWAS polygenic scores are used in concert, as they most often are to test a GxE interaction involving an index of contextual adversity (such as harsh punishment or divorce), what is most likely to emerge is a dual-risk finding. Risk number one, of course, is the polygenic score for some problem and risk number two is the adversity measure. As a result, reliance on a GWAS-derived polygenic score in GxE or GXI research typically involves testing the claim that children at high genetic risk for the problem in question, reflected in the polygenic score, will be the most likely to succumb to the effects of adversity.[26] In some respects, it would seem ill suited to testing for developmental plasticity, for better and for worse.

Despite this very real concern, of interest are the results of a GxE study that investigated the interaction of a GWAS-derived polygenic score for ADHD and maternal depression in predicting children's internalizing problems. Rather than revealing a dual-risk pattern as might be expected given the issue just raised involving reliance on two risk factors, one genetic and the other environmental, results proved consistent with the for-better-and-for-worse expectation of strong differential susceptibility.[27]

More noteworthy in light of the nature-of-nurture focus of this book are the results of Chinese research reliant on a GWAS-based genetic index of a pubertal-development outcome, the age at which girls first begin to develop breasts. Using threat and deprivation measures as predictors, results provided evidence of differential susceptibility. Intriguingly, evidence to the same effect emerged from this work in the case of boys, when the phenotype predicted was testicular volume.[28]

Now LET'S TURN from observational research to consider results of a few intervention studies that have relied on GWAS-based polygenic scores. One such inquiry took advantage of a long-standing investigation of economically disadvantaged children at high risk for developing behavior problems and underachieving in school. In this randomized control trial, only some first-grade classrooms in inner-city Baltimore were randomly assigned to participate in a prevention program that had been shown to be effective in achieving its goals. In two separate studies, researchers examined a GxI interaction predicting, separately, youth's age at first tobacco and first marijuana use. The polygenic predictor used in this work was based on GWAS findings related to tobacco use, as well as ease of smoking cessation. Results revealed that children who scored high on the polygenic score benefited the most from the intervention in terms of delayed age of first use of both tobacco and marijuana.[29]

Given concerns raised about relying on GWAS-derived polygenic indices based on behavioral, psychological, or even medical problems, one is forced to wonder whether there might be a way around this problem. One team of British investigators developed a quite creative strategy for doing so. Working with a sizable sample of identical twins—who share 100 percent of their genes—the researchers first distinguished twin pairs based on whether they manifested similar or different levels of emotional problems. Theorizing that this difference between the two sets of similar and dissimilar twins reflected the latter's greater genetic susceptibility to environmental influences and their exposure to different experiences while growing up (such as peer relations and school experiences), the investigators relied on GWAS to identify several thousand gene variants that distinguished the two groups of twins, those highly similar and those highly dissimilar in emotional problems, to create a (hypothesized) polygenic plasticity score.

With this measure in hand, the British team proceeded, using two new samples, to address a GxE question and also a GxI one in an effort to validate their GWAS-derived plasticity index. In the GxE inquiry, the empirical question was whether this index moderated or conditioned the effect of parenting on children's emotional symptoms in a manner consistent with differential susceptibility. Once the results provided evidence consistent with this expectation, thereby documenting the utility of the novel polygenic plasticity score, these same investigators turned to a different sample to test GxI. The intervention in question was designed to treat children and adolescents with anxiety disorders. This enabled evaluation of a second plasticity-related question: Would the polygenic plasticity score help to explain the differential efficacy of cognitive-behavioral therapy (CBT) carried out with varying intensity with children known to have emotional problems?

It turned out that it did! Select CBT effects were judged "clinically meaningful" in that they reflected real and significant changes in the well-being of the children. Children scoring high on polygenic plasticity achieved remission rates, meaning they no longer met criteria for an anxiety-related psychiatric diagnosis, of about 71 percent, 55 percent, and 41 percent when exposed, respectively, to individual, group, and brief parent-led CBT. These were rates higher than for children who scored low on the polygenic plasticity index.[30]

The success of this highly innovative approach for identifying and combining multiple plasticity genes stimulated another child-focused investigatory team to try it. Their GxI research involved a randomized control trial of another well-established and efficacious intervention, the Family Check-Up. Relying on the same twin-derived polygenic plasticity of the previous investigators, the question became whether it helped distinguish the children who benefited the most from the parenting intervention, in the case of economically disadvantaged ten-year-olds suffering from internalizing problems, from those who benefited much less or not at all. Consistent with differential susceptibility theorizing, it did. Children scoring highest on the polygenic plasticity score benefited the most from the treatment, whereas their similarly high-scoring counterparts in the control group manifest the most internalizing symptoms of all children involved in the research.[31] Yet once again a documented for-better-and-for-worse result!

In view of the fact that this book is principally about why, how, and for whom early-life conditions influence life history and children's development more generally, I will very briefly call attention to the only other intervention study that found this same plasticity index promising. I proposed and participated in this work that revealed that couples scoring high on the polygenic plasticity index benefited most from a program designed to improve marital quality and prevent divorce.[32]

One important note of caution is called for here, despite how excited I was by the creative effort to formulate a GWAS-derived polygenic plasticity score based on differences between identical twins on the particular phenotype of emotional problems. What remains unclear is how general the index might be in helping us understand which individuals are most susceptible to environmental influences. This is because, as just mentioned, it was originally based on differences between identical twins in emotional problems—and all the studies that used it evaluated its role in predicting functioning in realms not unrelated to emotional problems, including marital quality.

The question becomes: Just how domain-specific or domain-general is the GWAS-derived plasticity index? Does it principally reflect susceptibility to environmental effects on emotion-related phenotypes or does it operate similarly when subject to investigation of a much far wider range of phenotypes not related to emotional functioning? Whatever the eventual answer to the question just raised, it should be clear from this chapter that there is merit in considering the proposition central to my original differential susceptibility hypothesis—namely that natural selection has shaped human genomes to include genetic variants leading some children to be more developmentally plastic than others. There would also seem to be merit in seeking to identify plasticity genes, rather than just relying on those that have emerged in research principally designed to test dual-risk thinking.

WHEN WE CONSIDER the multiple plasticity factors that have been highlighted across this and the prior two chapters—temperament, physiology, and genetics— what still remain to be illuminated are the dynamic processes that instantiate enhanced susceptibility to environment influences. It is one thing to discover, based on empirical evidence, that this gene (or these multiple genes) or this temperament or that physiological phenotype is associated with greater or lesser developmental plasticity. But even evidence of this sort does not entirely illuminate *how* this comes to be the case—that is, the biological and psychological mechanisms related to identified plasticity factors that play a causal role in making individuals more and less developmentally plastic. It could have something to do with brain processes, epigenetics, immune function, the microbiome, or many other possibilities. Only future research can address these questions, as the "first wave" of differential susceptibility related inquiry discussed in this book was designed only to evaluate the differential susceptibility hypothesis and, in so doing, identify possible plasticity factors. As I trust I have made clear, this first stage work has proved very promising.

# Conclusion
## *Miles to Go Before I Sleep*

I<small>T IS BEYOND DISPUTE</small> that the Hubble Telescope, launched in 1990, radically transformed our understanding of the universe, affording insights that were simply not possible before this technological wonder was designed, manufactured, and sent into space. Given the speed of technological development, it has now been surpassed by the James Webb Space Telescope launched in 2021, a hundred times more powerful than its predecessor. To my way of thinking, when it comes to understanding life on planet Earth, Darwin's theory of adaptation by natural selection and Hamilton's insights on kin selection and inclusive fitness have functioned in a manner similar to these recent telescopic wonders. This is true not simply with respect to human nature, as long highlighted by many evolutionary-minded scholars, but specifically with regard to how early-life conditions shape, or fail to shape, child, adolescent, and even adult development.

This conclusion first provides a succinct summary of the take-home messages of Parts I and II of *The Nature of Nurture*. As will be emphasized again, it is important not to oversimplify these claims but to appreciate that development is complex and complicated. After considering some implications and applications of what has been covered in these pages, we will move on to some unknowns about the nature of nurture that are intriguing to ponder, and then bring the book to its close with some final comments.

## Summary

Let's review first what we discovered in Part I about the development of human reproductive strategies, before turning attention in Part II to differential susceptibility to environmental influences. Regarding the former, and thus the *why* and *how* of development highlighted in the book's subtitle, Part I made the case that humans evolved to respond to childhood experiences and environmental exposures, be they characterized by adversity or support, in ways that once increased, and perhaps even still do increase, their chances of passing genes on to the next generation (as dictated by biological gravity). More specifically, experiences of threat and harshness in childhood, themselves probabilistic markers of a life of continued adversity, including heightened risk of death, foster accelerated development (when energetics are sufficient). The resulting fast life history is characterized by an opportunistic, advantage-taking, and exploitative social orientation, a tendency to discount the future (so that a bird in the hand is preferred to two in the bush), early sexual maturity (especially in females) and sexual debut, unstable pair bonds, and the bearing of many children who experience limited parental investment. In contrast, a supportive rearing milieu, probabilistically foreshadowing a similar future, promotes a slow life history, characterized by developmental features that are the opposite of those just delineated. Even if the reproductive-fitness consequences that could once be expected from these contrasting reproductive strategies are no longer realized in the modern world (as a result, for example, of the prior century's revolution in birth control), the neurobiological and psychological machinery that evolved to serve those ends remains operative, resulting still in the developmental characteristics of each life history.

Reflecting on Part II, dealing with differential susceptibility to environmental influence, I further made the case that responsiveness to early-life conditions varies across individuals (for evolutionary reasons, this time pertaining to the inherent uncertainty of the future)—making some more developmentally plastic than others. As to which children appear most susceptible to the effects of their childhood experiences and environmental exposures, various things operate as plasticity factors, including negative emotionality in infancy, physiological reactivity in childhood, a hawk- or dove-like personality, being a highly sensitive person, genetic makeup, and likely others. The first two factors just listed may be either "born," a result of an individual's genetic makeup, or "made," the result of prenatal or early-life conditions. Finally, whether or not genetic (and other personal) differences between children influence their development depends on the familial, cultural, and even historical context in which they develop (that is, on their GxE interaction). In sum, biology is not destiny in any simplistic sense, because development is shaped probabilistically, not deterministically, by early-life conditions and genetics, in large part as a result of development's being context-dependent, with all this complexity evolving in the service of fostering reproductive fitness.

The moment we juxtapose variation in nurture-induced life history and differential susceptibility to environmental influences—and in so doing create the modern developmental synthesis of Darwinian adaptation, Hamiltonian inclusive fitness,

Mendelian genetics, and nurture broadly conceived—it becomes easy to imagine four prototypic reproductive strategies: fast and slow life histories that are born, and fast and slow life histories that are made. Some individuals will follow particular life histories because their development is disproportionately a function of their genetic makeup (these are *fixed* reproductive strategists), while the life histories of others will be disproportionately the result of their heightened developmental plasticity and thus early-life conditions (these are *plastic* reproductive strategists).

Just to be clear, development is probably even more diverse because variations in the character (fast versus slow) and origin (born versus made) of life histories are likely quite dimensional as opposed to categorical. Instead of individuals falling perfectly into the four prototypes, that is, their development likely ranges across two intersecting continuums, one reflecting developmental tempo (ranging from slowest to fastest) and the other reflecting the source of influence (ranging from purely born to wholly made). For example, one child might be strongly predisposed, for genetic reasons, to develop a fast life history while another might be somewhat less strongly predisposed genetically and, in consequence, more susceptible to environmental influences.

The fact that there are such variations in the degrees to which reproductive strategy is born versus made and in the extent to which childhood conditions shape development may help to explain why experiences and exposures within (or perhaps even following) the early years might deflect or redirect incipient development, speeding it up or slowing it down. This is most likely to occur when later experiences and exposures prove inconsistent with earlier ones, proving more or less supportive (such as increased or decreased threat, harshness, and support). This is likely true, then, both within and beyond the first five to seven years of life, the period most strongly regulating reproductive strategy, according to psychosocial acceleration theory.

However heuristically useful it is to speak of fast and slow life histories—and orchids and dandelions—it is, again, unlikely that all children can be sorted neatly into the four types of life histories referred to above. A child disposed to develop a slow life history due to supportive early-life conditions might have her development redirected—and thus accelerated—if later childhood conditions prove to be much less supportive, for whatever reason (such as parental divorce, neighborhood relocation). The same is true under the opposite environmental conditions, with an adversity-induced fast life history decelerated due to exposure to much more supportive contextual conditions, again for whatever reason (such as parent remarries, effective intervention).

Evidence consistent with such theorizing first emerged in collaborative work undertaken with Jeff Simpson of the University of Minnesota. In that research, we tested the hypothesis that early infant-parent attachment security would function as a protective factor mitigating the otherwise anticipated accelerating effect of early-life stress on age of menarche, finding this to be the case.[1] Similar results emerged in a large study of almost 2,000 individuals carried out in ten cities in nine countries (including China, Columbia, Italy, Jordan, Kenya, and the Philippines) when predicting fast life history behavior profiles based on aggression, impulsivity, and risk taking. Related evidence from China revealed that the accelerating effects of environmental harshness and unpredictability on life history were attenuated when parents were highly invested in their offspring and fully eliminated when their children were securely attached to a parent.[2] The fundamental point to be made, then, is that however disproportionately influential the early years are relative to later developmental epochs, or however adverse those conditions are, they will not always set the future life course in stone. Once again, we face the reality that development is probabilistic—and complicated.

My Dutch colleague Willem Frankenhuis has even hypothesized that inconsistent experiences in early life could delay what I would label *commitment* to a particular life history among those susceptible to being shaped by their developmental experiences and environmental exposures. He underscores the potential importance of the stability of the early environment in shaping a child's future development. Such commitment, Frankenhuis speculates, will be most likely when cues to adversity or supportiveness of the childhood environment prove consistent across the early years, thereby affording a kind of confidence that it makes strategic sense to develop a faster or slower life history. But when cues are not consistent, he theorizes, childhood conditions become ambiguous with regard to probabilistically forecasting the future; this makes it reproductively strategic for children to defer commitment to one reproductive strategy or another until more consistent—and convincing—evidence emerges as to what tomorrow is likely to bring.[3] This is most certainly not an issue I considered in my own theorizing.

Intriguingly, Frankenhuis's proposal would seem perfectly in line with Boyce and Ellis's U-shaped curve of the environmental conditions that foster plasticity and shape development, as discussed in Chapters 7 and 9. Recall that according to the biological sensitivity to context theory, high physiological reactivity and resulting increased developmental plasticity are most likely to characterize children who grow up in especially supportive and unsupportive childhood environments, not intermediate ones.[4] Might it be, then, that these extremely supportive and adverse environments exert the influence on plasticity that they do because of the consistency or stability of cues they provide the developing child, with far less consistency occurring in the intermediate childhood contexts? I suspect that may be the case.

Ultimately, evolutionary minded scholars must appreciate that the complexity of development outlined in the preceding paragraphs means that we should not expect childhood adversity to always predict an opportunistic, advantage-taking, and exploitative social orientation in childhood, early pubertal development, early age of sexual debut, or unstable pair bonds. Doing so risks the premature embracement of the null hypothesis when such "main effect" tests fail to prove in line with all-too-simplified theoretical expectations. This would seem to be especially true if no effort is made to take differential susceptibility and thus variation in developmental plasticity into account, along with the stability of early-life conditions. It is worth repeating yet again the English adage that the absence of evidence is not (necessarily) evidence of absence.

## Implications and Applications

In addition to enriching understanding about why, how, and for whom early life shapes later life, there are already several major implications and applications of the ideas discussed herein. As made clear in the introduction, it is simply time to stop characterizing some disciplines as "social science." Recall from the introduction that the very notion of social science emerged out of a desire to view ourselves as different from all other forms of life. So far, so good. But what we have failed to appreciate as a result of separating ourselves from other forms of life when it comes to effects of early life on later life is that we have much in common with all other living things, most notably the critical importance of passing on genes to future generations (that is, biological gravity) and how this may influence so much of how lives are lived.

This is why I believe psychology, sociology, anthropology, and probably economics, too, should be regarded as "life sciences." Evolutionary rules or principles that apply to all living things are also important to these fields of inquiry focused upon how we humans develop, think, and behave; how our families and societies are organized and function; why they are so different across cultures and throughout history; and even how we decide what to purchase, what to invest in, and with whom to share our resources. In repeating this assertion about the social sciences made in the book's introduction, I am once again only rephrasing a famous and controversial claim of the great evolutionary biologist, Edward O. Wilson, made in the last chapter of his book *Sociobiology*, published half a century ago.[5]

This critique is directly related to the first implication of the evo-devo perspective central to this book. By pathologizing ways of feeling, thinking and behaving—and developing—which mainstream society doesn't favor, we risk obscuring as much as illuminating that which we seek to understand and change.

I am referring here to the widespread tendency to treat so many effects of early life adversity, especially those central to psychosocial acceleration theory (such as opportunistic advantage-taking, early sexual debut, indiscriminate mating) as evidence of disturbance, dysfunction, dysregulation, if not downright diagnosable psychiatric disorder. Central to *The Nature of Nurture* is the claim that this traditional manner of thought risks getting in the way of understanding and even helping, because if understanding is off, so is the chance that an intervention could be off, too. After all, engineering follows understanding.

It is time to recognize that where we see consistent childhood patterns of developing and behaving across populations that we don't favor, understanding might begin by asking a core evolutionary question: Why might natural selection have shaped children to develop the way they often do in response to the early-life adversity they experienced? There is no guarantee that insight will follow, but neither is there a guarantee that it won't. If nothing else, recasting an issue usually considered from a medical or mental health perspective in this way turns the cylinders of one's mind in new ways. Could this be a strategy for keeping the mind sharp—a kind of mental exercise that delays or attenuates the cognitive deterioration that often accompanies aging? (I, for one, hope so!)

The second implication of evo-devo analysis is probably easier to embrace, even if quite related to what has just been stipulated. Because adversity appears to accelerate development—and not just in terms of puberty but regarding "biological aging," as well—there are limits to what the wear-and-tear perspective central to medical and mental health thinking can tell us. And this is so even if it is true that accelerated development of the kind discussed here undermines longer-term health and longevity, as evidence suggests is the case.

The truth remains that evolution by natural selection has privileged *reproduction*—the passing on of genes—more than it has favored health, wealth, happiness, or longevity. (This is not to say that these cannot serve as means to reproductive ends under some contextual conditions.) This, however, is not a case where what is hardest to see is what is right before our eyes (to return to Goethe's words from Chapter 7). It is a case of needing to look beyond what has become evident, even obvious—namely, that early-life adversity undermines health and longevity—to see more clearly why and how development operates the way it does.

BUT DOES this new way of looking at how nature (in the form of evolution) has shaped the effects of nurture—that is, childhood experiences and environmental exposures—actually "add value" to our understanding of child and adolescent development? In one sense, *yes,* but in another sense, *no.* The *yes* sense has already been addressed. It adds value by deepening and enriching our understanding of both the *why* and the *how* of development, fostering a modern developmental synthesis of Darwinian adaptation and Hamiltonian inclusive fitness with Mendelian genetics and nurture. But there is also a sense in which the answer is *no,* because many (though by no means all) of the implications of reproductive-strategy thinking are clearly in line with more traditional ideas about human development.

Both embrace the view that, if we don't value the consequences of some ways of growing up—such as becoming an opportunistic and exploitative advantage taker, initiating sex earlier rather than later, and having multiple mates and many children for whom parental investment is limited—then intervening earlier in life to improve a child's life conditions and prevent such "problematic" ways of developing can matter a lot. Deferring the timing of intervention may even reduce the efficacy of such preventative or remedial efforts, given theory and evidence that it is in the first five to seven years of life that reproductive strategy is most powerfully shaped by developmental experiences and environmental exposures. From this perspective, the standard way of thinking about nurture and the evolutionary nature-of-nurture ideas offered in Part I of this book reinforce each other, being quite complementary.

But the fact that evolutionary insight also led to appreciation of differential susceptibility "for better and for worse" takes us well beyond standard thinking in its implications. To begin with, it makes clear that individuals vary in their developmental plasticity and not just in terms of vulnerability to adversity, as long presumed by dual-risk thinking. In so doing, it also makes clear why what is fundamentally true about virtually all psychological and behavioral interventions—and no doubt many others—happens to be true. I am referring here to the reality of heterogeneous treatment effects, that not every person receiving a particular treatment benefits from it, even if the treatment proves effective *on average.*

In consequence—and just as with personalized medicine—there is a need to think in terms of more personalized interventions. What must be reiterated with respect to this issue is that even if we must acknowledge that some individuals may be far less affected by even the best efforts to prevent or remediate problems, that is no reason to disregard such children growing up under conditions of adversity who are less developmentally plastic than others. And there are at least two reasons for this. First, as previously stipulated, in an affluent society like our own, every child merits a life of safety and security—because its absence is unpleasant, being psychologically stressful, even painful, to say nothing of downright dangerous. Developmental science has for too long emphasized long-term consequences of childhood experience, inadvertently perhaps giving short shrift to the basic quality of everyday lives. It is well past time to reduce the emphasis on seeing children and childhood principally as means to future economic ends.

Efforts to improve the quality of children's lived lives should not be exclusively or even principally about downstream developmental payoffs. The todays, not just tomorrows, merit care and consideration. To also repeat, an affluent society like our own can afford it. What is required is the will, because the way is not difficult to appreciate. After all, we saw this in response to the COVID epidemic when the child poverty rate was cut substantially by giving needy families money to help them cope with lives that had become even more challenging. And we see it in many more putatively—and even less affluent—"socialist"—countries which have national policies of child and family support, such as paid parental leave for the care of infants and state-insured child health care.

The second reason not to view the limited plasticity of some children as grounds for not trying to improve their lives is that current knowledge about intervention efficacy remains limited.[6] Conceivably, more intensive interventions may be required for such children to realize the benefits that highly susceptible children achieve more readily. Furthermore, it might be the case, as some evidence indicates, that different children's development may be shaped by different factors and forces.[7] For some, the world of peers may be more influential than that of family, while the reverse may be true of yet others.[8] Or, as other research implies, some children's development may be shaped more by experiences of threat-harshness than deprivation, with the reverse being true for still others.[9] Findings such as these are consistent with Dante Cicchetti's thinking about "multifinality," which refers to the possibility that the very same experiences and exposures can lead to different developmental outcomes in different children.[10]

Collectively, the evidence and ideas just shared are also reasons not to turn our backs and throw up our hands in frustration, concluding that children who manifest limited susceptibility to environmental influences should be abandoned in favor of those for whom this is not the case. Just because efforts made today might not generate the kind or degree of benefit desired in the case of less developmentally plastic children does not mean that that will always and necessarily be the case. This might well turn out to be especially so if we proved able to target mediating mechanisms of environmental influence and change them. Imagine if we had understanding of brain, immune, epigenetic, or, as a final example, microbiome processes that are mechanistically responsible for how early-life conditions shape life history—and had the technology to modify them. Theoretically, we could thus turn a child on an accelerated-development trajectory into one developing more slowly—and thus more to our liking given our values. Before presuming this is far-fetched, just consider what the CRISPER revolution has already achieved, enabling medicine to change some genes and, thereby, some aspects of physical health. Consider as well how promising psychedelics appear, especially when linked with a supportive counselor, for reducing and perhaps even eliminating the adverse effects of PTSD.

CONSIDERATION OF some of the plasticity factors mentioned in Chapters 8, 9, and 10 also carry important implications, even applications, that are not well appreciated. To make this point, let's return to the case of highly negatively emotional and difficult infants. Recall that such babies are now regarded by most child development professionals as being at increased risk of developing problems if they grow up under adverse conditions. But what research inspired by evolutionary thinking has revealed is that the very same infants are also more likely than others to benefit when they experience support and enrichment. This should be an easy message for pediatricians to convey to parents seeking help who, understandably, complain about how challenging their baby is to care for. Why not alter the frame of reference from crisis to opportunity, by making clear that the child such parents have will be shaped by how she is treated more so than most other infants will.

By calling special attention to one personal attribute that seems to foster developmental plasticity in the preceding paragraph, I do not mean to reify it or regard negative emotionality as more important than others discussed in Part II of the book. Indeed, if anything, what I prefer to emphasize is that it is "open season" on plasticity factors. I doubt we are even close to documenting what are probably many genetic, physiological, temperamental, and other personal characteristics that heighten susceptibility to environmental influences. In fact, I purposefully avoided mentioning some that have emerged because the empirical work on them remains limited—and I didn't want to place even more demands on readers than I already have.

To be appreciated, then, is that there is some evidence that different brain factors affect developmental plasticity and so does positive emotionality, sometimes labeled "exuberance." The same appears to be true of the personality characteristics of impulsivity and even proneness to anger. My colleagues and I have also called attention to the possibility that androgens and the microbiome play a role in the degree to which a child is susceptible to environmental influence.[11]

RETURNING TO THE SUBJECT of implications of differential susceptibility thinking, let's reconsider current and widespread interest in the topic of resilience. One way of defining resilience is in terms of being protected against or buffered when it comes to the anticipated effects of adversity. Thus, the vulnerable child succumbs to negative effects of adversity but the resilient child does not. Recall now what intervention studies informed by the differential susceptibility hypothesis have revealed—that personal characteristics that make some individuals resilient in the face of adversity also make them more generally less developmentally plastic. In consequence, children who prove resilient to adversity turn out to be the least likely to benefit from support and enrichment. This insight should remind us of the context-dependent nature of development: the benefits or costs of different ways of developing, thinking, and behaving depend on the context of development. When faced with adversity, resilience is a benefit, but when faced with support and enrichment, it is not. This is why I previously characterized it as a double-edged sword.

The same of course is true of developmental plasticity more generally when viewed through the lens of evolution by natural selection and differential susceptibility—that is, from the perspective of a modern developmental synthesis. Being highly susceptible to environmental influences is great when the developmental milieu offers many diverse "nutrients," be they educational, social, economic and, of course, nutritional. But when these are lacking, we who live in the modern Western world understandably eschew the would-be "spoiled fruits" of plasticity, as they are certainly not "sweet." Even if it was once reproductively strategic—and perhaps even remains so today—to develop in response to adversity in the fast-life-history manner discussed in the first six chapters, this does not mean that we must enjoy living in a society in which certain environmental effects, given the nature of nurture, prove operative. Under developmental conditions of adversity, it would be more advantageous, probably, at least for the rest of us, for a child to be less rather than more developmentally plastic. The bottom line, then, is that developmental plasticity, just like resilience, is not an unmitigated good. This is something that was not appreciated before evolutionary thinking was brought to bear on the developmental science of why, how, and for whom early life shapes later life.

LET'S CONSIDER one final potential implication of differential susceptibility thinking having to do with effects of prenatal stress on the developing child. Over the past two decades, a great deal of research has focused on the adverse effects of prenatal stress on children's future development. Common stressors during pregnancy include, for example, financial strain, lack of social support, partner abuse, as well as maternal mood disorders such as depression and anxiety. Given the general developmental view that "bad things go together," it is perhaps not surprising that exposure to prenatal stress has been found to predict children's emotional problems,

ADHD, conduct disorder, and impaired cognitive development. But intriguingly, it also predicts heightened negative emotionality in infants and heightened physiological reactivity in children.[12] Remember those plasticity factors?

Consideration of the latter two consequences of prenatal stress led Michael Pluess and me to wonder whether prenatal stress might actually "program" heightened postnatal developmental plasticity. Could it be that prenatal stress predicts problematic child development in the first place because the source of prenatal stress (such as financial strain) often continues after birth, which then becomes the more proximate—and influential—force shaping children's development, as some evidence indicates? Might children exposed to prenatal distress develop poorly, then, because they have been primed to develop in accord with their (still stressful) postnatal experiences, as suggested by their increased probability of being highly negatively emotional and physiologically reactive?[13]

Working with Pluess and my next graduate student, Sarah Hartman, we tested this possibility in several investigations which yielded evidence consistent with it. Just as hypothesized, then, postnatal experiences shaped future development in a for-better-and-for-worse manner consistent with the differential susceptibility hypothesis. In fact, when the children of prenatally stressed mothers encountered a supportive postnatal environment, they were disproportionately likely to benefit from it. To take us beyond observational research and onto firmer ground in drawing truly causal conclusions, Hartman carried out an elegant study for her doctoral dissertation using rodents so that prenatal stress could be experimentally manipulated. This enabled her to determine whether it causally fostered postnatal developmental plasticity—in a for-better-and-for-worse manner—which it did.[14]

Only a single investigation has so far tested our prenatal-programming-of-plasticity hypothesis when focused on an outcome related to accelerated development. This Dutch work, in which I was involved, revealed that prenatal stress amplified (postnatal) parenting effects on change over time in telomeres in a differential susceptibility–related manner. Following prenatal stress, yet not in its absence, insensitive parenting forecast faster telomere erosion, whereas sensitive parenting induced the opposite. Such findings raise the possibility, consistent with Boyce and Ellis's BSC theorizing, that environmental exposures (in this case, to maternal prenatal stress) could influence children's postnatal susceptibility to environmental influences. There is even a basis for considering prenatal effects on particular brain regions known to be related to postnatal sensitive or critical periods during which susceptibility to environmental influences is heightened.[15] Intriguingly, the evidence cited raises the question of whether there could be reason to induce prenatal stress deliberately to foster postnatal developmental plasticity for some children, however far-fetched that might sound.

## Unknowns in the Nature of Nurture

This concluding chapter carries the same title—Miles to Go Before I Sleep—as the one in my previous book, *The Origins of You,* because, for me, this phrase from my favorite Robert Frost poem, "Stopping by the Woods on a Snowy Evening," captures the essence of scientific understanding. The journey must always go on, because *all knowledge is provisional.* Any conclusion is open to revision as new ideas and discoveries emerge, as they are wont to do over time. In the spirit of that sensibility, this book will close by raising some future directions for evolutionary-developmental psychology research, recognizing the ever-present limits to our knowledge.[16]

It is intriguing, for example, to wonder whether societies and cultures might vary in the proportion of individuals who are highly susceptible to environmental influences and highly unsusceptible, perhaps for Mendelian-genetic reasons. Might it be that, in locales where across evolutionary history environmental changes within a person's lifetime were uncommon, populations evolved to be more susceptible to effects of early-life conditions—and thus individuals were disproportionately likely to be plastic strategists? Given that a static situation would allow predictive adaptive responses to conditions to be quite accurate, the probability of a developing person's better fitting the future environment and being reproductively successful should increase.

And what if the situation were entirely different across long stretches of evolutionary history, so that early-life conditions, whether adverse or supportive, were unreliable harbingers of what was to come within a lifetime? In such populations, predictive-adaptive-response development would often have generated mismatches between early- and later life. Might natural selection have favored genes fostering more development of fixed than plastic strategists? In such contexts, what reason would there be to invest in developmental machinery enabling one to read and respond to early-life conditions to shape later development?

The question ultimately becomes whether different cultures or societies could be made up of different proportions of life histories that are born and made. I don't believe we can yet even address the hypotheses advanced about population genetics. While this is no doubt partly a result of not having yet identified with great certainty genes for plasticity, it is also because we have not to my knowledge considered the issue at hand.

Another unknown is raised by recent work carried out in Eastern Europe. In two different studies the issue was the same—and related to the question of how many generations of safety and security must a population experience before the legacy of historical trauma has been overcome. In each inquiry, one focused on what was then Czechoslovakia and the other Poland, select geographic locales were compared, two generations later, on markers of a fast life history (such as reduced life expectancy, more births outside of marriage, more rape). The "experimental" locales had been abandoned before and during the Second World War and then repopulated after the war by means of forced migrations of certain groups of people; the "control" locales had not experienced such population upheaval. Evidence revealed that even decades after the forced migrations, people living in the experimental areas showed more evidence of fast life histories, perhaps the result of the negative effects of the post-WWII experience on social cohesion which was still undermining social support and quality of interpersonal relations.[17] For how many generations to come might the same life history differences still prove evident?

The final unknown about the nature of nurture to be considered has long troubled me. In all my years studying children, parents, and families, as well as during my two decades raising my own sons, I have never heard a parent make reference to differential susceptibility to environmental influences, even if not in such jargony terms. Sure, I have known parents who speak of a stubborn child or one who doesn't listen, but these are characterizations of what I have referred to as "sensitivity," how the child reacts in an immediate situation, not "susceptibility," how she develops over the longer term. But never have I heard one discuss the fact that while they can exert long-term influence in the case of one or more of their offspring, there is one or more for whom this is simply not the case, or much less so.

The evolutionary-minded developmentalist in me finds this surprising. One might expect that natural selection would have shaped parents to be sensitive to differential susceptibility in their offspring because their efforts to influence their children would pay off differentially across them. Parental investment, after all, is expensive—in time, money, and effort. Shouldn't evolution, then, have equipped parents with neurobiological and psychological capabilities to detect susceptibility differences, not just sensitivity ones? Wouldn't this have resulted in the more efficient deployment of their limited resources—more directed at some offspring than others—in ways that would have enhanced the dispersion of their genes in future generations?

I gained some potential insight into why this does not appear to be the case some years ago when I raised the subject with two Swedish colleagues who had remarried each other and were raising a sizable brood of children. After some reflection on the matter, they shared a story of one child who often came to them about issues he was facing, seeking their counsel. But, they told me, irrespective of what they said to him, he seemed to go off and do whatever it was he had originally planned to do.

Reflecting further on this issue, I also recalled the frequent complaint of some children, including myself as a child, when a sibling appeared to get better treatment in some manner, shape, or form: "That's not fair!" Could this indignant objection, and the son's seeking but ignoring parental counsel, both function as tactics for disguising a child's limited susceptibility, increasing the likelihood that it would go undiscovered by his parents and thus help the child avoid getting less generous or supportive treatment? Sadly, my data-collection career ended upon my retirement, before I could recruit a student to test this perhaps long-shot hypothesis. I still wonder whether children more inclined to raise issues of fairness are actually the ones least susceptible—and are camouflaging that truth to keep parents from figuring out that their payoff from investing in this child is likely to be lower than with others.

## A Thought Experiment

Let me close this book with a thought experiment about differential susceptibility to environmental influences. As many know, Steve Jobs, the genius who created the world-changing company that has brought us so many useful technologies, was adopted as a child. His unplanned birth to his unmarried parents who were so busy working on their higher academic degrees that they did not feel they could give this child the love, attention, and care he deserved led to them giving him up for adoption—to a pair of much less educated individuals who were indisputably devoted to him. Lucky Steve.

Now let's imagine for the sake of this thought experiment that Steve was a highly susceptible child, for better and for worse. And let's also imagine that, because of his biological parents' other commitments, they would not have been anywhere near as devoted to their child as they would have wanted to be—and as his adopted parents proved to be. But now, let's imagine that Steve's extremely busy biological parents had never put him up for adoption, so that he did not experience the fruits of such parental commitment. Would our world look like it does today? It certainly seems plausible that it would not, even if there is no real way to know.

For me, this imaginative scenario brings home the cost—to a child, its family, our society, and perhaps even the entire world, and future history—of a highly developmentally plastic child growing up under conditions less sensitive to his individuality and less able or willing to provide as much support as Steve Jobs might have experienced. Economists refer to what I am referring to as "opportunity costs." These reflect lost opportunities; what could have been but won't be. Many think about children growing up poor and disadvantaged—at the family, school, and community levels—in terms of the cost their compromised development can impose on society. But what about the benefits the development of these highly developmentally plastic children might have yielded—again, to themselves, their families, and to society—because their childhood experiences and exposures fostered less rather than more valued ways of developing?

How many highly susceptible Steve Jobs types might end up unemployed, on drugs, in jail, or dead at an early age, despite their potential to be shaped in a development-enhancing manner by a supportive developmental context? Lacking that, how many end up developmentally compromised by unsupportive rearing conditions? Think about that the next time you hear arguments about how many children in America grow up in conditions of disadvantage. Does their doing so cost us even more than we imagine when only considering their being unemployed or underemployed; becoming a criminal and ending up in the prison system; or developing chronic health problems and consuming many Medicaid dollars? In other words, does the richest country that ever existed end up unnecessarily producing consumers rather than generators of tax revenue—or economic drivers? Think about the world in which a highly susceptible Steve Jobs was never adopted.

This is a case, of course, in which the evolutionary perspective that gave rise to the puberty and differential susceptibility hypotheses complements and extends the standard developmental canon, which romantically idealizes human development while failing to appreciate variation in children's developmental plasticity. Coming to grips with biological gravity and the inherent uncertainty of the future, the modern developmental synthesis on which *The Nature of Nurture* is based, demands a rethinking of how childhood experience shapes later life.

# Notes

## Introduction

1. E. O. Wilson, *Sociobiology: The New Synthesis* (Cambridge, MA: Belknap Press of Harvard University Press, 1975).

2. W. D. Hamilton, "The Genetical Evolution of Social Behaviour," *Journal of Theoretical Biology* 7, no. 1 (1964): 1–16.

3. Shenghao Ye, Jiayang Sun, Sienna R. Craig, et al., "Higher Oxygen Content and Transport Characterize High-Altitude Ethnic Tibetan Women with the Highest Lifetime Reproductive Success," *PNAS* 121, no. 45 (2024): e2403309121.

4. Jay Belsky, "The Nature of Nurture: Darwinian and Mendelian Perspectives," *Development and Psychopathology* 36, no. 5 (2024): 2197–2206.

5. Ernst Mayr, *The Growth of Biological Thought: Diversity, Evolution, and Inheritance* (Cambridge, MA: Belknap Press of Harvard University Press, 1982).

6. Jon Rolf, Ann S. Masten, Dante Cicchetti, Keith N. Nuechterlein, and Sheldon Weintraub, eds., *Risk and Protective Factors in the Development of Psychopathology* (New York: Cambridge University Press, 1990).

7. For more on supportive parenting, see An Ting Yang, Hui Jing Lu, and Lei Chang, "Environmental Harshness and Unpredictability, Parenting and Offspring Life History," *Evolutionary Psychological Science* 9 (2023): 451–462. For more on establishment of a secure attachment, see Sooyeon Sung, Jeffry A Simpson, Vladas Griskevicius, Sally I-Chun Kuo, Gabriel L Schlomer, and Jay Belsky, "Secure Infant-Mother Attachment Buffers the Effect of Early-Life Stress on Age of Menarche," *Psychological Science* 27 (2016): 667–674; Hui Jing Lu, Yuan Yuan Liu, and Lei Chang, "Child Attachment in Adjusting the Species-General Contingency between Environmental Adversities and Fast Life History Strategies," *Development and Psychopathology* 34 (2022): 719–730; Hui Jing Lu, Jennifer E. Lansford, Yuan Yuan Liu, et al., "Attachment Security, Environmental Adversity, and Fast Life History Behavioral Profiles in Human Adolescents," *Development and Psychopathology* (2025): DOI: 10.1017 / S0954579424001500.

8. Suniya S. Luthar, "The Culture of Affluence: Psychological Costs of Material Wealth," *Child Development* 74, no. 6 (2003): 1581–1593.

9. Jay Belsky, *The Origins of You: How Childhood Shapes Later Life* (Cambridge, MA: Harvard University Press, 2020).

10. Brian Klaas, *Fluke: Chance, Chaos, and Why Everything We Do Matters* (New York: Scribner, 2024).

11. Robert Plomin and C. S. Bergeman, "The Nature of Nurture: Genetic Influence on 'Environmental' Measures," *Behavioral and Brain Sciences* 14, no. 3 (2011): 373–386.

12. Lee Dugatkin, "Inclusive Fitness Theory from Darwin to Hamilton," *Genetics* 176 (2007): 1375–1380, 1376.

13. Hamilton, *"Genetical Evolution of Social Behaviour."*

14. David L. Olds, "The Nurse–Family Partnership: An Evidence-Based Preventive Intervention," *Infant Mental Health Journal* 27, no. 1 (2006): 5–25.

15. Ricki Pollycove, Frederick Naftolin, and James A. Simon, "The Evolutionary Origin and Significance of Menopause," *Menopause* 18, no. 3 (2012): 336–342; K. Hawkes, J. F. O'Connell, N. G. V. Jones, and E. L. Charnov, "Grandmothering, Menopause, and the Evolution of Life Histories," *PNAS* 95 (1998): 1336–1339.

16. Denys deCatanzaro, "Human Suicide: A Biological Perspective," *Behavioral and Brain Sciences* 3, no. 2 (1980): 265–272; Balázs Szentes and Caroline D. Thomas, "An Evolutionary Theory of Suicide," *Games* 4, no. 3 (2013): 426–436;

17. Robert Sapolsky, *Determined: A Science of Life without Free Will* (New York: Penguin, 2023).

18. Thomas Talheim, "The Rice Theory of Culture," *Online Readings in Psychology and Culture* 4, no. 1 (2022).

19. Beatrice B. Whiting, ed., *Six Cultures: Studies of Child Rearing* (New York: John Wiley, 1963); Jared Diamond, *Guns, Germs and Steel: The Fates of Human Societies* (New York: W.W. Norton, 1997); Klaas, *Fluke*.

20. Hamidreza Harati and Thomas Talhelm, "Cultures in Water-Scarce Environments Are More Long-Term Oriented," *Psychological Science* 34, no. 7 (2023): 754–770. See discussion of "study 4" at 763–767.

21. Steven Pinker, *The Language Instinct: How the Mind Creates Language* (New York: William Morrow, 1994).

22. Richard Dawkins, *The Genetic Book of the Dead* (New Haven: Yale University Press, 2024), 30.

23. Hrdy credits Robert Trivers for defining parental investment as "anything that a parent does to promote the survival of an offspring that also detracts from the parent's ability to invest in other offspring." Sarah Blaffer Hrdy, *Mother Nature: A History of Mothers, Infants, and Natural Selection* (New York: Pantheon, 1999), 37.

24. Peter S. Jensen, David Mrazek, Penelope K. Knapp, Laurence Steinberg, Cynthia Pfeffer, John Schowalter, and Theodore Shapiro, "Evolution and Revolution in Child Psychiatry: ADHD as a Disorder of Adaptation," *Journal of the Academy of Child and Adolescent Psychiatry* 36, no. 12 (1998): 1672–1679.

25. Objections to diagnoses and interventions related to ADHD are also raised by critics who are not looking through an evolutionary lens. See, for example, "ADHD Should Not Be Treated as a Disorder," *Economist*, October 30, 2024.

26. David L. Barack, Vera U. Ludwig, Felipe Parodi, Nuwar Ahmed, Elizabeth M. Brannon, Arjun Ramakrishnan, and Michael L. Platt, "Attention Deficits Linked with Proclivity to Explore while Foraging," *Proceedings of the Royal Society B* 291, no. 2 (2024): 20222584–20222584.

27. David W. Stephens and John R. Krebs, *Foraging Theory* (Princeton, NJ: Princeton University Press, 1986).

28. Kristopher J. Brazil, Ann H. Farrell, Abby Boer, and Anthony A. Volk, "Adolescent Psychopathic Traits and Adverse Environments: Associations with Socially Adaptive Outcomes," *Development and Psychopathology* 37, no. 1 (2025): 477–489.

29. Kristopher J. Brazil and Adelle E. Forth, "Psychopathy and Sexuality in Adolescent Males: Evidence of a Mating Strategy?," *Adaptive Human Behavior and Physiology* 10, no. 3 (2024): 368–388.

30. Bruce J. Ellis, Laura S. Abrams, Ann S. Masten, Robert J. Sternberg, Nim Tottenham, and Willem E. Frankenhuis, "Hidden Talents in Harsh Environments," *Development and Psychopathology* 34, no. 1 (2022): 95–113.

31. Willem E. Frankenhuis and Carolina de Weerth, "Does Early-Life Exposure to Stress Shape or Impair Cognition?," *Current Directions in Psychological Science* 22 (2013): 407–412; Willem E.

Frankenhuis and Daniel Nettle, "The Strengths of People in Poverty," *Current Directions in Psychological Science* 29, no. 1 (2020): 16–21; Carolyn Rieder and Dante Cicchetti, "Organizational Perspective on Cognitive Control Functioning and Cognitive-Affective Balance in Maltreated Children," *Developmental Psychology* 25, no. 3 (1989): 382–393.

32. See, for example, Seth D. Pollak, Shira Vardi, Anna M. Putzer Bechner, and John J. Curtin, "Physically Abused Children's Regulation of Attention in Response to Hostility," *Child Development* 76, no. 5 (2005): 968–977.

33. Natalie M. Saragosa-Harris, João F. Guassi Moreira, Yael Waizman, Anna Sedykin, Tara S. Peris, and Jennifer A. Silvers, "Early Life Adversity Is Associated with Greater Similarity in Neural Representations of Ambiguous and Threatening Stimuli," *Development and Psychopathology* 37, no. 2 (2025): 802–814.

34. Suping Sun, Quanlei Yu, Jinqi Ding, Yuxin Shi, Wanjun Zhou, Han Liu, Qingbai Zhao, and Junhua Dang. "Effects of Adverse Childhood Experiences on Creativity from Life History Theory," *Journal of Creative Behavior* 58, no. 4 (2024): 657–675.

35. Randolph M. Nesse and George C. Williams, *Why We Get Sick: The New Science of Darwinian Medicine* (New York: Vintage, 1996); Stephen C. Stearns and Ruslan Medzhitov, *Evolutionary Medicine* (Sunderland, MA: Sinauer, 2016).

## 1. A New World Order?

1. Patricia Draper and Henry Harpending, "Father Absence and Reproductive Strategy: An Evolutionary Perspective," *Journal of Anthropological Research* 38, no. 3 (1982), 255–273.

2. Denis Dutton, *The Art Instinct: Beauty, Pleasure, and Human Evolution* (London: Bloomsbury, 2010).

3. Will Storr, *The Status Game: On Human Life and How to Play It* (New York: HarperCollins, 2021).

4. Kerri Smith, "Brain Makes Decisions Before You Even Know It," *Nature News Online*, April 11, 2008, nature.com/news/2008/080411/full/news.2008.751.html.

5. Arline T. Geronimus "What Teen Mothers Know," *Human Nature* 7, no. 4 (1996), 323–352.

6. Arline Geronimus, *Weatherinng: The Extraordinary Stress of Ordinary Life in an Unjust Society* (New York: Little, Brown Spark, 2023).

7. Karl Popper, *Conjectures and Refutations: The Growth of Scientific Knowledge* [1963] (London: Routledge Classics, 2002), 77. Quoted in Noam Chomsky, Ian Roberts, and Jeffrey Watumull, "The False Promise of ChatGPT," *New York Times*, March 8, 2023.

8. Richard Dawkins, *The Selfish Gene* (Oxford: Oxford University Press, 1976); E. O. Wilson, *Sociobiology: The New Synthesis* (Cambridge, MA: Belknap Press of Harvard University Press, 1975).

9. Erik H. Erikson, *Childhood and Society* (New York: W. W. Norton, 1950).

10. John Bowlby, "Maternal Care and Mental Health," World Health Organization Monograph, Serial No. 2 (1950).

## 2. An Uncanny Prediction

1. Barry Bogin, *Patterns of Human Growth* 2nd ed. (Cambridge, UK: Cambridge University Press, 1999).

2. John Bowlby, *Attachment and Loss, Vol. 1: Attachment* (London: Hogarth Press and the Institute of Psycho-Analysis, 1969).

3. Sheri Madigan, Audrey-Ann Deneault, Robbie Duschinsky, Marian J. Bakermans-Kranenburg, Carlo Schuengel, Marinus H. van IJzendoorn, Anh Ly, R. M. Pasco Fearon, Rachel Eirich, and Marije L. Verhage, "Maternal and Paternal Sensitivity: Key Determinants of Child Attachment Security Examined through Meta-Analysis," *Psychological Bulletin* 150, no. 7 (2024): 839–872.

4. Marco Del Giudice, "Rethinking the Fast-Slow Continuum of Individual Differences," *Evolution and Human Behavior* 41 (2020): 536–549; Stephen C. Stearns, *The Evolution of Life Histories* (Oxford, UK: Oxford University Press, 1992).

5. Marco Del Giudice, Stephen W. Gangestad, and Hillard S. Kaplan, "Life History Theory and Evolutionary Psychology," in *The Handbook of Evolutionary Psychology*, Vol 1: Foundations, 2nd ed., ed. David M. Buss (New York: Wiley, 2015): 88–114.

6. Leah S. Richmond-Rakerd, Stephanie D'Souza, Signe Hald Andersen, Sean Hogan, Renate M. Houts, Richie Poulton, Sandhya Ramrakha, Avshalom Caspi, Barry J. Milne, and Terrie E. Moffitt, "Clustering of Health, Crime and Social-Welfare Inequality in Four Million Citizens from Two Nations," *Nature Human Behaviour* 4, no. 3 (2020): 255–264.

7. Marco Del Giudice, "Rethinking the Fast-Slow Continuum of Individual Differences," *Evolution and Human Behavior* 41 (2020): 536–549; Brendan P. Zietsch and Morgan J. Sidari, "A Critique of Life History Approach to Human Trait Covariation," *Evolution and Human Behavior* 41, no. 6 (2020): 527–535.

8. Kurt Lewin, "Constructs in Psychology and Psychological Ecology," *University of Iowa Studies in Child Welfare* 20 (1944): 3–29, 27; Arthur G. Bedeian, "A Note on the Aphorism 'There Is Nothing as Practical as a Good Theory,'" *Journal of Management History* 22, no. 2 (2016): 236–242.

9. Mary Margaret Thomes, "Children with Absent Fathers," *Journal of Marriage and Family* 30, no. 1 (1968): 89–96; Barbara Dafoe Whitehead, "Dan Quayle Was Right about Single Parents," *Atlantic Monthly*, April 1993, 47–85.

10. Thomas Kuhn, *The Structure of Scientific Revolutions* (Chicago: University of Chicago Press, 1962).

11. Naomi Oreskes, "The Dull Edge of Occam's Razor," *Scientific American*, 331, no. 4, October 15, 2024, 70.

12. Jay Belsky, Avshalom Caspi, Terrie E. Moffitt, and Richie Poulton, *The Origins of You: How Childhood Shapes Later Life* (Cambridge, MA: Harvard University Press, 2020).

13. Laurence Steinberg, *Age of Opportunity: Lessons from the New Science of Adolescence* (New York: Mariner Books, Houghton Mifflin Harcourt, 2015).

14. Richard Dawkins, *The Genetic Book of the Dead* (New Haven, CT: Yale University Press, 2024).

15. Michael Lewis, *Altering Fate: Why the Past Does Not Predict the Future* (New York: Guilford Press, 1997); John T. Bruer, *The Myth of the First Three Years: A New Understanding of Early Brain Development and Lifelong Learning* (New York: Free Press, 1999).

16. David C. Rowe, *The Limits of Family Influence: Genes, Experience, and Behavior* (New York: Free Press, 1995); Robert Plomin, *Blueprint: How DNA Makes Us Who We Are* (Cambridge, MA: MIT Press, 2019).

17. Peter D. Gluckman, Mark A. Hanson, and Hamish G. Spencer, "Predictive Adaptive Responses and Human Evolution," *Trends in Ecology and Evolution* 20, no. 10 (2005): 527–533; Daniel Nettle, Willem E. Frankenhuis, and Ian J. Rickard, "The Evolution of Predictive Adaptive Responses in Human Life History," *Proceedings of the Royal Society B*, 280 (2013): 20131343.

18. Stephen Jay Gould, "Sociology: The Art of Storytelling," *New Scientist*, November 16, 1978: 530–535.

## 3. Testing the Puberty Hypothesis

1. For extensive discussion of findings, see Jay Belsky, Avshalom Caspi, Terrie E. Moffitt, and Richie Poulton, *The Origins of You: How Childhood Shapes Later Life* (Cambridge, MA: Harvard University Press, 2020). For more about the Dunedin Study, see the project website maintained by Avshalom Caspi and Terrie Moffitt: https://moffittcaspi.trinity.duke.edu/research-topics/dunedin.

2. Terrie E. Moffitt, Avshalom Caspi, Jay Belsky, and Phil A. Silva, "Childhood Experience and the Onset of Menarche: A Test of a Sociobiological Model," *Child Development* 63, no. 1 (1992), 47–58.

3. Laurence Steinberg, "Reciprocal Relation Between Parent-Child Distance and Pubertal Maturation," *Developmental Psychology* 24, no. 1 (1988), 122–128.

4. Jay Belsky, Laurence Steinberg, and Patricia Draper, "Childhood Experience, Interpersonal Development and Reproductive Strategy: An Evolutionary Theory of Socialization," *Child Development*, 62, no. 4 (1991), 647–670; Robert A. Hinde, "When Is an Evolutionary Approach Useful," *Child Development* 62 (1991), 671–675; Eleanor E. Maccoby, "Different Reproductive Strategies in Males and Females," *Child Development* 62, no. 4 (1991), 676–681.

5. Bill Henry, Terrie E. Moffitt, Avshalom Caspi, John Langley, and Phil A. Silva, "On the 'Remembrance of Things Past': A Longitudinal Evaluation of the Retrospective Method," *Psychological Assessment* 6, no. 2 (1994), 92–101.

6. Vincent A. Felitti, Robert F. Anda, R.F., Dale Nordenberg, David F. Williamson, Alison M. Spitz, Valerie Edwards, Mary P. Koss, and James S. Marks, "Relationship of Childhood Abuse and Household Dysfunction to Many Leading Causes of Death in Adults: The Adverse Childhood Experiences (ACE) Study," *American Journal of Preventive Medicine* 14, no. 4 (1998), 245–258.

7. Jochen Hardt and Michael Rutter, "Validity of Adult Retrospective Reports of Adverse Childhood Experiences: Review of the Evidence," *Journal of Child Psychology and Psychiatry* 45, no. 2 (2004), 260–273.

8. Jessie R. Baldwin, Aaron Reuben, Joanne B. Newbury, and Andrea Danese, "Agreement between Prospective and Retrospective Measures Of Childhood Maltreatment: A Systematic Review and Meta-Analysis," *JAMA Psychiatry* 76, no. 6 (2019), 584–593.

9. Bruce J. Ellis, Steven McFadyen-Ketchum, Kenneth A. Dodge, Gregory S. Pettit, and John E. Bates, "Quality of Early Family Relationships and Individual Differences in the Timing of Pubertal Maturation in Girls: A Longitudinal Test of an Evolutionary Model," *Journal of Personality and Social Psychology* 77, no. 2 (1999), 387–401.

10. Tlotlo C. Thutoemang and Seth Oppong, "Fathers' Parental Involvement and Accessibility As Predictors Of Daughters' Age of Menarche: Testing the Life History Theory (LHT-P) in a Non-WEIRD Context," *Ghana Science Journal*, 20, no. 2 (2023), 213–228.

11. Bruce J. Ellis, "Timing of Pubertal Maturation in Girls: An Integrated Life History Approach," *Psychological Bulletin*, 130, no. 6 (2004), 920–958.

12. Bruce J. Ellis and Marilyn J. Essex, "Family Environments, Adrenarche, and Sexual Maturation: A Longitudinal Test of a Life History Model," *Child Development*, 78, no. 6 (2007), 1799–1817; P. Draper and H. Harpending, "Father Absence and Reproductive Strategy: An Evolutionary Perspective," *Journal of Anthropological Research* 38 (1982): 255–273.

13. Bruce J. Ellis, "Timing of Pubertal Maturation in Girls: An Integrated Life History Approach," *Psychological Bulletin*, 130, no. 6 (2004), 920–958.

14. Ellis and Essex, "Family Environments, Adrenarche and Sexual Maturation."

15. Molly M. Fox, Jennifer Hahn-Holbrook, Curt A. Sandman, Jessica A. Marino, Laura M. Glynn, and Elysia Poggi Davis, "Mothers' Prenatal Distress Accelerates Adrenal Pubertal Development in Daughters," *Psychoneuroendocrinology* 160 (2024), 106671.

16. Jacqueline M. Tither and Bruce J. Ellis, "Impact of Fathers on Daughters' Age of Menarche: A Genetically and Environmentally Controlled Sibling Study," *Developmental Psychology* 44, no. 5 (2008), 1409–1420.

17. Jane E. Costello, Minje Sung, Carol Worthman, and Adrian Angold, "Pubertal Maturation and the Development of Alcohol Use and Abuse," *Drug and Alcohol Dependence* 88S (2007), S50–S59.

18. Tamarra James-Todd, Parisa Tehranifar, Janet Rich-Edwards, Lina Titievsky, and Mary Beth Terry, "The Impact of Socioeconomic Status across Early Life on Age at Menarche among a Racially Diverse Population of Girls," *Annals of Epidemiology* 20, no. 11 (2010), 836–842.

19. Thea Senger-Carpenter, Julia Seng, Todd I. Herrenkohl, Deanna Marriott, Bingxin Chen, and Terri Voepel-Lewis, "Applying Life History Theory to Understand Earlier Onset of Puberty:

An Adolescent Brain Cognitive Development Cohort Analysis," *Journal of Adolescent Health* 74, no. 4 (2024), 682–688.

20. Anne Gaml-Sørensen, Nis Brix, Tine B. Henriksen, and Cecilia H Ramlau-Hansen, "Maternal Stress in Pregnancy and Pubertal Timing in Girls and Boys: A Cohort Study," *Fertility and Sterility* 122, no. 4 (2024), 715–726; E. V. Bräuner, T. Koch, A. Juul, D. A. Doherty, R. Hart, M. Hickey, "Prenatal Exposure to Maternal Stressful Life Events and Earlier Age at Menarche: The Raine Study," *Human Reproduction* 36, no. 7 (2021), 1959–1969.

21. Lauren Granata, Michaela Fanikos, and Heather C. Brenhouse, "Early Life Adversity Accelerates Hypothalamic Drive of Pubertal Timing in Female Rats with Associated Enhanced Acoustic Startle," *Hormones and Behavior* 159 (2024), 105478.

22. NICHD Early Child Care Research Network, *Child Care and Child Development: Results from the NICHD Study of Early Child Care and Youth Development* (New York: Guilford Press, 2005).

23. Jay Belsky, Laurence Steinberg, Renate M. Houts, Bonnie L. Halpern-Felsher, "The Development of Reproductive Strategy in Females: Early Maternal Harshness→Earlier Menarche→Increased Sexual Risk Taking," *Developmental Psychology* 46, no. 1 (2010), 120–128.

24. Avshalom Caspi, Donald Lynam, Terrie E. Moffitt, and Phil A. Silva, "Unraveling Girls' Delinquency: Biological, Dispositional, and Contextual Contributions to Adolescent Misbehavior," *Developmental Psychology* 29, no. 1 (1993), 19–30.

25. Marco Del Giudice, "Sex, Attachment, and the Development of Reproductive Strategies," *Behavioral and Brain Sciences* 32 (2009), 1–21; Jenee James, Bruce J. Ellis, Gabriel L. Schlomer, and Judy Garber, "Sex-Specific Pathways to Early Puberty, Sexual Debut and Sexual Risk-Taking: Tests of an Integrated Evolutionary-Developmental Model," *Developmental Psychology* 48, no. 3 (2012), 687–702.

26. Thomas J. Dishion, Thao Ha, and Marie-Hélène Veronneau, "An Ecological Analysis of the Effects of Deviant Peer Clustering on Sexual Promiscuity, Problem Behavior, and Childbearing from Early Adolescence to Adulthood: An Enhancement of the Life History Framework," *Developmental Psychology* 48, no. 3 (2012), 703–717; Lei Chang and Hui Jing Lu, "Resource and Extrinsic Risk in Defining Fast Life Histories of Rural Chinese Left-Behind Children," *Evolution and Human Behavior* 39, no. 1 (2018), 59–66; Anne Gaml-Sørensen, Nis Brix, Andreas Ernst, Lea Lykke Harrit Lunddorf, and Cecilia Høst Ramlau-Hansen, "Father Absence in Pregnancy or during Childhood and Pubertal Development in Girls and Boys: A Population Cohort Study," *Child Development* 92, no. 4 (2021), 1494–1508.

27. Ying Sun, Fiona K. Mensah, Peter Azzopardi, George C. Patton, and Melissa Wake, "Childhood Social Disadvantage and Pubertal Timing: A National Birth Cohort from Australia," *Pediatrics* 139, no. 6 (2017), e20164099.

28. Man-Kit Lei, Steven R. H. Beach, and Ronald L. Simons, "Childhood Trauma, Pubertal Timing, and Cardiovascular Risk in Adulthood," *Health Psychology* 37, no. 7 (2018), 613–617.

29. Jay Belsky, Renate M. Houts, R.M. Pasco Fearon, "Infant Attachment Security and Timing of Puberty: Testing an Evolutionary Hypothesis," *Psychological Science* 21, no. 9 (2010), 1195–1201.

30. Lei Zhang, Dandan Zhang, and Ying Sun, "Adverse Childhood Experiences and Early Pubertal Timing among Girls: A Meta-Analysis," *International Journal of Environmental Research and Public Health* 16, no. 16 (2019), 2887; Kathryn C. Monahan, Kevin M. King, Elizabeth P. Shulman, Elizabeth Cauffman, and Laurie Chassin, "The Effects of Violence Exposure on the Development of Impulse Control and Future Orientation across Adolescence and Early Adulthood: Time-Specific and Generalized Effects in a Sample of Juvenile Offenders," *Development and Psychopathology* 27, no. 4 (2015), 1267–1283.

## 4. Not So Fast

1. Marco Del Giudice, *Evolutionary Psychopathology: A Unified Approach* (New York: Oxford University Press, 2018).

2. Roy Otten, Thao Ha, Erika Westling, Kathryn Lemery-Chalfant, Melvin N. Wilson, and Daniel S. Shaw, "How Pubertal Timing and Self-Regulation Predict Adolescent Sexual Activity in Resource-Poor Environments," *Development and Psychopathology* 36 (2024): 1941–1947.

3. Carys Chainey, Kylie Burke, and Michele Haynes, "Does Parenting Moderate the Association Between Adverse Childhood Experiences and Adolescents' Future Orientation?" *Journal of Child and Family Studies* 31 (2022): 2359–2375.

4. Willem Frankenhuis and Alison Gopnik, "Early Adversity and The Development Of Explore-Exploit Tradeoffs," *Trends in Cognitive Sciences* 27 (2023): 616–630.

5. James S. Chisholm, "Death, Hope, and Sex: Life-History Theory and the Development of Reproductive Strategies," *Current Anthropology* 34 (1993): 1–24.

6. Daniel Nettle, "Dying Young and Living Fast: Variation in Life History across English Neighborhoods," *Behavioral Ecology* 21 (2010): 387–395.

7. Elena Brandt and Jon K. Maner, "Attitudes and Laws about Abortion Are Linked to Extrinsic Mortality Risk: A Life-History Perspective on Variability In Reproductive Rights," *Psychological Science* 35 (2024): 111–125.

8. Arline T. Geronimus, "What Teen Mothers Know," *Human Nature* 7 (1996): 323–352; Vladas Griskevicius, Andrew W. Delton, Theresa E. Robertson, and Joshua M. Tybur, "Environmental Contingency in Life History Strategies: The Influence of Mortality and Socioeconomic Status on Reproductive Timing," *Journal of Personality and Social Psychology* 100, no. 2 (2011): 241–254; Daniel Nettle, David A. Coall, and Thomas E. Dickins, "Early-Life Conditions and Age at First Pregnancy In British Women," *Proceedings of the Royal Society B: Biological Sciences* 278 (2011): 1721–1727.

9. Bruce J. Ellis, "Timing of Pubertal Maturation in Girls: An Integrated Life History Approach," *Psychological Bulletin* 30 (2004): 920–958.

10. Mairi Macleod, "Why Are Girls Growing Up So Fast?," *New Scientist,* February 7, 2007.

11. Elizabeth R. Baker, "Body Weight and the Initiation of Puberty," *Clinical Obstetrics and Gynecology* 28 (1985): 573–570.

12. Rose E. Frisch, "Body Fat, Menarche, Fitness and Fertility," *Human Reproduction* 2 (1987): 521–523.

13. Rose E. Frisch, Grace Wyshak, and Larry Vincent, "Delayed Menarche and Amenorrhea of Ballet Dancers," *New England Journal of Medicine* 303 (1980): 17–19.

14. Candace J. Black, Fiona S. McEwen, Demelza Smeeth, Cassandra M. Popham, Elie Karam, and Michael Pluess, "Effects of War Exposure on Pubertal Development In Refugee Children," *Developmental Psychology* 59 (2023): 1559–1572.

15. Bruce J. Ellis, "Timing of Pubertal Maturation in Girls: An Integrated Life History Approach," *Psychological Bulletin* 130 (2004): 920–958.

16. Bruce J. Ellis, Brie M. Reid, and Karen L. Kramer, "Two Tiers, Not One: Different Sources of Extrinsic Mortality Have Opposing Effects on Life History Traits," *Behavioral and Brain Sciences* (2025).

17. Ian J. Rickard, Willem Frankenhuis, and Daniel Nettle, "Why Are Childhood Family Factors Associated with Timing of Maturation? A Role for Internal Prediction," *Perspectives on Psychological Science* 9 (2014): 3–15.

18. Hui Jing Lu, Jennifer E. Lansford, Yuan Yuan Liu, Bin Bin Chen, Marc H. Bornstein, Ann T. Skinner, Kenneth A. Dodge, Laurence Steinberg, Kirby Deater-Deckard, W. Andrew Rothenberg, Dario Bacchini, Concetta Pastorelli, Liane Peña Alampay, Emma Sorbring, Sevtap Gurdal, Suha M. Al-Hassan, Paul Oburu, Saengduean Yotanyamaneewong, Sombat Tapanya, Laura Di Giunta, Liliana Maria Uribe Tirado, and Lei Chang, "Attachment Security, Environmental Adversity, and Fast Life History Behavioral Profiles in Human Adolescents," *Development and Psychopathology*, published online (2024): 1 9. doi10.1017 / S0951579414001500 (2025).

19. Grace M. Brennan, Terrie E. Moffitt, Kyle J. Bourassa, HonaLee Harrington, Sean Hogan, Renate Houts, Richie Poulton, Sandhya Ramrakha, and Avshalom Caspi, "The Continuity of Adversity: Negative Emotionality Links Early Life Adversity with Adult Stressful Life Events," *Clinical Psychological Science* 12, no. 6 (2024): 1111–1126.

20. Jay Belsky "Toward an Evo-Devo Theory of Reproductive Strategy, Health, and Longevity," *Perspectives in Psychological Science* 9 (2014): 16–18.

21. Sarah Hartman, Zhi Li, Daniel Nettle, and Jay Belsky, "External-Environmental and Internal-Health Early-Life Predictors of Adolescent Development," *Development and Psychopathology* 29 (2017): 1839–1849.

22. Jay Belsky, Paula L. Ruttle, W. Thomas Boyce, Jeffrey M. Armstrong, and Marilyn J. Essex, "Early Adversity, Elevated Stress Physiology, Accelerated Sexual Maturation and Poor Health in Females," *Developmental Psychology* 51 (2015): 816–822.

23. Lei Chang, Hui Jing Lu, Jennifer E. Lansford, Marc H. Bornstein, Laurence Steinberg, Bin-Bin Chen, Ann T. Skinner, Kenneth A. Dodge, Kirby Deater-Deckard, Dario Bacchini, Concetta Pastorelli, Liane Peña Alampay, Sombat Tapanya, Emma Sorbring, Paul Oburu, Suha M. Al-Hassan, Laura Di Giunta, Patrick S. Malone, Liliana Maria Uribe Tirado and Saengduean Yotanyamaneewong, "External Environment and Internal State in Relation to Life-History Behavioural Profiles of Adolescents in Nine Countries," *Proceedings of the Royal Society B, Biological Sciences* 286, no. 1917 (2019): 20192097.

24. Jay Belsky and Idan Shalev, "Contextual Adversity, Telomere Erosion, Pubertal Development, and Health: Two Models of Accelerated Aging—Or One?," *Development and Psychopathology* 28, no. 4 (2016): 1367–1383; Idan Shalev and Jay Belsky "Early-Life Stress and Reproductive Cost: A Two-Hit Developmental Model of Accelerated Aging? *Medical Hypotheses* 90 (2016): 41–47.

25. Jenna Alley, Jeffrey Gassen, and George M. Slavich, "The Effects of Childhood Adversity on Twenty-Five Disease Biomarkers and Twenty Health Conditions in Adulthood: Differences by Sex and Stressor Type," *Brain, Behavior, and Immunity* 123 (2025): 164–176.

26. Peter D. Gluckman, Mark A. Hanson, and Catherine Pinal, "The Developmental Origins of Adult Disease," *Maternal and Child Nutrition* 1, no. 3 (2005): 130–141.

27. Barbara J. Fuhrman, Steven C. Moore, Celia Byrne, Issam Makhoul, Cari M. Kitahara, and Amy Berrinton de González, "Associations of Age at Menarche with Site-Specific Cancer Risks in Pooled Data from Nine Cohorts," *Cancer Research* 15 (2021): 2246–2255.

28. Maria E. Bleil, Bradley M. Appelhans, Steven E. Gregorich, Robert A. Hiatt, Glenn I. Roisman, and Cathryn Booth-LaForce, "Pubertal Timing: A Life Course Pathway Linking Early Life Risk to Adulthood Cardiometabolic Risk," *PLOS One* 19, no. 3 (2024): p.e0299433-e0299433.

29. Vincent J. Felitti, Robert F. Anda, Dale Nordenberg, David F. Williamson, Alison M. Spitz, Valerie Edwards, Mary P. Koss, and James S. Marks, "Relationship of Childhood Abuse and Household Dysfunction to Many Leading Causes of Death in Adults: The Adverse Childhood Experiences (ACE) Study," *American Journal of Preventive Medicine* 14, no. 4 (1998): 245–258.

30. Bruce J. Ellis, Aurelio José Figueredo, Barbara H. Brumbach, and Gabriel L. Schlomer, "The Impact of Harsh Versus Unpredictable Environments on the Evolution and Development of Life History Strategies," *Human Nature* 20, no. 2 (2009): 204–268.

31. Katie A. McLaughlin and Margaret A. Sheridan, "Beyond Cumulative Risk: A Dimensional Approach to Childhood Adversity," *Current Directions in Psychological Science* 25, no. 4 (2016): 239–245.

32. Jay Belsky, Gabriel L. Schlomer, and Bruce J. Ellis, "Beyond Cumulative Risk: Distinguishing Harshness and Unpredictability As Determinants of Parenting and Early Life History Strategy," *Developmental Psychology* 48 (2012): 662–673; Katie A. McLaughlin and Margaret A. Sheridan, "Beyond Cumulative Risk: A Dimensional Approach to Childhood Adversity," *Current Directions in Psychological Science* 25, no. 4 (2016): 239–245.

33. Bruce J. Ellis, Margaret A. Sheridan, Jay Belsky, and Katie A. McLaughlin, "Why and How Does Early Adversity Influence Development? Toward an Integrated Model of Dimensions of Environmental Experience," *Development and Psychopathology* 34, no. 2 (2022): 447–471.

34. Maria Usacheva, Daniel Choe, Siwei Liu., Susan Timmer, and Jay Belsky, "Testing the Empirical Integration of Threat-Deprivation and Harshness-Unpredictability Dimensional Models of Adversity," *Development and Psychopathology* 34, no. 2 (2022): 513–526.

35. Jay Belsky, Gabriel L. Schlomer, and Bruce J. Ellis, "Beyond Cumulative Risk: Distinguishing Harshness and Unpredictability as Determinants of Parenting and Early Life History Strategy,"

*Developmental Psychology* 48 (2012): 662–673; Zhi Li, Siwei Liu, Sarah Hartman, and Jay Belsky, "Interactive Effects of Early-Life Income Harshness and Unpredictability on Children's Socioemotional and Academic Functioning in Kindergarten and Adolescence," *Developmental Psychology* 54, no. 11 (2018): 2101–2112.

36. Jeffry A. Simpson, Vladas Griskevicius, Sally I-Chun Kuo, Sooyeon Sung, and W. Andrew Collins, "Evolution, Stress, and Sensitive Periods: The Influence of Unpredictability in Early Versus Late Childhood on Sex and Risky Behavior," *Developmental Psychology* 48, no. 3 (2012): 674–686; Jay Belsky, Gabriel L. Schlomer, and Bruce J. Ellis, "Beyond Cumulative Risk: Distinguishing Harshness and Unpredictability as Determinants of Parenting and Early Life History Strategy," *Developmental Psychology* 48, no. 3 (2012): 662–673; Zhi Li, Siwei Liu, Sarah Hartman, and Jay Belsky, "Interactive Effects of Early-Life Income Harshness and Unpredictability on Children's Socioemotional and Academic Functioning in Kindergarten and Adolescence," *Developmental Psychology* 54, no. 11 (2018): 2101–2112; Jeffry A. Simpson, Vladas Griskevicius, Sally I-Chun Kuo, Sooyeon Sung, and W. Andrew Collins, "Evolution, Stress, and Sensitive Periods: The Influence of Unpredictability in Early Versus Late Childhood on Sex and Risky Behavior," *Developmental Psychology* 48, no. 3 (2012): 674–686.

37. Maria Usacheva, Daniel Choe, Siwei Liu, Susan Timmer, and Jay Belsky, "Testing the Empirical Integration of Threat-Deprivation and Harshness-Unpredictability Dimensional Models of Adversity," *Development and Psychopathology* 34 (2022): 513–526.

38. Natalie L. Colich, May L. Rosen, Eileen S. Williams, and Katie A. McLaughlin, "Biological Aging in Childhood and Adolescence Following Experiences of Threat and Deprivation: A Systematic Review and Meta-Analysis," *Psychological Bulletin* 146, no. 9 (2020): 721–764.

39. Jennifer A. Sumner, Natalie L. Colich, Monica Uddin, Don Armstrong, and Katie A. McLaughlin, "Early Experiences of Threat, But Not Deprivation, Are Associated with Accelerated Biological Aging in Children," *Biological Psychiatry* 85, no. 3 (2019), 268–278.

40. As examples of other threat-related research, see Tiffany C. Ho, Jessica Buthmann, Rajpreet Chahal, Jonas G. Miller, and Ian. H. Gotlib, "Exploring Sex Differences In Trajectories Of Pubertal Development and Mental Health following Early Adversity," *Journal of Psychoneuroendocrinology* 161 (2024): 106944; and Sofia Carozza, Joni Holmes, and Duncan E. Astle, "Testing Deprivation and Threat: A Preregistered Network Analysis of the Dimensions of Early Adversity," *Psychological Science* 33, no. 10 (2022): 1753–1766. For work focused on contextual harshness and unpredictability, see Maria Usacheva, Daniel Choe, Siwei Liu, Susan Timmer, and Jay Belsky, "Testing the Empirical Integration of Threat-Deprivation and Harshness-Unpredictability Dimensional Models of Adversity," *Development and Psychopathology* 34, no. 2 (2022): 513–526. Also see Jay Belsky, Gabriel L. Schlomer, and Bruce J. Ellis, "Beyond Cumulative Risk: Distinguishing Harshness and Unpredictability as Determinants of Parenting and Early Life History Strategy," *Developmental Psychology* 48, no. 3 (2012): 662–673; Zhi Li and Jay Belsky "Indirect Effects, via Parental Factors, of Income Harshness and Unpredictability on Kindergarteners' Socioemotional Functioning," *Development and Psychopathology* 34, no. 2 (2022): 635–646; and Michelle Shaul, Sarah Whittle, Timothy J. Silk, and Nandita Vijayakumar, "Pubertal Timing Mediates the Association between Threat Adversity and Psychopathology," *Development and Psychopathology* 54, no. 12 (2025): 3436–3446.

41. Gabriel J. Merrin, Joy Huanhuan Wang, Sarah M. Kiefer, Jesseca L. Jackson, Lauren A. Pascarella, Paige L. Huckaby, Corinne L. Blake, Michael D. Gomez, and Nicholas D. W. Smith, "Adverse Childhood Experiences and Bullying during Adolescence," *Adolescent Research Review* 9, no. 3 (2024): 513–541.

## 5. Even Faster?

1. Michael J. Meaney, "Maternal Care, Gene Expression, and the Transmission of Individual Differences in Stress Reactivity across Generations" *Annual Review Neuroscience* 24 (2001): 1161–1192.

2. Eleftheria Parasyraki, Medhavi Mallick, Victoria Hatch, . . . , Lars Schomacher, Debasish Mukherjee, Christof Niehrs "5-Formylcytosine is an Activating Epigenetic Mark For RNA Pol III during Zygotic Reprogramming" *Cell* 187 (2024): 6088–6103.

3. Sharon Begley, "Mom, Dad, DNA and Suicide," *Newsweek*, February 24, 2009.

4. Michael J. Meaney, "Maternal Care, Gene Expression, and the Transmission of Individual Differences in Stress Reactivity across Generations" *Annual Review Neuroscience* 24 (2001): 1161–1192.

5. Jay Belsky, Laurence Steinberg and Patricia Draper, "Childhood Experience, Interpersonal Development, and Reproductive Strategy: An Evolutionary Theory of Socialization," *Child Development* 62, no. 4 (1991): 647–670.

6. Daniel W. Belsky, Avshalom Caspi, Louise Arseneault, Andrea Baccarelli, David L. Corcoran, Xu Gao, Eiliss Hannon, Hona Lee Harrington, Line J. H. Rasmussen, Renate Houts, Kim Huffman, William E. Kraus, Dayoon Kwon, Jonathan Mill, Carl F. Pieper, Joseph A. Prinz, Richie Poulton, Joel Schwartz, Karen Sugden, Pantel Vokonas, Benjamin S. Williams, and Terrie E Moffitt, "Quantification of the Pace of Biological Aging in Humans Through a Blood Test, The DunedinPoAm DNA Methylation Algorithm," *Elife* 9 (2020): e54870.

7. Aaron Reuben, Karen Sugden, Louise Arseneault, David L. Corcoran, Andrea Danese, Helen L. Fisher, Terrie E. Moffitt, Joanne B. Newbury, Candice Odgers, Joey Prinz, Line J. H. Rasmussen, Ben Williams, Jonathan Mill, and Avshalom Caspi, "Association of Neighborhood Disadvantage in Childhood with DNA Methylation In Young Adulthood," *JAMA Network Open* 3 (2020): e206095.

8. Cyrielle Holuka, Giorgia Menta, Juan Carlos Caro, Claus Vögele, Conchita D'Ambrosio, and Jonathan D. Turner, "Developmental Epigenomic Effects of Maternal Financial Problems," *Development and Psychopathology* 37, no. 2 (2025): 1004–1017.

9. Laurel Raffington, Peter T. Tanksley, Aditi Sabhlok, Liza Vinnik, Travis Mallard, Lucy S. King, Bridget Goosby, K. Paige Hardent, and Elliot M. Tucker-Drob, "Socially Stratified Epigenetic Profiles Are Associated With Cognitive Functioning In Children and Adolescents," *Psychological Science* 34 (2023): 170–185.

10. Van den Oord, C.L.J.D, Copeland, W.E., Zhao, M., Xie, L.Y., Aberg, K.A., and van den Oord E, J.C. "DNA Methylation Signatures of Childhood Trauma Predict Psychiatric Disorders and Other Adverse Outcomes 17 Years After Exposure," *Molecular Psychiatry* 27 (2022): 3367–3373.

11. William E. Copeland, Lilly Shanahan, Jennifer Hinesley, Robin F. Chan, Karolina A. Aberg, John A. Fairbank, Edwin J. C. G. van den Oord, and E. Jane Costello, "Association of Childhood Trauma Exposure With Adult Psychiatric Disorders and Functional Outcomes," *JAMA Network Open* 1 (2018): e184493–e184493.

12. Jay Belsky, "Early-Life Adversity Accelerates Child-Adolescent Development," *Current Directions in Psychological Science*, 28 (2019): 241–246; Colich, N. L., Rosen, M. L., Williams, E. S., and McLaughlin, K. A. "Accelerated Biological Aging Following Childhood Experiences of Threat and Deprivation: A Meta-Analysis," *Psychological Bulletin* 146 (2020): 721–764.

13. Copeland, W.E., Shanahan, L., McGinnis, E.W., Aberg, K.A., and van den Oord, E.J.C.G., "Early Adversities Accelerate Epigenetic Aging into Adulthood: A 10-Year, Within-Subject Analysis," *Journal of Child Psychology and Psychiatry* 63 (2022): 1308–1315.

14. Barbara J. Fuhrman, Steven C. Moore, Celia Byrne, Issam Makhoul, Cari M. Kitahara, Amy Berrington de Gonzalez, Martha S. Linet, Elisabete Weiderpass, Hans-Olov Adami, Neal D. Freedman, Linda M. Liao, Charles E. Matthews, Rachael Z. Stolzenberg-Solomon, Mia M. Gaudet, Alpa V. Patel, I-Min Lee, Julie E. Buring, Alicja Wolk, Susanna C. Larsson, Anna E. Prizment, Kim Robien, Michael Spriggs, David P. Check, Neil Murphy, Marc J. Gunter, Harold L. Van Dusen Jr, Regina G. Ziegler, and Robert N. Hoover, "Association of the Age at Menarche with Site-Specific Cancer Risks in Pooled Data from Nine Cohorts," *Cancer Research* 15 (2021): 2246–2255.

15. Elizabeth Blackburn and Elissa Epel, *The Telomere Effect: A Revolutionary Approach to Living Younger, Healthier, Longer* (New York: Grand Central, 2017).

16. On general difficulties, see Sonja Entringer, Elissa S. Epel, Jue Lin, Claudia Buss, Babak Shahbaba, Elizabeth H. Blackburn, Hyagriv N. Simhan, and Pathik D. Wadhwa, "Maternal Psychosocial Stress during Pregnancy Is Associated with Newborn Leukocyte Telomere Length," *American Journal of Obstetrics and Gynecology* 208, no. 2 (2013): 134.e1–134.e7. On depression, see Michelle Bosquet Enlow, Valentina Bollati, Georgios Sideridis, Julie D. Flom, Mirjam Hoxha, Michele R. Hacker, and Rosalind J. Wright, "Sex Differences in Effects of Maternal Risk and Protective Factors in Childhood and Pregnancy on Newborn Telomere Length," *Psychoneuroendocrinology* 95 (2018): 74–85. On low socioeconomic status, see Dries S. Martens, Bram G. Janssen, Esmée M. Bijnens, Diana B. P. Clemente, Paolo Vineis, Michelle Plusquin, and Tim S. Nawrot, "Association of Parental Socioeconomic Status and Newborn Telomere Length," *JAMA Network Open* 3 (2020): e204057.

17. On low-income backgrounds, see Martens et al., "Association of Parental Socioeconomic Status and Newborn Telomere Length." On maltreatment, see Xiao Yan Chen, Camilla K. M. Lo, Ko Ling Chan, Wing Cheong Leung, and Patrick Ip, "Association between Childhood Exposure to Family Violence and Telomere Length: A Meta-Analysis," *International Journal of Environmental Research and Public Health* 19, no. 19 (2022): 12511. On acute traumatic experiences, see Andreas Lorenz Kuffer, Aoife O'Donovan, Andrea Burri, and Andreas Maercker, "Posttraumatic Stress Disorder, Adverse Childhood Events, and Buccal Cell Telomere Length in Elderly Swiss Former Indentured Child Laborers," *Frontiers in Psychiatry* 7 (2016): 147.

18. Jesse L. Coe, Teresa Daniels, Lindsay Huffhines, Ronald Seifer, Carmen J. Marsit, Hung-Teh Kao, Barbara Porton, Stephanie H. Parade, and Audrey R. Tyrka, "Examining the Biological Impacts of Parent-Child Relationship Dynamics on Preschool-Aged Children Who Have Experienced Adversity," *Developmental Psychobiology* 66, no. 2 (2024): e22463.

19. Camille Moeckel, Lauren Gaydosh, Lisa Schneper, Colter Mitchell, and Daniel A. Notterman, "Material Hardship and Telomere Length in Children," *Child Development* 95 (2024): 2232–2240.

20. Idan Shalev, Terrie E. Moffitt, K. Sugden, Benjamin Williams., Renate M. Houts, A. Danese, J. Mill, Louise Arseneault, and Avshalom Caspi, "Exposure to Violence during Childhood Is Associated with Telomere Erosion from 5 to 10 Years of Age: A Longitudinal Study," *Molecular Psychiatry* 18 (2013): 576–581.

21. Gillian V. Pepper, Melissa Bateson, and Daniel Nettle "Telomeres as Integrative Markers of Exposure to Stress and Adversity: A Systematic Review and Meta-Analysis," *Royal Society Open Science* 5 (2018), 180744.

22. Shlomit Fogel-Yaakobi, Ilanit Gordon, Michal Lavidor, Or Burstein, Neta Salomon, Dana Shai, "The Association between Parenting Quality and Offspring's Biological Aging Evaluated by Telomere Length: A Systematic Review and Meta-Analysis," *Development and Psychopathology* (2025): doi:10.1017 / S095457942500015.

23. Kalsea J. Koss, Lisa M. Schneper, Jeanne Brooks-Gunn, Sara McLanahan, Colter Mitchell, and Daniel A. Notterman, "Early Puberty and Telomere Length in Preadolescent Girls and Mothers," *Journal of Pediatrics* 222 (2020): 193–199.

24. Daniel W. Belsky, Terrie E. Moffitt, Alan A. Cohen, David L. Corcoran, Morgan E. Levine, Joseph A. Prinz, Jonathan Schaefer, Karen Sugden, Benjamin Williams, Richie Poulton, and Avshalom Caspi, "Eleven Telomere, Epigenetic Clock, and Biomarker-Composite Quantifications of Biological Aging: Do They Measure the Same Thing?," *American Journal of Epidemiology* 187 (2018): 1220–1230; Mei Ling Ong, Man-Kit Lei, Eric Klopack, Mark Berg, Yue Zhang, Robert Philibert, Steven S. R. Beach, and Ronald L. Simons, "Unstable Childhood, Adult Adversity, and Smoking Accelerate Biological Aging Among Middle-Age African Americans: Similar Findings for GrimAge and PoAm," *Journal of Aging Health* 34 (2022): 487–498.
Kusters, C.D.J. & Horvath, S. (2025). Quantification of Epigenetic Aging in Public Health. *Annual Review Public Health*, 46, 91–110.

25. Steven R. H. Beach, Frederick X. Gibbons, Sierra E. Carter, Mei Ling Ong, Justin A. Lavner, Man-Kit Lei, Ronald L. Simons, Meg Gerrard, and Robert A. Philibert, "Childhood Adversity

Predicts Black Young Adults' DNA Methylation-Based Accelerated Aging: A Dual Pathway Model," *Development and Psychopathology* 34 (2022): 689–703; Laurel Raffington, Daniel W. Belsky, Meeraj Kothari, Margherita Malanchini, Elliot M. Tucker-Drob, and K. Paige Harden, "Socioeconomic Disadvantage and the Pace of Biological Aging in Children," *Pediatrics* 147, no. 6 (2021): e2020024406.

26. Tanja Jovanovic, L. Alexander Vance, Dorthie Cross, Anna K. Knight, Varun Kilaru, Vasiliki Michopoulos, Torsten Klengel, and Alicia K. Smith, "Exposure to Violence Accelerates Epigenetic Aging in Children," *Scientific Reports* 7 (2017): 8962–8967

27. Makeda K. Austina, Edith Chena, Kharah M. Rossc, Lisa M. McEwend, Julia L. MacIsaacd, Michael S. Kobord, and Gregory E. Miller, "Early-Life Socioeconomic Disadvantage, Not Current, Predicts Accelerated Epigenetic Aging of Monocytes," *Psychoneuroendocrinology* 97 (2018): 131–134.

28. Olivia D. Chang, Helen C. S. Meier, Kathryn Maguire-Jack, Pamela Davis-Kean, and Colter Mitchell, "Childhood Maltreatment and Longitudinal Epigenetic Aging: NIMHD Social Epigenomics Program," *JAMA Network Open* 7 (2024): e2421877.

29. Gabriel L. Schlomer, "Epigenetic Age Acceleration and Reproductive Outcomes in Women," *Evolution and Human Behavior* 45 (2024): 91–98.

30. Anthony S. Zannas, Janine Arloth, Tania Carrillo-Roai, Stella Iurato, Simone Röh, Kerry J. Ressler, Charles B. Nemeroff, Alicia K. Smith, Bekh Bradley, Christine Heim, Andreas Menke, Jennifer F. Lange, Tanja Brück, Marcus Ising, Naomi R. Wray, Angelika Erhardt, Elisabeth B. Binder, and Divya Mehta, "Lifetime Stress Accelerates Epigenetic Aging In An Urban, African American Cohort: Relevance of Glucocorticoid Signaling," *Genome Biology* 16 (2015): 266.

31. Steven R. H. Beach, Mei Ling Ong, Man-Kit Lei, Eric Klopack, Sierra E. Carter, Ronald L. Simons, Frederick X. Gibbons, Justin A. Lavner, Robert A. Philibert, and Kaixiong Ye, "Childhood Adversity Is Linked to Adult Health Among African American Via Adolescent Weight Gain and Effects Are Genetically Moderated," *Development and Psychopathology* 33 (2021): 803–820.

32. Steven R. H. Beach, Frederick X. Gibbons, Sierra E. Carter, Mei Ling Ong, Justin A. Lavner, Man-Kit Lei, Ronald L. Simons, Meg Gerrard, and Robert A. Philibert, "Childhood Adversity Predicts Black Young Adults' DNA Methylation-Based Accelerated Aging: A Dual Pathway Model," *Development and Psychopathology* 34 (2021): 689–703; Beach, S.R.H., Gibbons, F.,X., Carter, S.E., Ong, M.L., Lavner, J.A., Lei, M-K., Simons, R.L., Gerrard, M., and Philibert, R.A., and "Childhood Adversity Predicts Black Young Adults' DNA Methylation-Based Accelerated Aging: A Dual Pathway Model," *Development and Psychopathology* 34 (2021): 689–703.

33. Daniel W. Belsky, Avshalom Caspi, David L. Corcoran, Karen Sugden, Richie Poulton, Louise Arseneault, Andrea Baccarelli, Kartik Chamarti, Xu Gao, Ellis Hannon, Hona Lee Harrington, Renate Houts, Meeraj Kothari, Dayoon Kwon, Jonathan Mill, Joel Schwartz, Pantel Vokonas, Cuicui Wang, Benjamin S. Williams, and Terrie E. Moffitt "DunedinPACE, a DNA Methylation Biomarker of Pace of Aging," *eLife* 11 (2022): e73420.

34. Daniel W. Belsky, Avshalom Caspi, Harvey J. Cohen, William E. Kraus, Sandhya Ramrakha, Richie Poulton, and Terrie E. Moffitt "Impact of Early Personal-History Characteristics on Pace of Aging," *Aging Cell* 16, no. 4 (2017): 644–651.

35. Alexandra D. W. Sullivan, Sarah M. Merrill, Chaini Konwar, Michael Coccia, Luisa Rivera, Julia L. MacIsaac, Alicia F. Lieberman, Michael S. Kobor, and Nicole R. Bush, "Intervening after Trauma: Child-Parent Psychotherapy Treatment Is Associated with Lower Pediatric Epigenetic Age Acceleration," *Psychological Science* 35, no. 9 (2024): 1062–1073.

36. Alexandra M. Binder, Camila Corvalan, Verónica Mericq, Ana Pereira, José Luis Santos, Steve Horvath, John Shepherd, and Karin B. Michels, "Faster Ticking Rate of the Epigenetic Clock Is Associated with Faster Pubertal Development in Girls," *Epigenetics* 13, no. 1 (2018): 85–94.

37. Emma Bolhuis, Jay Belsky, Willem E. Frankenhuis, Idan Shalev, Waylon J. Hastings, Marieke S. Tollenaar, Kieran J. O'Donnell, Megan G. McGill, Irina Pokhvisneva, David T. S. Lin, Julia L.

MacIsaac, Michael S. Kobori, Carolina de Weerth, and Roseriet Beijers, "Attachment Insecurity and the Biological Embedding of Reproductive Strategies: Investigating the Role of Cellular Aging," *Biological Psychology* 175 (2022): 108446.

38. Schlomer, "Epigenetic Age Acceleration and Reproductive Outcomes in Women."

39. Matthew W. Gillman, "Developmental Origins of Health and Disease," *New England Journal of Medicine* 353, no. 17 (2005): 1848–1850.

40. J. Kathie Xie, Avshalom Caspi, Kathleen M., Harris, Allison E., Aiello, HonaLee Harrington, Renate Houts, Daniel W. Belsky, Laurel L. Raffington, Jay Belsky, Sandhya Ramrakha, R. F. Theodore, and Terrie E. Moffitt, *"Do Children Who Develop Faster Go on to Age Faster in Midlife? Testing Competing Hypotheses in Two Longitudinal Studies,"* Manuscript under Review (2025).

41. Ursula A. Tooley, Danielle S. Bassett, and Allyson P. Mackey, "Environmental Influences on the Pace of Brain Development," *Nature Reviews Neuroscience* 22 (2021): 372–384.

42. Anna Tyborowska, Inge Volman, Hannah C. M. Niermann, J. Loes Pouwels, Sanny Smeekens, Antonius H. N. Cillessen, Ivan Toni, and Karin Roelofs, "Early-Life and Pubertal Stress Differentially Modulate Grey Matter Development in Human Adolescents," *Scientific Reports* 8, no. 1 (2018): 9201–9211.

43. Daniel S. Busso, Katie A. McLaughlin, Stephanie Brueck, Matthew Peverill, Andrea L. Gold, and Margaret A. Sheridan, "Child Abuse, Neural Structure, and Adolescent Psychopathology: A Longitudinal Study," *Journal of the American Academy of Child and Adolescent Psychiatry* 56 (2017): 321–328.

44. On institutional care, see Natalie L. Colich, Eileen Williams, Tiffany Cheing Ho, Lucy S. King, et al. "The Association between Early Life Stress and Prefrontal Cortex Activation during Implicit Emotion Regulation Is Moderated by Sex in Early Adolescence," *Development and Psychopathology* 29, no. 5 (2017): 1851–1864. On traumatic experience, see Meichen Yu, Kristin A. Linn, Russell T. Shinohara, Desmond J. Oathes, Philip A. Cook, et al., "Childhood Trauma History Is Linked to Abnormal Brain Connectivity in Major Depression," *PNAS: Biological Sciences* 116, no. 17 (2019): 8582–8590; Taylor J. Keding, Justin D. Russell, Xioajin Zhu, Quanfa He, James J. Li, and Ryan J. Herringa, "Diverging Effects of Violence Exposure on Psychiatric Symptoms on Amygdala-Prefrontal Maturation during Childhood and Adolescence," *Biological Psychiatry: Cognitive Neuroscience and Neuroimaging*. 10, no. 5 (2025): 450–462. On harsh parenting, see Sandra Thijssen, Ryan L. Muetzel, Marian J. Bakermans-Kranenburg, Vincent W. V. Jaddoe, Henning Tiemeier, Frank C. Verhulst, Tonya White, Marinus H. Van Ijzendoorn, "Insensitive Parenting May Accelerate the Development of the Amygdala-Medial Prefrontal Cortex Circuit," *Development and Psychopathology* 29, no. 2 (2017): 505–518.

45. Dylan G. Gee, Kathryn L. Humphreys, Jessica Flannery, Bonnie Goff, Eva H. Telzer, Mor Shapiro, Todd A. Hare, Susan Y. Bookheimer, and Nim Tottenham, "A Developmental Shift from Positive to Negative Connectivity in Human Amygdala-Prefrontal Circuitry," *Journal of Neuroscience* 33, no. 10 (2013): 4584–4593.

46. Laurence Steinberg, *Age of Opportunity: Lessons from the New Science of Adolescence* (Boston: Houghton Mifflin Harcourt, 2014).

47. Shi Yu Chan, Zhen Ming Ngoh, Zi Yan Ong, and Ai Ling Teh, "The Influence of Early-Life Adversity on the Coupling of Structural and Functional Brain Connectivity across Childhood. *Nature Mental Health* 2 (2024): 52–62.

48. Gabriele Ciceri, Arianna Baggiolini, Hyein S. Cho, Meghana Kshirsagar, et al., "An Epigenetic Barrier Sets the Timing of Human Neuronal Maturation," *Nature* 626 (2024): 881–890.

49. Natalie L. Colich, Maya L. Rosen, Eileen S. Williams, and Katie A. McLaughlin, "Biological Aging in Childhood and Adolescence following Experiences of Threat and Deprivation: A Systematic Review and Meta-Analysis," *Psychological Bulletin* 146, no. 9 (2020): 721–764.

50. Ursula A. Tooley, Aidan Latham, Jeanette K. Kenley, Dimitrios Alexopoulos, Tara A. Smyser, Ashley N. Nielsen, et al., "Prenatal Environment Is Associated with the Pace of Cortical

Network Development over the First Three Years of Life," *Nature Communications* 15, 7932 (2024). https://doi.org/10.1038/s41467-024-52242-4.

51. Muriel M. K. Bruchhage, Giang-Chau Ngo, Nora Schneider, Viren D'Sa, and Sean C. L. Deoni, "Functional Connectivity Correlates of Infant and Early Childhood Cognitive Development," *Brain Structure and. Function* 225, no. 2 (2020): 669–681.

52. Jonas G. Miller, Peter D. Gluckman, Marielle V. Fortier, Yap Seng Chong, Y.S., Michael J. Meaney, Ai Peng Tan, and Ian H. Gotlib, "Faster Pace of Hippocampal Growth Mediates the Association between Perinatal Adversity and Childhood Depression," *Developmental Cognitive Neuroscience* 67 (2024): 101392.

53. Sebastian Moguilner, Sandra Baez, Hernan Hernandez, Joaquin Migeot, et al., "Brain Clocks Capture Diversity and Disparities in Aging and Dementia across Geographically Diverse Populations," *Nature Medicine* 30, no. 12 (2024): 3646–3657.

54. Dani Beck, Lucy Whitmore, Niamh MacSweeney, Alexis Brieant, Valerie Karl, Ann-Marie G. de Lange, Lars T. Westlye, Kathryn L. Mills, and Christian K. Tamnes, "Dimensions of Early-Life Adversity Are Differentially Associated with Patterns of Delayed and Accelerated Brain Maturation," *Biological Psychiatry* 97, no. 1 (2005): 64–72.

55. Cassidy L. McDermott, Katherine Hilton, Anne T. Park, Ursula A. Tooley, Austin L. Boroshok, Muralidhar Mupparapu, JoAnna M. Scott, Erin E. Burmann, E., and Allyson P. Mackey, "Early Life Stress Is Associated with Earlier Emergence of Permanent Molars," *PNAS* 118, no. 24 (2021): e2105304118; X. Lu, X. Yu, Y. Zhang, J. Pan, B. Zhao, Y. Sun, and X. Chen, "Longitudinal Associations between Early-Life Adversity and Accelerated Molar Eruption," *BMC Oral Health*, in press (2025).

56. Begona Ruiz, Jonathan M. Broadbent, William Murray Thomson, Sandhya Ramrakha, Joseph Boden, John Horwood, and Richie Poulton, "Is Childhood Oral Health the 'Canary in the Coal Mine' for Poor Adult General Health? Findings from Two New Zealand Birth Cohort Studies," *Community Dentistry and Oral Epidemiology* 51, no. 5 (2023): 838–846.

## 6. A Genetic Illusion?

1. Robert Plomin, Robin Corley, J. C. DeFries, and D. W. Fulker, "Individual Differences in Television Viewing in Early Childhood: Nature as Well as Nurture," *Psychological Science* 1, no. 6 (1990): 371–377.

2. On pubertal timing, see Brian Mustanski, Richard J. Viken, Jaakko Kaprio, Lea Pulkkinen, and Richard J. Rose, "Genetic and Environmental Influences on Pubertal Development: Longitudinal Data from Finnish Twins at Ages 11 and 14," *Developmental Psychology*, 40, no. 6 (2004): 1188–1198; Felix R. Day, Deborah J. Thompson, Hannes Helgason, Daniel I. Chasman, et al., "Genomic Analyses Identify Hundreds of Variants Associated with Age at Menarche and Support a Role for Puberty Timing in Cancer Risk," *Nature Genetics*, 49, no. 6 (2017): 834–841; Jia Zhu, Temitope O. Kusa, and Yee-Ming Chan, "*Genetics of Pubertal Timing*," *Current Opinion in Pediatrics* 30, no. 4 (2018): 532–540. On age of first sex, see N. G. Martin, L. J. Eaves, and H. J. Eysenck, "Genetical, Environmental and Personality Factors Influencing the Age of First Sexual Intercourse in Twins," *Journal of Biosocial Science* 9 (1977): 91–97; Melinda C. Mills, Felix C. Tropf, David M. Brazel, Natalie van Zuydam, et al., "Identification of 371 Genetic Variants for Age at First Sex And Birth Linked to Externalising Behaviour," *Nature Human Behaviour* 5, no. 12 (2021): 1717–1730. On stability of intimate relationships, see Beth A. Jerskey, Matthew S. Panizzon, Kristen C. Jacobson, Michael C. Neale, et al., "Marriage and Divorce: A Genetic Perspective," *Personality and Individual Differences* 49, no. 5 (2010): 473–478; Matt McGue and David T. Lykken, "Genetic Influence on Risk of Divorce," *Psychological Science* 3, no. 6 (1992): 368–373; Brian M. D'Onofrio, Eric Turkheimer, Robert E. Emery, Wendy S. Slutske, et al., "A Genetically Informed Study of

Marital Instability and Its Association with Offspring Psychopathology," *Journal of Abnormal Psychology* 114, no. 4 (2005): 570–586. On number of children born, see Iain Mathieson, I., Felix R. Day, Felix C. Tropf, David M. Brazel, et al., "Genome-Wide Analysis Identifies Genetic Effects on Reproductive Success and Ongoing Natural Selection at the FADS Locus," *Nature Human Behavior* 7, no. 5 (2023): 790–801.

3. Claire Prince, Gemma C. Sharp, Laura D. Howe, Abigail Fraser, and Rebecca C. Richmond, "The Relationships between Women's Reproductive Factors: A Mendelian Randomisation Analysis," *BMC Medicine* 20, no. 1 (2022): 103.

4. Robert Plomin and C. S. Bergeman: "The Nature of Nurture: Genetic Influence on 'Environmental' Measures," *Behavioral and Brain Sciences* 14, no. 3 (1991): 373–386.

5. Jasmin Wertz: Jay Belsky, Terrie E. Moffitt, Daniel W. Belsky, et al., "Genetics of Nurture: A Test of the Hypothesis that Parents' Genetics Predict Their Observed Caregiving," *Developmental Psychology* 55, no. 7 (2019): 1461–1472; Jana Runze, Marian J. Bakermans-Kranenburg, Charlotte A. M. Cecil, Marinus H. van IJzendoorn, and Irene Pappa, "The Polygenic and Reactive Nature of Observed Parenting," *Genes Brain and Behavior* 22, no. 6 (2023): e12874; Jasmin Wertz, Terrie E. Moffitt, Jessica Agnew-Blais, Louise Arseneault, et al., "Using DNA from Mothers and Children to Study Parental Investment in Children's Educational Attainment," *Child Development* 91, no. 5 (2020): 1745–1761.

6. Jasmin Wertz, Terrie E. Moffitt, Louise Arseneault, J. C. Barnes, Michel Boivin, et al., "Genetic Associations with Parental Investment from Conception to Wealth Inheritance in Six Cohorts," *Nature Human Behaviour* 7, no. 8 (2023): 1388–1401.

7. Jay Belsky, Laurence Steinberg, Renate M. Houts, Bonnie L. Halpern-Felsher, et al., "The Development of Reproductive Strategy in Females: Early Maternal Harshness→Earlier Menarche→Increased Sexual Risk Taking," *Developmental Psychology* 46, no. 1 (2010): 120–128.

8. Lauren Gaydosh, Daniel W. Belsky, Benjamin W. Domingue, Jason D. Boardman, and Kathleen Mullan Harris, "Father Absence and Accelerated Reproductive Development in Non-Hispanic White Women in the United States," *Demography* 55, no. 4 (2018): 1245–1267.

9. Gabriel L. Schlomer and Kristine Marceau, "Father Absence, Age at Menarche, and Genetic Confounding: A Replication and Extension Using a Polygenic Score," *Development and Psychopathology* 34, no. 1 (2022): 355–366.

10. Jacqueline M. Tither and Bruce J. Ellis, "Impact of Fathers on Daughters' Age of Menarche: A Genetically and Environmentally Controlled Study," *Developmental Psychology* 44, no. 5 (2008): 1409–1420.

11. George B. Richardson, Daniel Bates, Amy Ross, Hexuan Liu, and Brian B. Boutwell, "Is Reproductive Development Adaptively Calibrated to Early Experience? Evidence From a National Sample of Females," *Developmental Psychology* 60, no. 2 (2024): 306–321.

12. Michael P. Grosz, Adam Ayaita, Ruben C. Arslan, Susanne Buecker, Tobias Ebert, et al., "Natural Experiments: Missed Opportunities for Causal Inference in Psychology," *Advances in Methods and Practices in Psychological Science* 7, no. 1 (2024).

13. Pauline Anderson, "Long-Term Data Reveal Psychiatric, Physical Fallout For Children of 9 / 11," *Medscape Medical News*, May 20, 2019.

14. Anu-Katriina Pesonen, Katri Räikkönen, Kati Heinonen, Eero Kajantie, Tom Forsén, and Johan G. Eriksson, "Reproductive Traits following a Parent-Child Separation Trauma during Childhood: A Natural Experiment during World War II," *American Journal of Human Biology* 20, no. 3 (2008): 345–351.

15. Qiguo Lian, Xiayun Zuo, Yanyan Mao, Yan Zhang, Shan Luo, et al., "The Impact of the Wenchuan Earthquake on Early Puberty: A Natural Experiment," *PeerJ* 6 (2018): e5085.

16. Jeffry A. Simpson, Vladas Griskevicius, Sally I-Chun Kuo, Sooyeon Sung, and W. Andrew Collins, "Evolution, Stress, and Sensitive Periods: The Influence of Unpredictability in Early Versus Late Childhood on Sex and Risky Behavior," *Developmental Psychology* 48, no. 3 (2012): 674–686.

17. Espen Røysamb, Terrie E. Moffitt, Avshalom Caspi, Eivind Ystrøm, and Ragnhild Bang Nes, "Worldwide Well-Being: Simulated Twins Reveal Genetic and (Hidden) Environmental Influences," *Perspectives on Psychological Science* 18, no. 6 (2023): 1562–1574.

18. Douglas Teixeira Leffa, Arthur Caye, Sintia I. Belangero, Ary Gadelha, Pedro Maria Pan, et al., "The Synergistic Effect of Genetic and Environmental Factors in the Development of Attention-Deficit / Hyperactivity Disorder Symptoms in Children and Adolescents," *Development and Psychopathology* 36, no. 3 (2024): 1134–1144.

19. M. P. Dunne, N. G. Martin, D. J. Statham, W. S. Slutske, S. H. Dinwiddie, et al., "Genetic and Environmental Contributions to Variance in Age at First Sexual Intercourse," *Psychological Science* 8, no. 3 (1997): 211–216; Melinda C. Mills, et al., "Identification of 371 Genetic Variants for Age at First Sex And Birth Linked to Externalising Behaviour."

20. Mary Waldron, Andrew C. Heath, Eric N. Turkheimer, Robert E. Emery, et al., "Childhood Sexual Abuse Moderates Genetic Influences on Age at First Consensual Sexual Intercourse in Women," *Behavior Genetics* 38, no. 1 (2008): 1–10.

21. Jennie G. Noll, Penelope K. Trickett, Jeffrey D. Long, Sonya Negriff, et al., "Childhood Sexual Abuse and Early Timing of Puberty," *Journal of Adolescent Health* 60, no. 1 (2017): 65–71.

22. Elizabeth A. Shewark, Alexandra Y. Vazquez, Amber L. Pearson, Kelly L. Klump, and S. Alexandra Burt, "Neighborhood Features Moderate Genetic and Environmental Influences on Children's Social Information Processing," *Developmental Psychology* 60, no. 4 (2024): 610–623.

23. On toddlers, see Elliot M. Tucker-Drob, Mijke Rhemtulla, K. Paige Harden, Eric Turkheimer, and David Fask," *Psychological Science* 22, no. 1 (2011): 125–133. On preschoolers, see Eric Turkheimer, Andreana Haley, Mary Waldron, Brian D'Onofrio, and Irving I. Gottesman, "Socioeconomic Status Modifies the Heritability of IQ in Young Children," *Psychological Science* 14, no. 6 (2003): 623–628. On adolescents, see K. Paige Harden, Eric Turkheimer, and John C. Loehlin, "Genotype by Environment Interaction in Adolescents' Cognitive Aptitude," *Behavior Genetics* 37, no. 2 (2007): 273–283.

24. Elliot M. Tucker-Drob and Timothy C. Bates, "Large Cross-National Differences in Gene × Socioeconomic Status Interaction on Intelligence," *Psychological Science* 27, no. 2 (2016): 138–149.

25. Jay Belsky, "The Nature of Nurture: Darwinian and Mendelian Perspectives," *Development and Psychopathology* 36, no. 5 (2024): 2197–2206.

26. Ryutaro Uchiyama, Rachel Spicer, and Michael Muthukrishna, "Cultural Evolution of Genetic Heritability," *Behavioral and Brain Sciences* 45 (2022): e152.

27. Urie Bronfenbrenner and Stephen J. Ceci, "Nature-Nurture Reconceptualized in Developmental Perspective: A Bioecological Model," *Psychological Review* 101, no. 4 (1994): 568–586.

28. Sharon Niv, Catherine Tuvblad, Adrian Raine, and Laura A. Baker, "Aggression and Rule-Breaking: Heritability and Stability of Antisocial Behavior Problems in Childhood and Adolescence," *Journal of Criminal Justice* 41, no. 5 (2013): 285–291.

29. Isabella Badini, Yasmin Ahmadzadeh, Daniel L. Wechsler, Torkild H. Lyngstad, et al., "Socioeconomic Status and Risk for Child Psychopathology: Exploring Gene–Environment Interaction in the Presence of Gene–Environment Correlation Using Extended Families in the Norwegian Mother, Father and Child Birth Cohort Study," *Journal of Child Psychology and Psychiatry* 65, no. 2 (2024): 176–187.

## 7. For Better and for Worse

1. Matthew L. Maciejewski, David E. Arterburn, Lynn Van Scoyoc, Valerie A. Smith, William S. Yancy, Hollis J. Weidenbacher, Edward H. Livingston, and Maren K. Olsen, "Bariatric Surgery and Long-term Durability of Weight Loss," *JAMA Surgery* 151 (2016): 1046–1055.

2. Earl Hunt and Franca Agnoli, "The Whorfian Hypothesis: A Cognitive Psychology Perspective," *Psychological Review* 98 (1991): 377–389.

3. Jay Belsky, "Variation in Susceptibility to Rearing Influences: An Evolutionary Argument," *Psychological Inquiry* 8 (1997): 182–186; Jay Belsky, Marian Bakermans-Kranenburg, and Marinus van IJzendoorn, "For Better *and* for Worse: Differential Susceptibility to Environmental Influences," *Current Directions in Psychological Science* 16 (2007): 305–309; Jay Belsky and Michael Pluess, "Beyond Diathesis-Stress: Differential Susceptibility to Environmental Influences," *Psychological Bulletin* 135 (2009): 885–908; Jay Belsky and Michael Pluess, "Beyond Risk, Resilience, and Dysregulation: Phenotypic Plasticity and Human Development," *Development and Psychopathology* 25 (2013): 1243–1261.

4. Esther Nederhof and Mathias V. Schmidt, "Mismatch or Cumulative Stress: Toward an Integrated Hypothesis of Programming Effects," *Physiology & Behavior* 106 (2012): 691–700; Andrew Sih, "Effects of Early Stress on Behavioral Syndromes: An Integrated Adaptive Perspective," *Neuroscience and Biobehavioral Reviews* 35 (2011): 1452–1465.

5. Jay Belsky, "Differential Susceptibility to Rearing Influence: An Evolutionary Hypothesis and Some Evidence," in *Origins of the Social Mind: Evolutionary Psychology and Child Development*, ed. Bruce J. Ellis and David F. Bjorklund, 139–163 (New York: Guilford, 2005).

6. Marian J. Bakermans-Kranenburg and Marinus H. van IJzendoorn, "Interventions: Gene X Environment Experiments from a Differential Susceptibility Perspective," *Annual Review of Psychology* 66 (2015): 381–409.

7. Jay Belsky, "Conditional and Alternative Reproductive Strategies: Individual Differences in Susceptibility to Rearing Experience," in *Genetic Influences on Human Fertility and Sexuality: Theoretical and Empirical Contributions from the Biological and Behavioral Sciences*, ed. J. Rodgers, D. Rowe, and W. Miller, 127–146 (Boston: Kluwer, 2000).

8. Patricia J. Williams, "Torn Apart," *New York Review of Books*, November 6, 2024.

9. Rosalind J. Neuman, Elizabeth Lobos, Wendy Reich, Cynthia H. Henderson, Ling-Wei Sun, and Richard D. Todd, "Prenatal Smoking Exposure and Dopaminergic Genotypes Interact to Cause a Severe ADHD Subtype," *Biological Psychiatry* 61, no. 12 (2007): 1320–1328.

10. Michael Pluess, Jay Belsky, and Rosalind J. Neuman, "Prenatal Smoking and ADHD: DRD4-7R as a Plasticity Gene," *Biological Psychiatry* 66 (2009): e5–e6.

11. W. Thomas Boyce and Bruce J. Ellis, "Biological Sensitivity to Context: I. An Evolutionary-Developmental Theory of the Origins and Functions of Stress Reactivity," *Development and Psychopathology* 17 (2005): 271–301.

12. W. Thomas Boyce, Margaret Chesney, Abbey Alkon, Jeanne M. Tschann, Sally Adams, Beth Chesterman, Frances Cohen, Pamela Kaiser, Susan Folkman, and Diane Wara, "Psychobiologic Reactivity to Stress and Childhood Respiratory Illnesses: Results of Two Prospective Studies," *Psychosomatic Medicine* 57 (1995): 411–422.

13. Bruce J. Ellis, W. Thomas Boyce, Jay Belsky, Marian J. Bakermans-Kranenburg, and Marinus H. van IJzendoorn, "Differential Susceptibility to the Environment: A Neurodevelopmental Theory," *Development and Psychopathology* 23 (2011): 7–28.

14. Marco Del Giudice, Bruce J. Ellis, and E. A. Shirtcliff, "The Adaptive Calibration Model of Stress Responsivity," *Neuroscience and Biobehavioral Reviews* 35 (2011): 1562–1592.

15. E. Aron, *The Highly Sensitive Person: How to Thrive When the World Overwhelms You* (New York: Broadway Books, 1997); E. Aron, *The Highly Sensitive Person: How to Survive and Thrive in a World That Doesn't Understand You* (New York: Harper Collins, 2016).

16. E. N. Aron and E. Aron, "Sensory-processing Sensitivity and Its Relation to Introversion and Emotionality," *Journal of Personality and Social Psychology* 73 (1997): 345–368.

17. J. Maynard Smith and G. R. Price, "The Logic of Animal Conflict," *Nature* 246 (1973): 15–18; S. L. Lima and L. M. Dill, "Behavioral Decisions Made Under the Risk of Predation: A Review and Prospectus," *Canadian Journal of Zoology* 68 (1990): 619–640.

18. Brian R. Smith and Daniel T. Blumstein, "Behavioral Types as Predictors of Survival in Trinidadian Guppies (*Poecilia reticulata*)," *Behavioral Ecology* 19 (2008): 19–28.

19. Patrick T. Davies, Rochelle F. Hentges, Jesse L. Coe, Lucia Q. Parry, and Melissa L. Sturge-Apple, "Children's Dove Temperament as a Differential Susceptibility Factor in Child Rearing Contexts," *Developmental Psychology* 57 (2021): 1274–1290.

## 8. The Difficult Infant

1. Stephen J. Suomi, "Uptight and Laid-Back Monkeys: Individual Differences in the Response to Social Challenges," in *Plasticity of Development*, ed. S. E. Brauth, W. S. Hall, and R. J. Dooling, 27–56 (Cambridge, MA: MIT Press, 1991).

2. Dennis Golm and Valerie Brandt, "The Longitudinal Association Between Infant Negative Emotionality, Childhood Maltreatment, and ADHD Symptoms," *Development and Psychopathology* 36, no. 3 (2024): 1231–1238.

3. Susan B. Crockenberg, "Infant Irritability, Mothers' Responsiveness, and Social Support Influences on the Security of Infant-Mother Attachment," *Child Development* 52, no. 3 (1981): 857–865.

4. Grazyna Kochanska, "Toward a Synthesis of Parental Socialization and Child Temperament in Early Development of Conscience," *Child Development* 64, no. 2 (1993): 325–347.

5. Jay Belsky, Kuang-Hua Hsieh, and Keith Crnic, "Mothering, Fathering, and Infant Negativity as Antecedents of Boys' Externalizing Problems and Inhibition at Age 3: Differential Susceptibility to Rearing Influence?" *Development and Psychopathology* 10, no. 2 (1998): 301–319.

6. Michael Pluess and Jay Belsky, "Differential Susceptibility to Rearing Experience: The Case of Childcare," *Journal of Child Psychology and Psychiatry* 50 (2009): 396–404; NICHD Early Child Care Research Network, "Does Quality of Childcare Affect Child Outcomes at Age 4½?" *Developmental Psychology* 39 (2003): 451–469.

7. Margarete Bolten, Irina Nast, Marta Skrundz, Christina Stadler, Dirk H. Hellhammer, and Gunther Meinlschmidt, "Prenatal Programming of Emotion Regulation: Neonatal Reactivity as a Differential Susceptibility Factor Moderating the Outcome of Prenatal Cortisol Levels," *Journal of Psychosomatic Research* 75, no. 4 (2013): 351–357.

8. Martina Pitzer, Christine Jennen-Steinmetz, Guenter Esser, Martin H. Schmidt, and Manfred Laucht, "Differential Susceptibility to Environmental Influences: The Role of Early Temperament and Parenting in the Development of Externalizing Problems," *Comprehensive Psychiatry* 52 (2011): 650–658.

9. Xiaoya Zhang, Kristina Sayler, Sarah Hartman, and Jay Belsky, "Infant Temperament, Early-Childhood Parenting, and Early-Adolescent Development: Testing Alternative Models of Parenting-X-Temperament Interaction," *Development and Psychopathology* 34 (2022): 784–795; Jay Belsky, Michael Pluess, and Keith F. Widaman, "Confirmatory and Competitive Evaluation of Alternative Gene-Environment Interaction Hypotheses," *Journal of Child Psychology and Psychiatry* 54, no. 10 (2013): 1135–1143.

10. M. Lynn Chapieski and Karen D. Evankovich, "Behavioral Effects of Prematurity," *Seminars in Perinatology* 21, no. 3 (1997): 221–239; Julie Poehlmann, A. J. M. Schwichtenberg, Rebecca J. Shlafer, Emily Hahn, Jon-Paul Bianchi, and Rachael Warner, "Emerging Self-Regulation in Toddlers Born Preterm or Low Birth Weight: Differential Susceptibility to Parenting?" *Development and Psychopathology* 23, no. 1 (2011): 177–193; Noa Gueron-Sela, Naama Atzaba-Poria, Gal Meiri, and Kyla Marks, "Temperamental Susceptibility to Parenting Among Preterm and Full-Term Infants in Early Cognitive Development," *Infancy* 21, no. 3 (2015): 312–331; Dafna A. Windhorst, Ralph C. A. Rippe, Viara R. Mileva-Seitz, Frank C. Verhulst, Vincent W. V. Jaddoe, Gerard Noppe, Elisabeth F. C. van Rossum, Erica L. T. van den Akker, Henning Tiemeier, and Marian J. Bakermans-Kranenburg, "Mild Perinatal Adversities Moderate the Association between Maternal Harsh Parenting and Hair Cortisol: Evidence for Differential Susceptibility," *Developmental Psychobiology* 59, no. 3 (2017): 294–337; Tobey Nichols, Julia Jaekel, Peter Bart-

mann, and Dieter Wolke, "Differential Susceptibility Effects of Maternal Sensitivity in Childhood on Small for Gestational Age Adults' Wealth," *Development and Psychopathology* 32, no. 1 (2020): 197–203.

11. Robert H. Bradley and Robert F. Corwyn, "Security and Closeness with Mothers and Fathers in the Transition to Adolescence: Differences by Temperament," *Journal of Family Psychology* 35, no. 7 (2021): 950–960.

12. Theodore Dix and Ni Yan, "Mothers' Depressive Symptoms and Infant Negative Emotionality in the Prediction of Child Adjustment at Age 3," *Development and Psychopathology* 26, no. 1 (2013): 111–124.

13. Jay Belsky, "Early Human Experience: A Family Perspective," *Developmental Psychology* 17, no. 1 (1981): 3–23; Rochelle F. Hentges, Patrick T. Davies, and Dante Cicchetti, "Temperament and Interparental Conflict: The Role of Negative Emotionality in Predicting Child Behavior Problems," *Child Development* 86, no. 5 (2015): 1333–1350.

14. Jay Belsky, Margaret Fish, and Russell A. Isabella, "Continuity and Discontinuity in Infant Negative and Positive Emotionality: Family Antecedents and Attachment Consequences," *Developmental Psychology* 27, no. 3 (1991): 421–431.

15. Meike Slagt, Judith S. Dubas, Maja Deković, and Marcel A. G. van Aken, "Differences in Sensitivity to Parenting Depending on Child Temperament: A Meta-Analysis," *Psychological Bulletin* 142 (2016): 1068–1110.

16. Russell A. Isabella and Jay Belsky, "Interactional Synchrony and the Origins of Infant-Mother Attachment: A Replication Study," *Child Development* 62 (1991): 373–384; Russell A. Isabella, Jay Belsky, and A. von Eye, "The Origins of Infant-Mother Attachment: An Examination of Interactional Synchrony During the Infant's First Year," *Developmental Psychology* 25 (1989): 12–21; Marianne S. De Wolff and Marinus H. van Ijzendoorn, "Sensitivity and Attachment: A Meta-Analysis on Parental Antecedents of Infant Attachment," *Child Development* 68 (1997): 571–591; Sheri Madigan, Audrey-Ann Deneault, Robbie Duschinsky, Marian J. Bakermans-Kranenburg, Carlo Schuengel, Marinus H. van Ijzendoorn, Ahh Ly, R. M. P. Fearon, Rachel Eirich, and Marije L. Verhage, "Maternal and Paternal Sensitivity: Key Determinants of Child Attachment Security Examined Through Meta-Analysis," *Psychological Bulletin* 150 (2024): 839–872.

17. Jay Belsky, "Theory Testing, Effect-Size Evaluation, and Differential Susceptibility to Rearing Influence: The Case of Mothering and Attachment," *Child Development* 64 (1997): 598–600; D. C. van den Boom, "The Influence of Temperament and Mothering on Attachment and Exploration: An Experimental Manipulation of Sensitive Responsiveness Among Lower-Class Mothers with Irritable Infants," *Child Development* 65, no. 5 (1994): 1457–1477.

18. Esther M. Leerkes and Nan Zhou, "Maternal Sensitivity to Distress and Attachment Outcomes: Interactions with Sensitivity to Nondistress and Infant Temperament," *Journal of Family Psychology* 32, no. 6 (2018): 753–761; van den Boom, "Influence of Temperament."

19. Jude Cassidy, Susan S. Woodhouse, Laura J. Sherman, Brandi Stupica, and C. W. Lejuez, "Enhancing Infant Attachment Security: An Examination of Treatment Efficacy and Differential Susceptibility," *Development and Psychopathology* 23, no. 1 (2011): 131–148.

20. Juyoung Kim and Grazyna Kochanska, "Considering Heterogeneity within Negative Emotionality Can Inform the Distinction between Diathesis-Stress and Differential Susceptibility: Children's Early Anger and Fear as Moderators of Effects of Parental Socialization on Antisocial Conduct," *Development and Psychopathology* (2025): 1–13.

21. Susan B. Crockenberg and Esther M. Leerkes, "Negative Infant Emotionality and the Development of Family Relationships in Infancy and Early Childhood," in *Children's Influence on Family Dynamics: The Neglected Side of Family Relationships*, ed. A. C. Crouter and A. Booth, 57–78 (Mahwah, NJ: Erlbaum, 2003); S. Kim and G. Kochanska, "Family Sociodemographic Resources Moderate the Path from Toddlers' Hard-to-Manage Temperament to Parental Control to Disruptive Behavior in Middle Childhood," *Development and Psychopathology* 33 (2021): 160–172.

22. A. Bhutta, M. Cleves, P. H. Casey, M. M. Cradock, and K. Anand, "Cognitive and Behavioral Outcomes of School-Aged Children Who Were Born Preterm," *JAMA* 288 (2002): 728–737.

23. Nathan A. Fox, Selin Zeytinoglu, Emilio A. Valadez, George A. Buzzell, Santiago Morales, and Heather A. Henderson, "Annual Research Review: Developmental Pathways Linking Early Behavioral Inhibition to Later Anxiety," *Journal of Child Psychology and Psychiatry* 64 (2023): 537–561; Heather M. Joseph, Nicole E. Lorenzo, Nadiyah Fisher, Danielle R. Novick, Cassandra Gibson, Scott D. Rothenberger, Jill E. Foust, and Andrea Chronis-Tuscano, "Research Review: A Systematic Review and Meta-Analysis of Infant and Toddler Temperament as Predictors of Attention-Deficit / Hyperactivity Disorder," *Journal of Child Psychology and Psychiatry* 64 (2023): 715–735.

24. Jay Belsky, Kuang-Hua Hsieh, and Keith Crnic, "Infant Positive and Negative Emotionality: One Dimension or Two?" *Developmental Psychology* 32 (1996): 289–298.

## 9. Physiological Reactivity and Sensory-Processing Sensitivity

1. Bruce Ellis, Marilyn J. Essex, and W. Thomas Boyce, "Biological Sensitivity to Context: II. Empirical Explorations of an Evolutionary–Developmental Theory," *Development and Psychopathology* 17 (2005): 303–328.

2. Nila Shakiba, Bruce J. Ellis, Nicole R. Bush, and W. Thomas Boyce, "Biological Sensitivity to Context: A Test of the Hypothesized U-Shaped Relation Between Early Adversity and Stress Responsivity," *Development and Psychopathology* 32 (2019): 641–660.

3. Bruce J. Ellis, Elizabeth A. Shirtcliff, W. Thomas Boyce, Julianna Deardorff, and Marilyn J. Essex, "Quality of Early Family Relationships and the Timing and Tempo of Puberty: Effects Depend on Biological Sensitivity to Context," *Development and Psychopathology* 23 (2011): 85–99.

4. Darby Saxbe, Gayla Margolin, Lauren A. Spies Shapiro, and Brian R. Baucom, "Does Dampened Physiological Reactivity Protect Youth in Aggressive Family Environments?" *Child Development* 83 (2012): 821–830.

5. Joanna Pearson, Patrick Davies, and Melissa Sturge-Apple, "The Moderating Role of Adrenocortical Reactivity in the Associations Between Interparental Conflict, Emotional Reactivity, and School Adjustment," *Development and Psychopathology* 35 (2023): 1878–1890; Jelena Obradović, Nicole R. Bush, and W. Thomas Boyce, "The Interactive Effect of Marital Conflict and Stress Reactivity on Externalizing and Internalizing Symptoms," *Development and Psychopathology* 23 (2011): 101–114; Marilyn J. Essex, Jeffrey M. Armstrong, Linnea R. Burk, H. Hill Goldsmith, and W. Thomas Boyce, "Biological Sensitivity to Context Moderates the Effects of the Early Teacher-Child Relationship on the Development of Mental Health by Adolescence," *Development and Psychopathology* 23 (2011): 49–61; Danielle S. Roubinow, Nicole R. Bush, Melissa J. Hagan, Jason Thompson, and W. Thomas Boyce, "Associations Between Classroom Climate and Children's Externalizing Symptoms: The Moderating Effect of Kindergarten Children's Parasympathetic Reactivity," *Development and Psychopathology* 32 (2020): 661–672; Jelena Obradović, Ximena A. Portilla, and Parissa J. Ballard, "Biological Sensitivity to Family Income: Differential Effects on Early Executive Functioning," *Child Development* 87 (2016): 374–384.

6. Nicolle M. van de Wiel, Stephanie H. van Goozen, Walter Matthys, Heddeke Snoek, and Herman van Engeland, "Cortisol and Treatment Effect in Children with Disruptive Behavior Disorder: A Preliminary Study," *Journal of the American Academy of Child and Adolescent Psychiatry* 43 (2004): 1011–1018.

7. Elaine N. Aron, Arthur Aron, and Jadzia Jagiellowicz, "Sensory Processing Sensitivity: A Review in the Light of the Evolution of Biological Responsivity," *Personality and Social Psychology Review* 16 (2002): 262–282.

8. Meike Slagt, Judith Semon Dubas, Marcel A. G. van Aken, Bruce J. Ellis, and Maja Deković, "Sensory Processing Sensitivity as a Marker of Differential Susceptibility to Parenting," *Developmental Psychology* 54 (2017): 543–558.

9. Alessandra Sperati, Bianca P. Acevedo, Antonio Dellagiulia, Mirco Fasolo, Maria Spineli, Giulio D'Urso, and Francesca Lionetti, "The Contribution of Sensory Processing Sensitivity and Internalized Attachment Representations on Emotional Regulation Competencies of School-Age Children," *Frontiers in Psychology* 15 (2024): 1357808.

10. Alessandra Sperati, Maria Spinelli, Mirco Fasolo, Massimiliano Pastore, Michael Pluess, and Francesca Lionetti, "Investigating Sensitivity through the Lens of Parents: Validation of the Parent-Report Version of the Highly Sensitive Child Scale," *Development and Psychopathology* 36, no. 1 (2024): 415–428.

11. Samantha M. Brown, Galena K. Rhoades, Michael Pluess, Elizabeth S. Allen, and Scott M. Stanley, "Genetic and Subjective Sensitivity, Relationship Dynamics, and Psychological Distress in Couples," *Journal of Family Psychology* 38, no. 5 (2024): 743–750.

12. Elham Assary, Helena M. S. Zavos, Eva Krapohl, Robert Keers, and Michael Pluess, "Genetic Architecture of Environmental Sensitivity Reflects Multiple Heritable Components: A Twin Study with Adolescents," *Molecular Psychiatry* 26, no. 9 (2021): 4896–4904.

13. Francesca Lionetti, Elaine N. Aron, Arthur Aron, Daniel N. Klein, and Michael Pluess, "Observer-rated Environmental Sensitivity Moderates Children's Response to Parenting Quality in Early Childhood," *Developmental Psychology* 55 (2019): 2389–2402.

14. Zhi Li, Melissa L. Sturge-Apple, Hannah R. Jones-Gordils, and P. T. Davies, "Sensory Processing Sensitivity Behavior Moderates the Association Between Environmental Harshness, Unpredictability, and Child Socioemotional Functioning," *Development and Psychopathology* 34 (2022): 675–688.

15. Rabia R. Chhangur, Joyce Weeland, Geertjan Overbeek, W. Matthys, Bram Orobio de Castro, Danielle van der Giessen, and Jay Belsky, "Genetic Moderation of Intervention Efficacy: Dopaminergic Genes, the Incredible Years, and Externalizing Behavior in Children," *Child Development* 88 (2017): 796–811.

16. Michael Pluess and Ilona Boniwell, "Sensory-Processing Sensitivity Predicts Treatment Response to a School-Based Depression Prevention Program," *Personality and Individual Differences* 82 (2015): 40–45.

17. Chieko Kibe, Miki Suzuki, Mari Hirano, and Ilona Boniwell, "Sensory Processing Sensitivity and Culturally Modified Resilience Education: Differential Susceptibility in Japanese Adolescents," *PLOS One* 15 (2020): e0239002.

18. Annalaura Nocentini, Ersilia Menesini, and Michael Pluess, "The Personality Trait of Environmental Sensitivity Predicts Children's Positive Response to a School-Based Antibullying Intervention," *Clinical Psychological Science* 6 (2018): 848–859.

19. Xiaozi Gao, Frank Tian-Fang Ye, Kerry Lee, Alfredo Bautista, Kuen-Fung Sin, and Lan Yang, "Parents Differ in Their Sensitivity to the Environment: An Investigation of the Relationship Between Socioeconomic Status, Social Support, and Child Maltreatment Risks," *Child Abuse and Neglect* 158 (2024): 107131; Beverly H. Brummett, Stephen H. Boyle, Ilene C. Siegler, Cynthia M. Kuhn, Allison Ashley-Koch, Charles R. Jonassaint, Stephan Zuchner, Ann Collins, and Redford B. Williams, "Effects of Environmental Stress and Gender on Associations among Symptoms of Depression and the Serotonin Transporter Gene Linked Polymorphic Region (5-HTTLPR)," *Behavior Genetics* 38 (2008): 34–43.

## 10. The Genetics of Developmental Plasticity

1. Jay Belsky, C. Jonassaint, Michael Pluess, M. Stanton, B. Brummet, and R. Williams, "Vulnerability Genes or Plasticity Genes?" *Molecular Psychiatry* 14 (2009): 746–754.

2. Jay Belsky and Michael Pluess, "Beyond Diathesis-Stress: Differential Susceptibility to Environmental Influences," *Psychological Bulletin* 135 (2009): 885–908; Jay Belsky and Michael Pluess, "Beyond Risk, Resilience, and Dysregulation: Phenotypic Plasticity and Human Development," *Development and Psychopathology* 25 (2013): 1243–1261.

3. Stephen B. Manuck, Anna E. Craig, Janine D. Flory, Indrani Halder, and Robert E. Ferrell, "Reported Early Family Environment Covaries with Menarcheal Age as a Function of Polymorphic Variation in Estrogen Receptor-Alpha Gene," *Development and Psychopathology* 23 (2011): 69–83.

4. Sarah Hartman, Keith F. Widaman, and Jay Belsky, "Genetic Moderation of Effects of Maternal Sensitivity on Girls' Age of Menarche: Replication of Manuck et al. (2011)," *Development and Psychopathology* 27 (2015): 747–756.

5. Avshalom Caspi, Ahmad R. Hariri, Andrew Holmes, Rudolf Uher, and Terrie E. Moffitt, "Genetic Sensitivity to the Environment: The Case of the Serotonin Transporter Gene and Its Implications for Studying Complex Diseases and Traits," *American Journal of Psychiatry* 167 (2010): 509–527.

6. Vanessa Babineau, Cathryn G. Green, Alexis Jolicoeur-Martineau, Andrée-Anne Bouvette-Turcot, Klaus Minde, Roberto Sassi, Martin St-André, Normand Carrey, Leslie Atkinson, James L. Kennedy, John Lydon, Meir Steiner, Helene Gaudreau, Robert Levitan, Michael Meaney, Ashley Wazana, and MAVAN Project, "Prenatal Depression and 5-HTTLPR Interact to Predict Dysregulation from 3–36 Months—A Differential Susceptibility Model," *Journal of Child Psychology and Psychiatry* 56 (2015): 21–29.

7. Jinni Su, Andrew J. Supple, Esther M. Leerkes, and Sally I-Chun Kuo, "Latent Trajectories of Alcohol Use from Early Adolescence to Young Adulthood: Interaction Effects Between 5-HTTLPR and Parenting Quality and Gender Differences," *Development and Psychopathology* 31 (2018): 457–469; Gene H. Brody, Steven R. Beach, Yi-Fu Chen, Ezemenari Obasi, Robert A. Philibert, Steven M. Kogan, and Ronald L. Simons, "Perceived Discrimination, Serotonin Transporter Linked Polymorphic Region Status, and the Development of Conduct Problems," *Development and Psychopathology* 23 (2011): 617–627; Jonathan Daw, Michael Shanahan, Kathleen Mullan Harris, Andrew Smolen, Brett Haberstick, and Jason D. Boardman, "Genetic Sensitivity to Peer Behaviors: 5HTTLPR, Smoking and Alcohol Consumption," *Journal of Health and Social Behavior* 54 (2013): 92–108

8. Marinus H. van Ijzendoorn, Jay Belsky, and Marian J. Bakermans-Kranenburg, "Serotonin Transporter Genotype 5HTTLPR as a Marker of Differential Susceptibility? A Meta-Analysis of Child and Adolescent Gene-by-Environment Studies," *Translational Psychiatry* 2 (2012): e147.

9. Rodolfo A. Bulatao, and Norman B. Anderson, eds., *Understanding Racial and Ethnic Differences in Health in Late Life: A Research Agenda* (Washington, DC: National Academies Press, 2004); Carolyn E. Sartor, Elliot C. Nelson, Michael T. Lynskey, Pamela A. F. Madden, Andrew C. Heath, and Kathleen K. Bucholz, "Are There Differences Between Young African-American and European-American Women in the Relative Influences of Genetics Versus Environment on Age at First Drink and Problem Alcohol Use?" *Alcohol: Clinical and Experimental Research* 37 (2013): 1939–1946; Kit K. Elam, Kaitlin E. Bountress, Thao Ha, Daniel S. Shaw, Melvin N. Wilson, Fazil Aliev, Danielle M. Dick, and Kathryn Lemery-Chalfant, "Developmental Genetic Effects on Externalizing Behavior and Alcohol Use: Examination Across Two Longitudinal Samples," *Development and Psychopathology* 36 (2024): 82–91.

10. Marian J. Bakermans-Kranenburg, Marinus H. van IJzendoorn, Femke T. A. Pijlman, Judi Mesman, and Femmie Juffer, "Experimental Evidence for Differential Susceptibility: Dopamine D4 Receptor Polymorphism (DRD4 VNTR) Moderates Intervention Effects on Toddlers' Externalizing Behavior in a Randomized Trial," *Developmental Psychology* 44 (2008): 293–300.

11. Barak Morgan, Robert Kumsta, Pasco Fearon, Dirk Moser, Sarah Skeen, Peter Cooper, Lynne Murray, Greg Moran, and Mark Tomlinson, "Serotonin Transporter Gene (SLC6A4) Polymorphism and Susceptibility to a Home-Visiting Maternal-Infant Attachment Intervention Delivered by Community Health Workers in South Africa: Re-Analysis of a Randomized Controlled Trial," *PLOS Medicine* 14 (2017): e1002237.

12. Zoë H. Brett, Kathryn L. Humphreys, Anna T. Smyke, Mary Margaret Gleason, Charles A. Nelson, Charles H. Zeanah, Nathan A. Fox, and Stacy S. Drury, "5HTTLPR Genotype Moderates the Longitudinal Impact of Early Caregiving on Externalizing Behavior," *Development and*

*Psychopathology* 27 (2015): 7–18; Stacy S. Drury, Mary M. Gleason, Katherine P. Theall, Anna T. Smyke, Charles A. Nelson, Nathan A. Fox, and Charles H. Zeanah, "Genetic Sensitivity to the Caregiving Context: The Influence of 5HTTLPR and BDNF Val66 Met on Indiscriminate Social Behavior," *Physiology and Behavior* 106 (2012): 728–735.

13. Stephen V. Faraone, Roy H. Perlis, Alysa E. Doyle, Jordan W. Smoller, Jennifer J. Goralnick, Meredith A. Holmgren, and Pamela Sklar, "Molecular Genetics of Attention-Deficit / Hyperactivity Disorder," *Biological Psychiatry* 57 (2005): 1313–1323.

14. Henry Harpending and Gregory Cochran, "In Our Genes," *PNAS* 99 (2002): 10–12.

15. Michael Pluess, Jay Belsky, and R. J. Neuman, "Prenatal Smoking and ADHD: DRD4-7R as a Plasticity Gene," *Biological Psychiatry* 66 (2009): e5–e6; D.Berry, K. Deater-Deckard, K. McCartney, Z. Wang, and S. A. Petrill, "Gene-Environment Interaction Between Dopamine Receptor D4 7-Repeat Polymorphism and Early Maternal Sensitivity Predicts Inattention Trajectories Across Middle Childhood," *Development and Psychopathology* 25 (2013): 291–306.

16. Katrin Zohsel, Arlette F. Buchmann, Dorothea Blomeyer, Erika Hohm, Martin H. Schmidt, Günter Esser, Daniel Brandeis, Tobias Banaschewski, and Manfred Laucht, "Mothers' Prenatal Stress and Their Children's Antisocial Outcomes: A Moderating Role for the Dopamine D4 Receptor (DRD4) Gene," *Journal of Child Psychology and Psychiatry* 55 (2014): 69–76; Annelies Janssens, Wim van den Noortgate, Luc Goossens, Hilde Colpin, Karine Verschueren, Stephan Claes, and Karla van Leeuwen, "Externalizing Problem Behavior in Adolescence: Parenting Interacting with DAT1 and DRD4 Genes," *Journal of Research on Adolescence* 27 (2017): 278–297; Ariel Knafo, Salomon Israel, and Richard P. Ebstein, "Heritability of Children's Prosocial Behavior and Differential Susceptibility to Parenting by Variation in the Dopamine Receptor D4 Gene," *Development and Psychopathology* 23 (2011): 53–67.

17. Marian J. Bakermans-Kranenburg and Marinus H. van Ijzendoorn, "Differential Susceptibility to Rearing Environment Depending on Dopamine Genes," *Development and Psychopathology* 23 (2011): 39–52.

18. Marian J. Bakermans-Kranenburg, Marinus H. van Ijzendoorn, F. T. A. Pijlman, J. Mesman, and F. Juffer, "Experimental Evidence for Differential Susceptibility: Dopamine D4 Receptor Polymorphism (DRD4 VNTR) Moderates Intervention Effects on Toddlers' Externalizing Behavior in a Randomized Controlled Trial," *Developmental Psychology* 44 (2008): 293–300.

19. Stephen R. H. Beach, Gene H. Brody, Man-Kit Lei, and Robert A. Philibert, "Differential Susceptibility to Parenting among African American Youths," *Journal of Family Psychology* 24 (2010): 513–521; Gene H. Brody, Yi-fu Chen, Steven R. H. Beach, Steven M. Kogan, Tianyi Yu, Ralph J. Diclemente, Gina M. Wingood, Michael Windle, and Robert A. Philibert, "Differential Sensitivity to Prevention Programming: A Dopaminergic Polymorphism-Enhanced Prevention Effect on Protective Parenting and Adolescent Substance Use," *Health Psychology* 33 (2014): 182–191.

20. Rita Baião, Pasco Fearon, Jay Belsky, Pedro Teixeira, Isabel Soares, and Ana Mesquita, "Does 5-HTTLPR Moderate Effects of the Quality of Environmental Context on Maternal Sensitivity? Testing the Differential Susceptibility Hypothesis," *Psychiatric Genetics* 30 (2020): 49–56; A. Sperati, M. E. Persico, R. Palumbo, M. Fasolo, M. Spinelli, Michael Pluess, G. D'Urso, and F. Lionetti, "The Role of Individual Differences in Environmental Sensitivity in Teachers' Stress and Burnout at Work," *Stress and Health* 40 (2024): e3491.

21. Jay Belsky and M. Beaver, "Cumulative-Genetic Plasticity, Parenting and Adolescent Self-Control / Regulation," *Journal of Child Psychology & Psychiatry* 52 (2011): 619–626.

22. Cathryn Gordon Green, Vanessa Babineau, Alexia Jolicoeur-Martineau, Andrée-Anne Bouvette-Turcot, Klaus Minde, Roberto Sassi, Martin St-André, Normand Carrey, Leslie Atkinson, James L. Kennedy, Meir Steiner, John Lydon, Helene Gaudreau, Jacob A. Burack, Robert Levitan, Michael J. Meaney, Ashley Wazana, and Maternal Adversity, Vulnerability, and Neurodevelopment Research Team, "Prenatal Maternal Depression and Child Serotonin

Transporter Linked Polymorphic Region (5-HTTLPR) and Dopamine Receptor D4 (DRD4) Genotype Predict Negative Emotionality from 3 to 36 Months," *Development and Psychopathology* 29 (2017): 901–917; R. L. Simons, M. K. Lei, S. R. H. Beach, G. H. Brody, R. Philibert, and F. X. Gibbons, "Social Environmental Variation, Plasticity Genes, and Aggression: Evidence for the Differential Susceptibility Hypothesis," *American Sociological Review* 76 (2011): 883–912; Patrick T. Davies, Dante Cicchetti, Morgan J. Thompson, Sonnette M. Bascoe, and E. Mark Cummings, "The Interplay of Polygenic Plasticity and Adrenocortical Activity as Sources of Variability in Pathways Among Family Adversity, Youth Emotional Reactivity, and Psychological Problems," *Development and Psychopathology* 32 (2020): 587–603; April S. Masarik, Rand D. Conger, M. Brent Donnellan, Michael C. Stallings, Monica J. Martin, Thomas J. Schofield, Tricia K. Neppl, Laura V. Scaramella, Andrew Smolen, and Keith F. Widaman, "For Better and for Worse: Genes and Parenting Interact to Predict Future Behavior in Romantic Relationships," *Journal of Family Psychology* 28 (2014): 357–367.

23. Emily Rauscher, "Plastic and Immobile: Unequal Intergenerational Mobility by Genetic Sensitivity Score Within Sibling Pairs," *Social Science Research* 65 (2017): 112–129.

24. The Incredible Years parenting intervention was developed by psychologist Carolyn Webster-Stratton. Carolyn Webster-Stratton and M. Jamila Reid, "The Incredible Years Parents, Teachers, and Children Training Series: A Multifaceted Treatment Approach for Young Children with Conduct Problems," in John R. Weisz and Alan E. Kazdin, eds., *Evidence-Based Psychotherapies for Children and Adolescents* third edition (New York: Guilford Press, 2018): 122–141; *The Incredible Years: Parents and Children Videotape Series: A Parenting Course (BASIC)* (Seattle, WA: Incredible Years, 2001).

25. Rabia R. Chhangur, Joyce Weeland, Geertjan Overbeek, Walter Matthys, Bram Orobio de Castro, Danielle van der Giessen, and Jay Belsky, "Genetic Moderation of Intervention Efficacy: Dopaminergic Genes, the Incredible Years, and Externalizing Behavior in Children," *Child Development* 88 (2017): 796–811.

26. X. Zhang and Jay Belsky, "Three Phases of Gene-X-Environment Interaction Research: Theoretical Assumptions Underlying Gene Selection," *Development and Psychopathology* 34 (2022): 295–306.

27. L. M. Chen, M. S. Tollenaar, S. A. Hari Dass, A. A. Bouvette-Turcot, I. Pokhvisneva, H. Gaudreau, C. Parent, J. Diorio, L. M. McEwen, J. L. MacIsaac, M. S. Kobor, R. Beijers, C. de Weerth, P. P. Silveira, S. Karama, M. J. Meaney, K. J. O'Donnell, and MAVAN Study Team, "Maternal Antenatal Depression and Child Mental Health: Moderation by Genomic Risk for Attention Deficit / Hyperactivity Disorder," *Development and Psychopathology* 32 (2020): 1810–1821.

28. Ying Sun, Jiao Fang, Yuhui Wan, Puyu Su, and Fangbiao Tao, "Association of Early-Life Adversity with Measures of Accelerated Biological Aging Among Children in China," *JAMA Network Open* 3 (2020): e2013588.

29. Rashelle J. Musci, Katherine E. Masyn, George Uhl, Brion Maher, Sheppard G. Kellam, and Nicholas S. Ialongo, "Polygenic Score x Intervention Moderation: An Application of Discrete-Time Survival Analysis to Model the Timing of First Tobacco Use Among Urban Youth," *Development and Psychopathology* 27 (2015): 111–122; Rashelle J. Musci, Brian Fairman, Katherine E. Masyn, George Uhl, Brion Maher, Danielle Y. Sisto, Sheppard G. Kellam, and Nicholas S. Ialongo, "Polygenic Score × Intervention Moderation: An Application of Discrete-Time Survival Analysis to Model the Timing of First Marijuana Use Among Urban Youth," *Prevention Science* 19 (2018): 6–14.

30. Robert Keers, Jonathan R. I. Coleman, Kathryn J. Lester, Susanna Roberts, Gerome Breen, Mikael Thastum, Susan Bögels, Silvia Schneider, Einar Heiervang, Richard Meiser-Stedman, Maaike Nauta, Cathy Creswell, Kerstin Thirlwall, Ronald M. Rapee, Jennifer L. Hudson, Cathryn Lewis, Robert Plomin, Thalia C. Eley, "A Genome-Wide Test of the Differential Susceptibility Hypothesis Reveals a Genetic Predictor of Differential Response to Psychological Treatments for Child Anxiety Disorders," *Psychotherapy and Psychosomatics* 85 (2016): 146–158.

31. Kathryn Lemery-Chalfant, Sierra Clifford, Thomas J. Dishion, Daniel S. Shaw, and Melvin N. Wilson, "Genetic Moderation of the Effects of the Family Check-Up Intervention on Children's Internalizing Symptoms: A Longitudinal Study with a Racially / Ethnically Diverse Sample," *Development and Psychopathology* 30 (2018): 1729–1747.

32. Michael Pluess, Galena Rhoades, Rob Keers, Kayla Knopp, Jay Belsky, Howard Markman, and Scott Stanley, "Genetic Sensitivity Predicts Long-Term Psychological Benefits of a Relationship Education Program for Married Couples," *Journal of Consulting and Clinical Psychology* 90 (2022): 195–207.

## Conclusion

1. Sooyeon Sung, Jeffrey A. Simpson, Vladas Griskevicius, Sally I-Chun Kuo, Gabriel L. Schlomer, and Jay Belsky, "Secure Infant-Mother Attachment Buffers the Effect of Early-Life Stress on Age of Menarche," *Psychological Science* 27 (2016): 667–674.

2. Hui Jing Lu, Jennifer E. Lansford, Yuan Yuan Liu, Bin Bin Chen, Marc H. Bornstein, Ann T. Skinner, . . . and Lei Chang, "Attachment Security, Environmental Adversity, and Fast Life History Behavioral Profiles in Human Adolescents," *Development and Psychopathology* (2025); An Ting Yang, Hui Jing Lu, and Lei Chang, "Environmental Harshness and Unpredictability, Parenting and Offspring Life History," *Evolutionary Psychological Science* 9 (2023): 451–446; Hui Jing Lu, Yuan Yuan Liu, and Lei Chang, "Child Attachment in Adjusting the Species-General Contingency Between Environmental Adversities and Fast Life History Strategies," *Development and Psychopathology* 34 (2022): 719–730.

3. Willem E. Frankenhuis and Karthik Panchanathan, "Individual Differences in Developmental Plasticity May Result from Stochastic Sampling," *Perspectives on Psychological Science* 6 (2011): 336–347.

4. Nila Shakiba, Bruce J. Ellis, Nicole R. Bush, and W. Thomas Boyce, "Biological Sensitivity to Context: A Test of the Hypothesized U-shaped Relation Between Early Adversity and Stress Responsivity," *Development and Psychopathology* 32 (2019): 641–660.

5. E. O. Wilson, *Sociobiology: The New Synthesis* (Cambridge, MA: Belknap Press of Harvard University Press, 1975).

6. Angelica Ronald, "Editorial: Are Government Early Years Learning and Development Frameworks Evidence Based? A Scientist's Perspective," *Journal of Child Psychology and Psychiatry* 65 (2024): 591–593.

7. Jay Belsky, Xiaoya Zhang, and Kristina Sayler, "Differential Susceptibility 2.0: Are the Same Children Affected by Different Experiences And Exposures?" *Development and Psychopathology* 34 (2022): 1025–1033; Cassidy L. McDermott, Katherine Taylor, Sophie D. S. Sharp, David Lydon-Staley, Julia A. Leonard, and Allyson P. Mackey, "Sensitivity to Psychosocial Influences at Age 3 Predicts Mental Health in Middle Childhood," *Developmental Science* 27 (2024): e13531; Noam Markovitch, Yuval Hart, and Ariel Knafo-Noam, "Environmental Susceptibility for All: A Data-Driven Approach Suggests Individual Differences in Domain-General and Domain-Specific Patterns of Environmental Susceptibility," *Development and Psychopathology* 36 (2024): 1520–1536.

8. Kristina Sayler, Xiaoya Zhang, Laurence Steinberg, and Jay Belsky, "Parenting, Peers and Psychosocial Adjustment: Are the Same—or Different—Children Affected by Each?" *Journal of Youth and Adolescence* 51 (2022): 443–457; Noam Markovitch and Ariel Knafo-Noam, "Sensitivity, but to Which Environment? Individual Differences in Sensitivity to Parents and Peers Show Domain-Specific Patterns and a Negative Genetic Correlation," *Developmental Science* 24 (2021): e13136.

9. Kristina Sayler, Katie A. McLaughlin, and Jay Belsky, "Early-life Threat and Deprivation: Are Children Similarly Affected by Exposure to Each?" *Child Development* 96 (2025): 606–618.

10. Dante Cicchetti and Fred A. Rogosch, "Equifinality and Multifinality in Developmental Psychopathology," *Development and Psychopathology* 8 (1996): 597–600.

11. Brain factors: Camille Deane, Nandita Vijayakumar, Nicholas B. Allen, Orli Schwartz, Julian G. Simmons, Chad A. Bousman, Christos Pantelis, and Sarah Whittle, "Parenting x Brain Development Interactions as Predictors of Adolescent Depressive Symptoms and Well-Being: Differential Susceptibility or Diathesis-Stress?" *Development and Psychopathology* 32 (2019): 139–150; Arianna M. Gard, Daniel S. Shaw, Erika E. Forbes, and Luke W. Hyde, "Amygdala Reactivity as a Marker of Differential Susceptibility to Socioeconomic Resources during Early Adulthood," *Developmental Psychology* 54 (2018): 2341–2355; Sarah Whittle, Marie B. H. Yap, Lisa Sheeper, Paul Dudgeon, Murat Yucel, Christos Pantelis, Julian G. Simmons, and Nicholas B. Allen, "Hippocampal Volume and Sensitivity to Maternal Aggressive Behavior: A Prospective Study of Adolescent Depressive Symptoms," *Development and Psychopathology* 23 (2011): 115–129. Positive emotionality: Natalie V. Miller, Kathryn A. Degnan, Amie A. Hane, Nathan A. Fox, and Andrea Chronis-Tuscano, "Infant Temperament Reactivity and Early Maternal Caregiving: Independent and Interactive Links to Later Childhood Attention-Deficit / Hyperactivity Disorder Symptoms," *Journal of Child Psychology and Psychiatry* 60 (2019): 43–53; Stella Tsotsi, Birit F. P. Broekman, Lynette P. Shek, Kok Hian Tan, Yap Seng Chong, Helen Chen, Michael J. Meaney, and Anne E. Rifkin-Graboi, "Maternal Parenting Stress, Child Exuberance, and Preschoolers' Behavior Problems," *Child Development* 90 (2018): 136–146. Impulsivity and anger proneness: Liliana J. Lengua, Sharlene A. Wolchik, Irwin N. Sandler, and Stephen G. West, "The Additive and Interactive Effects of Parenting and Temperament in Predicting Adjustment Problems in Children of Divorce," *Child Psychology and Psychiatry* 29 (2000): 232–244. Androgens and microbiota: Marco Del Giudice, Emily S. Barrett, Jay Belsky, Sarah Hartman, Michelle M. Martel, Susanne Sangenstedt, and Christopher W. Kuzawa, "Individual Differences in Developmental Plasticity: A Role for Early Androgens?" *Psychoneuroendocrinology* 90 (2018): 168–173; Sarah Hartman, K. Sayler, and Jay Belsky, "Prenatal Stress Enhances Postnatal Plasticity: The Role of Microbiota," *Developmental Psychobiology* 61 (2019): 729–738.

12. Vivette Glover, "Annual Research Review: Prenatal Stress and the Origins of Psychopathology," *Journal of Child Psychology and Psychiatry* 52 (2011): 356–367; Irene Tung, Alison E. Hipwell, Philip Grosse, Lindsey Battaglia, Elena Cannova, Gabrielle English, Allysa D. Quick, Bianca Llamas, Megan Taylor, and Jill E. Foust, "Prenatal Stress and Externalizing Behaviors in Childhood and Adolescence: A Systematic Review and Meta-Analysis," *Psychological Bulletin* 150 (2024): 107–131; Elysia Poggi Davis, Laura M. Glynn, Christine Dunkel Schetter, Calvin Hobel, Aleksandra Chicz-Demet, and Curt A. Sandman, "Prenatal Exposure to Maternal Depression and Cortisol Influences Infant Temperament," *Journal of the American Academy of Child and Adolescent Psychiatry* 46, no. 6 (2007): 737–746; Barbara M. Gutteling, Carolina de Weerth, and Jan K. Buitelaar, "Prenatal Stress and Children's Cortisol Reaction to the First Day of School," *Psychoneuroendocrinology* 30 (2005): 541–549.

13. Jay Belsky and Michael Pluess, "The Nature (and Nurture?) of Plasticity in Early Human Development," *Perspectives in Psychological Science* 4 (2009): 345–351; Michael Pluess and Jay Belsky, "Prenatal Programming of Postnatal Plasticity?" *Development and Psychopathology* 23 (2011): 29–38; Chiara Sacchi, Pietro De Carli, Camilla Gregorini, Catherine Monk, and Alessandra Simonelli, "In the Pandemic from the Womb: Prenatal Exposure, Maternal Psychological Stress and Mental Health in Association with Infant Negative Affect at 6 Months of Life," *Development and Psychopathology* 36 (2024): 810–820; Rebecca Lipschutz, Paulina A. Kulesz, Guillaume Elgbeili, Brian Biekman, David P. Laplante, David M. Olson, Suzanne King, and Johanna Bick, "Maternal Mental Health Mediates the Effect of Prenatal Stress on Infant Temperament: The Harvey Mom Study," *Development and Psychopathology* 36 (2024): 893–907.

14. Sarah Hartman, Jay Belsky, and Michael Pluess, "Prenatal Programming of Environmental Sensitivity," *Translational Psychiatry* 13 (2023): 161; Sarah Hartman and Jay Belsky, "Prenatal

Programming of Postnatal Plasticity Revisited—and Extended," *Development and Psychopathology* 30 (2018): 825–842; Sarah Hartman, Espen Moen Eilertsen, Eivind Ystrom, Jay Belsky, and Line C. Gjerde, "Does Prenatal Stress Amplify Effects of Postnatal Maternal Depressive and Anxiety Symptoms on Child Problem Behavior?" *Developmental Psychology* 56 (2020): 128–137; Sarah Hartman, Sara M. Freeman, Karen L. Bales, and Jay Belsky, "Prenatal Stress as a Risk—and Opportunity—Factor," *Psychological Science* 29 (2018): 572–580.

15. Roseriet Beijers, Sarah Hartman, Idan Shalev, Waylon Hastings, Brooke C. Mattern, Carolina de Weerth, and Jay Belsky, "Testing Three Hypotheses about Effects of Sensitive-Insensitive Parenting on Telomeres," *Developmental Psychology* 56 (2020): 237–250; W. Thomas Boyce and Bruce J. Ellis, "Biological Sensitivity to Context: I. An Evolutionary-Developmental Theory of the Origins and Functions of Stress Reactivity," *Development and Psychopathology* 17 (2005): 271–301; Emma T. Margolis and Laurel J. Gabard-Durnam, "Prenatal Influences on Postnatal Neuroplasticity: Integrating DOHaD and Sensitive / Critical Period Frameworks to Understanding Biological Embedding in Early Development," *Infancy* 30 (2025): e12588.

16. Jay Belsky, Avshalom Caspi, Terrie E. Moffitt, and Richie Poulton, *The Origins of You: How Childhood Shapes Later Life* (Cambridge, MA: Harvard University Press, 2020).

17. Slobodan Koljević, "Historical Population Displacement Is Associated with Faster Life History in Czechia," *Adaptive Human Behavior and Physiology* 10 (2024): 324–334; Slobodan Koljević, "Life History Strategy in Poland: Population Displacement as a Life History Accelerating Event," *Evolutionary Psychological Science* 10 (2024): 100–109.

# Acknowledgments

This book has been thirty-plus years in the making, and there is no shortage of individuals to whom I am intellectually indebted. My first thanks go to my one-time Penn State colleague, Pat Draper, and her late husband, Henry Harpending, for opening my eyes to the potential utility of viewing nurture through the lens of Darwinian and Hamiltonian nature. Next in line is my long-time friend and colleague Larry Steinberg, whose many discussions with me in graduate school about his work on the effects of pubertal timing on family relations most likely planted the seed for my eventual thinking that reversed his frame of reference, resulting in my puberty hypothesis, the focus of this book's first part.

Just as important, but in a much different way, is Bruce Ellis. As I am wont to say, without Bruce's very early interest in my original theorizing about what he came to label as "psychosocial acceleration theory," my ideas might have died on the vine. He more than anyone else took them seriously, proceeding to test the puberty hypothesis and working to further develop the evolutionary-developmental perspective on which this volume is based. Fellow evo-devo travelers Marco Del Giudice and Willem Frankenhuis have also played critical roles in the further development of this theoretical perspective and have thereby shaped my thinking. Not to be forgotten are wonderful friends Temi Moffit and Avshalom Caspi, who were the first to offer to test my puberty prediction, providing the initial empirical evidence that convinced me to pursue my evolutionary ideas further. Let me mention also Marinus van IJzendoorn and Marian Bakermans-Kranenburg, who took my differential susceptibility ideas seriously, testing them rigorously in experimental research.

Not only do scientists stand on the shoulders of giants who came before—in my case, Darwin, Hamilton, Dawkins, E. O. Wilson, Draper, and Harpending—they also rely on hard-working graduate students and post docs. In the latter category, several have been central to the work described in this volume. They have made important contributions to the nature-of-nurture research on effects of early-life conditions on reproductive development, as well as differential susceptibility to environmental influences. Let me especially acknowledge Michael Pluess from my days at Birkbeck University of London, and Zhi Li, Sarah Hartman, Xioaya Zhang, and Kristina Sayler from my UC Davis years.

Last but not least, I thank the two anonymous reviewers of my manuscript and my editor at Harvard University Press, Grigory Tovbis, all of whom offered what I like to call "appreciative critiques." Despite not buying into everything I had to say in prior drafts of *The Nature of Nurture,* these readers offered valuable and encouraging feedback that most certainly improved the final product.

# Index

distal conditions. *See* environmental
exposures
disturbance. *See* disorder
dopamine receptor gene (DRD4), 153,
157–159, 160, 161, 162
Draper, Pat, 30, 32, 36, 47, 53, 57
DRD4, 153, 157–159, 160, 161, 162
dual benefit, 112–113, 117–118, 120–121, 128.
*See also* differential susceptibility for better
and for worse
dual risk: defined, 111; and difficult infants,
131, 135, 138–139; and dual benefit, 112–113,
117–118, 120–121; and genetic studies,
152–153, 157, 163; and temperament,
138–139. *See also* differential susceptibility
for better and for worse
dysfunction. *See* disorder
dysregulation. *See* disorder

early-life / later-life mismatch, 71, 72, 89,
113–116, 178
Ellis, Bruce: on biological sensitivity to
context, 122–124, 128, 140, 142, 143, 177; on
dimensions of adversity and development,
75, 146, 170; on hidden talents, 22; on
puberty and genetics, 99; and puberty
hypothesis, support for, 56–58; on
reproductive development, 70–71
emotion regulation, 38, 133, 145, 146, 154–155
environmental exposures: and biological
aging, 25; defined, 5–6; and developmental
plasticity, 111, 115, 124, 154, 168, 170,
177; and disorder, 21; and evolution, 36;
examples of, 34; importance of in early
years of life, 102, 173; as independent
variables, 79; as not masking genetic
explanations for development, 98–102,
106; and pubertal timing, 47–48; and
reproductive strategies, 102, 167–168; and
sensory-processing sensitivity, 145–146.
*See also* adverse childhood experiences
(ACEs); differential susceptibility
hypothesis; epigenetics; psychosocial
acceleration theory; puberty hypothesis
Environmental-Risk Study, 81–82
epigenetics: and adverse childhood experiences
(ACEs), 81–82, 90; and brain aging, 90;
defined, 79; in development, study of,
78–79, 80–81; and DNA methylation, 80,
82, 85–86; and epigenetic clocks, 85–88, 90;
and heritability, 103–104; and interventions,

potential for, 59; and psychosocial
acceleration theory, 80–81
Erikson, Erik, 37
evolution: as alternative to psychological
explanation for development, 8, 13, 14;
and development, study of, 75; and
developmental plasticity, 40, 50, 116–117;
and disorder as adaptation, 21–24, 105; and
evolutionary-developmental perspective,
3–4, 25, 30, 36, 50, 54–55, 62, 77, 171–172;
and gene-culture coevolution, 15;
and phenotypes, 40; and reproductive
fitness, as driver of, 11–12, 30, 104. *See also*
adaptations; development, reproductive
fitness explanation for; reproductive fitness
evolutionary theory of socialization, 25,
46–49, 50–51, 52, 57. *See also* psychosocial
acceleration theory; puberty hypothesis

family size, 18–19
father absence: developmental responses
to, 30–31, 32–33, 39; extensions to study
of, 47, 48, 77; vs. father behavior, 57; and
life history theory, 42, 43; and menarche,
53, 57, 63; study of developmental
consequences of, 30, 32, 43–44; and
telomere length, 84
5-HTTLPR (serotonin transporter gene),
153, 154–157, 160, 161
fixed strategists, 124, 141–142, 178. *See also*
dandelions
Frankenhuis, Willem, 22, 170
Freud, Sigmund, 29–30, 37

gene-by-environment research, 94–95,
102–106, 110, 121. *See also* genetics of
differential susceptibility
gene-by-intervention research: and anxiety
treatment, 164; and first tobacco and
marijuana use, 163–164; and parenting
interventions, 156–157, 158–159, 162, 164–165
gene-culture coevolution, 15
gene expression. *See* epigenetics
genetics: and adaptations, 5; and culture, 15;
and developmental plasticity, 117, 121, 123,
127; and early pubertal development, 59, 163;
and eugenics, 34–35; individual variations
in, 4; and parenting, 97–98, 155, 156,
157–158, 162; and penetrance, 102–104; and
phenotypes, measuring influence on, 95–96;
and reproductive fitness, 7–8, 9, 11–12, 14,